# Frank G. Raichle
## Pre-Law Studies Collection

D1557305

The Poor in Court

# The Poor in Court

## THE LEGAL SERVICES PROGRAM AND SUPREME COURT DECISION MAKING

*Susan E. Lawrence*

PRINCETON UNIVERSITY PRESS

PRINCETON, NEW JERSEY

Copyright © 1990 by Princeton University Press
Published by Princeton University Press, 41 William Street,
Princeton, New Jersey 08540
In the United Kingdom: Princeton University Press, Oxford

*Library of Congress Cataloging-in-Publication Data*

Lawrence, Susan E., 1957-
The poor in court : the legal services program and Supreme Court decision making /
Susan E. Lawrence.
p. cm.

Includes bibliographical references (p. ).
Based on the author's thesis, Johns Hopkins, 1986.

ISBN 0-691-07855-6 (alk. paper)

1. Legal assistance to the poor—United States. 2. Legal aid—United States. I. Title.
KF336.L35   1990   344.73′03258—dc20   [347.3043258]   90-34925 CIP

This book has been composed in Times Roman

Princeton University Press books are printed on acid-free paper,
and meet the guidelines for permanence and durability of the
Committee on Production Guidelines for Book Longevity of the
Council on Library Resources

Printed in the United States of America by Princeton University Press,
Princeton, New Jersey

10  9  8  7  6  5  4  3  2  1

I, ———, DO SOLEMNLY SWEAR that I will administer justice without respect to persons, and do equal right to the poor and to the rich, and that I will faithfully and impartially discharge and perform all the duties incumbent upon me as ——— Justice of the Supreme Court of the United States according to the best of my abilities and understanding, agreeably to the Constitution and laws of the United States.

So help me God.

Oath of Office
United States Supreme Court

# Contents

# Preface

LINCOLN once remarked, "God must have loved poor people, he made so many of them." Not surprisingly, in a legal system where the ability to retain and compensate an attorney is, effectively, a prerequisite to participation in judicial decision making, the bar and the courts have been somewhat less enamored of the indigent. Throughout most of our history, few of the poor have been able to turn to the courts for redress of their grievances and participate in the judicial development of law and policy.

In the late 1960s, the Supreme Court suddenly began to give substantial attention to poverty issues outside the criminal justice process, using the due process and equal protection clauses to supervise the state's interaction with the less fortunate among us. The Legal Services Program (LSP), created in 1965 as part of the Office of Economic Opportunity, played a seminal role in precipitating this change in the Court's agenda and doctrinal development. By providing counsel to the poor and litigating well over a million civil cases, including 164 that percolated up the appellate ladder to the Supreme Court between 1966 and 1974, the LSP changed the parameters of access to one of our major governing institutions. The poor, represented by Legal Services attorneys, provided the Supreme Court with a new set of opportunities for decision. This book examines why the LSP's provision of counsel to the poor resulted in litigation before the Supreme Court; why the justices were so responsive to the opportunities for decision presented by the poor in LSP cases; and how these opportunities for decision affected the course of our constitutional jurisprudence.

During the writing of this book, I was fortunate to have many sources of support and I owe much to them all. J. Woodford Howard, Jr., and Francis E. Rourke at the Johns Hopkins University provided guidance and artfully mixed critiques with encouragement. Lawrence Baum, Milton Heumann, and Doris Marie Provine patiently read drafts, in whole or in part, and provided many thoughtful suggestions. John Kingdon helped stimulate my thoughts on explaining the Legal Services Program's success.

I had the pleasure of spending two years at the Brookings Institution while working on this project. Many thanks to Governmental Studies Directors Martha Derthick and Paul Peterson for their comments and the financial support Brookings provided. Robert A. Katzmann, Gilbert Y. Steiner, and Kent Weaver were also quite helpful. Ellen Hope's assistance in mastering the Brookings computer system was invaluable. A very special thanks and acknowledgment goes to my fellow Fellows of 1983–84: Charles Cameron, Phil Mundo, and Barry Rabe.

I am also indebted to the American Judicature Society for its generous grant during the early stages of this project. The Rutgers University Research Council provided support for its completion. Under the Chairmanships of Richard Mansbach and Mike Aronoff, the Rutgers University Department of Political Science provided a hospitable climate for the polishing of this manuscript. Thanks to Phyllis Moditz who did an expert job of word processing many more drafts than she or I care to remember. Joe Cammarano, Siobhan Moroney, and William Strazza provided assistance in some final data collection and bibliography preparation. My gratitude also goes to Gail Ullman of Princeton University Press and her staff who guided this book to completion.

A very special thank you goes to all the former Legal Services Program attorneys who donated their time to discuss the Program and this project with me. Of course, they were promised anonymity.

There are a number of people who freely gave of their own unique talents as this work progressed. Each left his or her imprint and I am deeply indebted to each of them for their contributions: Yvonne Chilik; Tom Gais; Cathy Johnson; Mark Peterson; H. W. Perry, Jr.; Pris Regan; Dana Runestad; Wayne Sulfridge; Wendy Wyatt; and especially Daniel N. Hoffman who provided much-appreciated encouragement and enthusiasm during the final stages of this endeavor.

My most enduring debts are to my undergraduate professors, Donald P. Aiesi, James Guth, and Ernest J. Walters, Jr., who set me upon the path that led to these pages; to Milton Heumann, who took time to mentor when time was a very precious commodity for him; and to J. Woodford Howard, Jr., my dissertation advisor, whose most valuable lessons are taught through the example he sets.

# List of Tables

# The Poor in Court

# Introduction: Access to the U.S. Supreme Court

> "Each age brings the Court its own special anxieties and concerns.
> The main outlines of the life of the nation are mirrored in the cases
> filed with us."
>
> Justice William O. Douglas[1]

THE U.S. SUPREME COURT has become an integral part of the national policy-making and implementing process. Unlike Congress and the Presidency, the Court is not officially constrained by electoral accountability. Consequently, we often focus on judicial attitudes, values, and behaviors in explaining judicial outcomes when simple reference to "the law" fails us.[2] But agenda setting and decision making in the Court, as in Congress and in the executive branch, is also affected by changing patterns of access and participation.[3] Agenda setting in the Court, and the resulting development of constitutional and statutory doctrine, are influenced by who has access to the Court's jurisdictional docket. Much as who has access to the franchise and the other tools of electoral politics ultimately affects Congressional and executive policy making, who has access to legal counsel willing to pursue cases through the appellate courts ultimately affects the Supreme Court's doctrinal development. Clients and lawyers create the mirror effect Justice Douglas writes of. Litigation is the means by which the people set judicial agendas and participate in decision making by an unelected judiciary. Adjudication provides a different set of procedures for participatory government and carries with it its own set of limitations on access. The parameters of access to the Supreme Court translate into parameters on the Court's opportunities for decision and thereby shape the development of law and policy by the Court.[4]

[1] Douglas, "The Supreme Court," p. 140.

[2] Much of this literature is summarized in Grossman, "Symposium"; Grossman and Tanenhaus, *Frontiers*. See also Spaeth, *Supreme Court Policy Making*. Another child of the legal realist movement, critical legal studies, emerged in the law schools in the 1970s. Generally, these scholars attribute the patterns of judicial decision making to the hegemony of liberal capitalism. See especially Smith, "All Critters"; "A Bibliography of Critical Legal Studies."

[3] See Cobb and Elder, *Participation*; Verba and Nie, *Participation*, esp. pp. 334–43; Jacob, *Debtors*; Zemans, "Legal Mobilization."

[4] Wells and Grossman, "The Concept of Judicial Policy-Making," and, later, Casper, *Lawyers Before the Warren Court*, similarly use the term "occasions for decision." I use "opportunities" rather than "occasions" to acknowledge the enormous discretion the justices have in selecting cases for review from the pool of cases litigants place before them.

## LIMITATIONS ON ACCESS

The Supreme Court is a passive institution in that it depends upon litigants to provide opportunities for decision. The justices are powerless to act without a case. Although the concept of equality of access to the policy-making process is an important element of our political ideology, in reality the judicial process is not open to all equally.[5]

The primary formal prerequisite is a justiciable controversy. The Court will not render advisory opinions; it will not decide "political questions"; the parties must have standing; the controversy must be live. Nonetheless, even as early as 1832, Tocqueville observed that, "scarcely any political question arises in the U.S. that is not resolved, sooner or later, into a judicial question." While, more recently, the Burger and Rehnquist Courts have restricted the Warren Court's flexible application of these doctrines, skillful attorneys can still transform almost any policy issue into at least an arguably justiciable controversy.[6] But, access to attorneys is not evenly distributed. Because attorneys play a central role in translating client problems into legal controversies and presenting such claims to the courts, which political controversies become judicial questions and when, is in part determined by the availability of counsel. The de facto requirement that one be represented by an attorney to carry one's case to court is the most severe limitation on equal access to the judicial process.

We can identify three analytically distinct, but in practice often overlapping, categories of people upon which the de facto assistance of counsel requirement works a particular hardship. The first category includes those who, for a variety of sociological and psychological reasons, do not perceive the law (and lawyers) as useful in resolving their disputes.[7] Lawyers, who act as

[5] On litigation, or legal mobilization, as a form of political participation, see Zemans, "Legal Mobilization"; see also Black, "Mobilization of Law"; Lawrence, "Participation."

[6] On the Burger Court's limiting of the formal rules of access, see Rathjen and Spaeth, "Denying Access"; Gunther, *Cases*, 10th ed., pp. 1604–1717. See also Bickel, *The Supreme Court and the Idea of Progress*, pp. 106–7.

[7] The Civil Litigation Research Project at the University of Wisconsin has addressed the question of *why* individuals do or do not turn to lawyers and litigation. See especially Bumiller, *Civil Rights Society*; Bumiller, "Victims"; Coates and Penrod, "Social Psychology"; Felstiner et al., "Emergence and Transformation"; Grossman et al., "Dimensions"; Miller and Sarat, "Grievances"; Trubek et al., *Civil Litigation*. See also Galanter, "Reading the Landscape of Disputes."

There is also a body of work which argues that increasing access to courts does not increase justice. While this may be true, my argument here is that changing access does change judicial agendas and the legal doctrines and policies emanating from the courts. See, for example, Grossman, "Access to Justice"; Hazard, "Social Justice"; Abel, "Law Without Politics"; Galanter, "The Duty *NOT* to Deliver"; Scheingold, *Politics of Rights*. But see Abel, "Informalism." Scheingold has pointed out that while court decisions do not automatically lead to political and social change, through the "politics of rights," court decisions can be powerful tools in the battle for political mobilization and social change.

gatekeepers for the courts, seldom become aware of the problems of these people that the courts could fruitfully address. The second category includes those who cannot afford to retain counsel. While devices such as contingency fees, *pro bono publico* assistance, early legal aid societies, and in forma pauperis provisions have given some of those unable to pay lawyers' traditional hourly rates access to civil trial courts, historically few comparable mechanisms have provided legal assistance for civil appeals. Furthermore, the financial burden associated with appellate litigation prevents many of those who can afford trial court litigation from pursuing their civil claims further. The third category of people who are often unable to effectively participate in the judicial process because of their inability to retain counsel includes those who are, themselves, politically unpopular, or who espouse politically unpopular causes.[8] To the extent that the de facto assistance of counsel requirement works to deny these various categories of people access to the courts, the range of possible judicial choice is constrained.

## OVERCOMING THE LIMITS

Of course, anyone who has even a passing familiarity with Supreme Court doctrine can point to a number of cases brought by litigants who fall into at least one of these three categories. Occasionally, private attorneys' *pro bono* work has extended to Supreme Court litigation for poor clients or the Court has appointed counsel to represent a petitioner who filed in forma pauperis.[9] But, more often, the sociologically or psychologically alienated, the financially constrained, and the politically unpopular have been represented in the Court by interest groups that were using litigation as an instrument of reform.

### Interest Groups

The NAACP Legal Defense Fund's (LDF) attack on Plessy v. Ferguson, which culminated in Brown v. Board of Education, provides the prototype for such

[8] See Auerbach, *Unequal Justice*, pp. 241–58; Casper, *Lawyers Before the Warren Court*, esp. pp. 134, 172, 176, 180–84.

[9] Approximately half of the petitions filed with the U.S. Supreme Court each year are filed in forma pauperis. For these litigants, the filing fee and the requirement that multiple printed copies of the briefs be submitted are waived. In the 1980s about 80 percent of these petitions were filed by criminal defendants and prisoners and less than 1 percent were accepted for review. Frequently, these petitions are filed without the assistance of counsel. Consequently, the issues are generally perceived as either "trivial" or poorly framed. Baum, *The Supreme Court*, pp. 89–90. Occasionally, the Supreme Court will appoint counsel for litigants too poor to afford their own. During a five-year period running from 1983 through 1987, the Supreme Court appointed counsel in fifty-five cases. Appointed counsel represented the appellant/petitioner in only 30 percent (17) of the cases and only 13 percent (7) of the fifty-five cases were civil claims. Andreosky, "Appointment of Counsel."

group litigation and illustrates the role of interest groups in representing people burdened by the de facto counsel requirement. For a myriad of reasons, prior to 1954, most blacks were unlikely to see the courts as providing any solution to the problem of state-mandated segregation. Indeed, there was no "legal remedy" to this problem until the NAACP LDF created one through a series of Supreme Court test cases. NAACP LDF attorneys had to seek out and educate clients willing to participate in these cases. Even if blacks had seen their problems as amenable to a legal resolution, few would have been able to bear the financial burden of appellate litigation on their own. Further, even with the money to pay an attorney, it was extremely difficult for blacks to convince southern lawyers to represent them in court in any type of case, never mind one as politically unpopular as a challenge to segregation. It is hard to imagine the Supreme Court playing the seminal role in the development of civil rights policy that it has, if the NAACP LDF had not brought these issues to the Court. Indeed, even Plessy was sponsored by an interest group.[10]

Other groups have played similar roles in providing access to the Supreme Court and shaping the development of constitutional doctrine. The American Civil Liberties Union (ACLU) has a long history of supporting the legal claims of political dissidents. More recently, the ACLU has provided counsel to litigants through its special projects in such areas as juvenile rights, women's rights, prisoners' rights, military law, amnesty, abortion, and sexual privacy.[11] Various areas of constitutional law have developed largely at the invitation of litigants represented by organized interest groups. For example, Sorauf's examination of constitutional decisions on church-state separation describes the role of interest groups in bringing these cases to court, especially the ACLU, the American Jewish Congress, and Protestants and Other Americans United for Separation of Church and State.[12] O'Connor and Epstein found that women's rights groups, especially the ACLU Women's Rights Project, provided counsel in 29 percent of the sixty-three gender-based discrimination cases decided by the Burger Court during the 1969–1980 Terms.[13] Elsewhere, O'Connor and Epstein report that during the 1969–1980 Terms, interest groups sponsored 20 percent of the 1370 full opinion cases heard by the U.S. Supreme Court.[14] Studying an earlier era, 1957 to 1966, Casper

[10] Between 1930 and 1956 the LDF argued forty-two racial discrimination cases before the Supreme Court. See Hahn, "NAACP Legal Defense and Education Fund"; Kluger, Simple Justice; Tushnet, NAACP's; Greenberg, "Litigation for Social Change"; Vose, "Litigation"; Vose, Caucasians Only; Vose, Constitutional Change.

[11] Rabin, "Lawyers for Social Change"; Note, "Private Attorneys-General"; Cowan, "Women's Rights"; Halpern, "ACLU Chapters"; Donahue, The Politics of the American Civil Liberties Union; Dorsen, "The American Civil Liberties Union."

[12] Sorauf, Wall; see also Manwaring, Render Unto Caesar.

[13] The ACLU Women's Rights Project sponsored all but two of the twenty-eight cases brought by groups. O'Connor and Epstein, "Beyond Legislative Lobbying," p. 139.

[14] Of these 272 cases, 265 were sponsored by liberal groups and seven by conservative groups.

found that, outside the area of criminal justice, only five of the fifty-four attorneys who argued civil liberties and civil rights claims before the U.S. Supreme Court perceived themselves as primarily representing their particular client rather than a group or societal interest. Indeed, the majority of the remaining forty-nine attorneys were officially affiliated with a formal interest group.[15]

Generally, interest groups' provision of counsel to litigants is part of their larger attempts to influence the course of public policy. Interest groups, as their name would imply, tend to represent interests rather than clients. Interest groups' emphasis on achieving ideological or policy goals rather than providing representation to individual clients is reflected in their methods of participation in the judicial forum. The growing literature on interest groups' use of the courts reveals that the filing of amicus curiae, or friend of the court, briefs is their most common method of participation in Supreme Court decision making. While amicus briefs may influence the Court's decisions and serve as a participation vehicle, they do not involve the direct representation of clients. Groups provide counsel generally only when they believe that the control afforded by sponsorship is essential to achieving their broader goals and they have the financial resources to sustain protracted litigation. Historically, the most active and prominent interest groups before the Supreme Court, including the NAACP and ACLU, did not initially restrict their policy-oriented activity to litigation. Further, the emerging literature suggests that groups that are involved in a whole panoply of lobbying techniques are increasingly also participating in the judicial policy process.[16]

Studies of interest group litigation often rest on a characterization of courts as yet another arena for pluralist conflict. These studies frequently begin by

Although one would postulate that liberal groups would be more likely than conservative groups to represent the three categories of people who are most often excluded from court by the de facto counsel requirement, this remains an untested assumption. Of course, interest groups also participate in Supreme Court decision making through the filing of amicus curiae briefs. During the 1969–1980 Terms, groups participated either through sponsorship or through amicus filings in 49.3 percent of the cases decided. O'Connor and Epstein, "The Rise of Conservative Interest Group Litigation," pp. 481, 482.

[15] Casper, *Lawyers Before the Warren Court*, pp. 79, 156–63, 179–84.

[16] See especially Epstein, *Conservatives*; O'Connor, *Women's Organizations*; O'Connor and Epstein, "Amicus Curiae"; O'Connor and Epstein, "The Rise of Conservative Interest Group Litigation"; and O'Connor and Epstein, "Beyond Legislative Lobbying"; Gates and McIntosh, "Classical Liberalism"; Bruer, "Washington Interest Group"; Bruer, "Washington Organizations and Public Policy Litigation"; Olson, *Clients and Lawyers*; Rabin, "Lawyers for Social Change." Occasionally, interest groups are drawn into representing clients whose cases are not part of their litigation strategies. For instance, this was the case when the NAACP LDF represented defendants in the sit-in cases because there was no other source of counsel available. Such representation may be considered analogous to a private law firm's *pro bono publico* work. Hahn, "The NAACP Legal Defense and Education Fund."

tracing their intellectual history to Arthur Bentley and David Truman.[17] Group litigation is seen as an extension of pressure group politics, not as a device that broadens popular participation in government decision making. Interest group, and more broadly, public interest, litigation is defined by the group's conscious selection and pursuance of "socially desirable" goals rather than by whom they represent. Indeed, some commentators have questioned whether public interest lawyers really represent any client, in the traditional sense, and whether the clienteles' interests are really as homogeneous as they are presented by interest group lawyers.[18] Whether or not one accepts the full implications of these critiques, it is clear that interest groups do not function as traditional law firms minus the fee requirement.[19] This is not to suggest that there is something illegitimate about interest group litigation in a democratic regime. Indeed, it is perfectly appropriate and necessary in a system of democratic pluralism. In the courts and in the political branches, interest groups are important mechanisms for the aggregation of interests and provision of useful information to policy makers. Interest group activity supplements the ballot and provides the citizenry with an additional method of participation in governmental decision making. Group representation can best contribute to self-government when it accompanies, rather than replaces, direct participation by the people, either through voting or litigating.[20]

In providing representation in court, interest groups serve largely as "trustees" for their clientele rather than as "delegates" of their clients. While interest groups have expanded access to the Supreme Court and had a substantial effect on the development of Supreme Court doctrine, their representation of individual litigants burdened by the de facto assistance of counsel requirement is largely incidental to their pursuance of ideological or policy goals.

## The Legal Services Program

In the 1960s, the parameters of access to the U.S. Supreme Court changed substantially. American scholars and politicians rediscovered poverty and the War on Poverty was launched.[21] The poor, who had been largely excluded from the civil courts because they could not afford to hire an attorney, were provided with legal counsel through the federally-financed Legal Services Pro-

---

[17] Bentley, *The Process of Government*; and Truman, *The Governmental Process*. See especially Cortner, "Strategies and Tactics"; Epstein, *Conservatives*; O'Connor and Epstein, "Beyond Legislative Lobbying"; O'Connor and Epstein, "Amicus Curiae"; Olson, "Interest Group Litigation"; Vose, "Litigation."

[18] For example, see Breger, "Accountability," and sources cited therein; Bell, "Serving Two Masters."

[19] See Casper, *Lawyers Before the Warren Court*, p. 194.

[20] See Loomis and Cigeler, "Introduction"; Verba and Nie, *Participation*, esp. pp. 341–42.

[21] Patterson, *America's Struggle*, pp. 99–154. See also Heclo, "The Political Foundations of Antipoverty Policy."

gram (LSP). The LSP was established in 1965 as part of the Office of Economic Opportunity. Lawyers had come to be seen as important weapons in the War on Poverty. Like the other Great Society Programs, the LSP was a federal grant-dispensing agency. It provided funds to local Legal Services projects whose staff attorneys provided legal assistance to the poor in civil cases. As we will see, the distinctive development of the national Legal Services Program and the decentralization that characterizes grant-making agencies resulted in a Program that, in practice, mixed both individual client service and "law reform," particularly through appellate advocacy. Society's renewed interest in poverty resulted in an expansion of the poor's access to the U.S. Supreme Court. Through the LSP's representation of indigent litigants, the nation's newfound concern with the plight of the poor came to be mirrored in the Supreme Court's docket.

Unlike litigants represented by interest groups, LSP clients were accepted because they met the indigency requirements of the Program rather than because their cases fit into a litigation strategy. The LSP's representation of the poor was direct, rather than incidental to the pursuance of specified policy goals. It was closer to the "delegate" model of representation. Much like private attorneys providing vigorous counsel to paying clients, and unlike the earlier legal aid lawyers, LSP attorneys pursued their clients' cases through the court system, occasionally reaching the U.S. Supreme Court.

Before the mid-sixties, none of the interest groups that had occasionally represented indigent clients focused on poverty per se. As a result, the Supreme Court had been provided with few opportunities to develop civil poverty case law. The LSP's representation of the poor in appellate tribunals, including the U.S. Supreme Court, was largely responsible for the development of poverty law as a distinct legal subfield. A major law and poverty casebook published in 1969 cited only six Supreme Court cases decided before the LSP brought its first appeal during the 1966 Term.[22] During its nine-year tenure, 1965 through 1974, the LSP sponsored 164 cases before the Supreme Court, 119 of which were accepted for review. The eighty LSP cases that received plenary consideration represent 7 percent of all written opinions handed down by the Supreme Court during this era. Many LSP cases became important com-

[22] Dodyk, *Law and Poverty*. This case book (like the LSP) focuses primarily on civil law and therefore lists some, but not all, of the criminal cases that involved indigency related claims. There is no evidence that legal aid organizations participated in any of the six pre-LSP cases: Barrows v. Jackson (1953), granted third party standing in racially restrictive covenant cases; Edwards v. California (1941), struck down state criminal restriction on importation of indigents; Flemming v. Nestor (1960), declined to declare a right to Social Security payments; Mapp v. Ohio (1961), criminal proceedings; Shelley v. Kraemer (1948), restrictive covenants; and Sherbert v. Verner (1963), states may not apply unemployment eligibility provisions so as to constrain a worker to abandon his religious convictions respecting the day of rest. The Supreme Court decided its first LSP case, *Thorpe v. Housing Authority of the City of Durham* (1967) on 17 April 1967.

ponents in the Court's development of its due process and equal protection jurisprudence. The Supreme Court's first decision in favor of welfare recipients was an LSP case, *King v. Smith* (1968).[23] In 1969, the Supreme Court invalidated residency requirements for welfare recipients in a landmark case sponsored by the LSP, *Shapiro v. Thompson*. LSP attorneys had filed similar cases in over twenty jurisdictions. Prior to the establishment of the LSP, there had only been one reported constitutional challenge to these long-standing residency requirements in the lower courts, Heydenreich v. Lyons (1940), although it was estimated that at least one hundred thousand persons annually were denied aid because of residence laws.[24] The dearth of case law was not the result of a lack of legal problems among the poor, but rather, it was the result of their inability to retain counsel and their resulting de facto exclusion from the appellate courts.[25]

Supreme Court litigation was but a small part of the services provided by LSP attorneys, and, perhaps, from the perspective of the poor as a class, it was not the most important or helpful.[26] But, an examination of the LSP's Supreme Court litigation allows us to assess the effect of a change in the parameters of access to that forum on outcomes. The LSP significantly changed the distribution of access to legal counsel willing to pursue cases through the appellate courts to the U.S. Supreme Court. The LSP provided access to at least one of the categories of people burdened by the de facto counsel requirement—the poor. This book focuses on how poor litigants, represented by Legal Services attorneys, participated in and helped to shape Supreme Court decisions during the Program's nine-year tenure. How does a change in who litigates before the Supreme Court affect agenda setting and policy development in that institution

[23] Rosenblatt, "Legal Entitlements," p. 269. Throughout, LSP sponsored cases are set in italics for easy identification.

[24] Greenberg, "Litigation for Social Change," p. 362; Piven and Cloward, *Regulating the Poor*, p. 309. Also, prior to the establishment of the LSP the legality of "midnight searches" and "suitable home" policies had not been tested. Note, "Federal Judicial Review of State Welfare Practices," p. 86.

[25] The emergence of poverty law as an important subfield in the 1960s and early 1970s is further evidenced by the publication of several poverty law casebooks and the addition of poverty law courses and clinical programs to law school curriculums. In 1967, the LSP told Congress that at least thirty-six law schools had instituted courses on law and poverty and an estimated two hundred law schools were helping the LSP. Earl Johnson testified, "Two years ago there probably wasn't a law school in the country that offered a course in welfare law or legal problems of the poor." U.S. Congress, Senate, Committee on Labor and Public Welfare, *Legal Services Program of the Office of Economic Opportunity, Hearings before the Subcommittee on Employment, Manpower, and Poverty*. 91st Cong., 2d sess., 7 and 9 October 1970, p. 7. Law and poverty issues also received increased attention in established legal journals. In 1970, the *Index to Legal Periodicals* adopted "poverty law" as a separate subheading. In the mid-1960s the Commercial Clearinghouse began publishing a *Poverty Law Reporter*.

[26] For one sympathetic assessment of the LSP's contribution to social reform through litigation, see Johnson, *Justice and Reform*, pp. 192–224.

and what can that tell us about the processes of Supreme Court decision making?

## ASSESSING A CHANGE IN ACCESS TO THE COURT

To assess the importance and effect of the LSP's introduction of a new set of litigant claims to the Court, I view Supreme Court decision making as a process that begins with litigant petitions. I question the common assumption that the Court's vast discretion in case selection and its freedom from electoral accountability allow Supreme Court decision making to be explained exclusively, or even primarily, in terms of the justices' values and attitudes.[27] Judicial attributes are, of course, an important determinate of the Court's decisions. Though they affect which cases are selected for review and what decisions are reached, the traditional judicial behavior variables neglect the importance of the earlier portion of the Court's policy-making process. This study focuses on the importance of variations in the opportunities for decision placed before the justices.

My purpose is to evaluate the extent, effect, and content of the LSP's expansion of the poor's access to the Supreme Court. I examine why the LSP presented a wide range of opportunities for decision to the Court, how the LSP fared in the processes of Supreme Court decision making, and the role of the LSP's cases in the development of Supreme Court doctrine. I attempt to incorporate litigant claims into a comprehensive picture of the factors that influence Supreme Court decision making. I suggest some ways in which both litigant access and judicial decision making are affected by the political and social climate of the era, or the "temper of the times." Of course, given the difficulty of measurement, attempts to attribute judicial decisions to the prevailing political winds run the risk of tautology and post hoc explanation.[28] On the other

[27] Other works that challenge this assumption and look at the role of litigants and lawyers in presenting occasions or opportunities for decision include Casper's *Lawyers Before the Warren Court*; and Grossman, "A Model for Judicial Policy-Analysis."

[28] In studying some policy areas or in reference to some groups of litigants, some salient features of the "temper of the times" are measurable. For instance, congressional interest in controlling judicial policy making in an area through jurisdictional changes or constitutional amendment is measurable. For example, see Nagel, "Court-Curbing." However, precise measurement of the effect of even such overt responses is more difficult, though the biographies of justices certainly do suggest that such connections are sometimes made. See Howard, "Judicial Biography and the Behavioral Persuasion." The difficulty of attempting to statistically measure the effect of political climate on judicial decision making is illustrated by the attempts to correlate patterns of judicial decision making with realigning elections. See Adamany, "Law and Society: Realigning Elections and the Supreme Court"; Funston, "The Supreme Court and Critical Elections"; Beck, "Critical Elections and the Supreme Court"; Canon and Ulmer, "The Supreme Court and Critical Elections"; Lasser, "The Supreme Court in Periods of Critical Realignment." See also Dahl, "Decision-Making in a Democracy"; Casper, "The Supreme Court and National Policy Making." On lower court judges' responsiveness to local political climates, see Cook, "Sentenc-

hand, ignoring the environment in which the Supreme Court operates leads to the mistaken impression that it conducts its work in a vacuum. Such an approach misses much of the complexity of the interaction between our separate branches and the richness of judicial decision making.

I focus on the first national Legal Services Program because it marked the beginning of the poor's direct and substantial participation in the Supreme Court's civil docket. I limit my study to the LSP because, as described in chapters 2 and 3, the Program was the initiator of such litigation and was, far and away, the dominant poverty law litigator during this time period. Also, as shown in chapter 3, the LSP's decentralized structure and combining of the client server and reformer roles prevented the Program from implementing a litigation strategy and allowed it to represent poor clients rather than a group interest.

This study focuses on the LSP's Supreme Court litigation during the October Terms of 1966 through 1974.[29] The LSP brought its first case to the Supreme Court during the 1966 Term.[30] The 1974 Term coincided with the year between passage of the Legal Services Corporation Act and the Legal Services Corporation's (LSC) first board of directors meeting.[31] The Corporation (LSC) brought with it a fundamentally different attitude toward appellate litigation. While the national LSP actively advocated appellate challenges, the Corporation was, at best, lukewarm on the notion and did little to encourage local projects to pursue such litigation. By examining the LSP, one views legal services at its pinnacle and one sees the potential inherent in a move toward equalization of access to one of our policy-making forums.[32]

ing Behavior of Federal Judges''; Cook, ''Public Opinion and Federal Judicial Policy''; Cook, ''Judicial Policy''; Kritzer, ''Political Correlates of the Behavior of Federal District Judges''; Kritzer, ''Federal Judges and Their Political Environments''; Kuklinski and Stanga, ''Political Participation and Government Responsiveness.''

[29] The Legal Services Program was established, without explicit congressional authorization, as part of the Office of Economic Opportunity. The Program was launched with the appointment of its first director on 25 September 1965. Johnson, *Justice and Reform*, pp. 67–71. As early as mid-1973, the Legal Services Program issued new guidelines that stated, ''Law reform will no longer be a primary or separate goal of the program or the chief criterion in evaluating or refunding projects.'' *Poverty Law Reporter*, 2:9787. On 25 July 1974, President Nixon signed the Legal Services Corporation Act establishing the entity which replaced the LSP. The Corporation put considerably less emphasis on appellate litigation. In October 1975, the LSP officially ended, and the new Corporation took over the delivery of legal services to the poor. Johnson, *Justice and Reform*, pp. ix–xxiii; George, ''Development''; Champagne, ''Legal Services''; *Legal Services Corporation Act*, United States Code Annotated, 96th Cong., 2d sess., 1980, Title 42.

[30] *Thorpe v. Housing Authority of the City of Durham*, 386 U.S. 670 (1967). Decided 17 April 1967.

[31] 25 July 1975. The official transfer from the LSP to the Corporation occurred 90 days later, on 12 October 1975.

[32] To the contention that I have chosen the best case to demonstrate litigant influence, I plead mea culpa but with a caveat. Although I may have chosen one of the best cases, many have argued that the LSP does not provide a very good example of appellate advocacy. It lacked the organiza-

In examining the LSP, I seek to explain the Supreme Court's response to the poor's claims, rather than to retill ground covered by Earl Johnson's comprehensive history of the politics, administration, and demise of the LSP.[33] When relevant to my focus on the LSP's role in influencing the Supreme Court's agenda and its decisions on the merits, I draw on his work, as well as on the works of many other students of the Program's operation and its attorneys, especially Champagne; Finman; Handler, Hollingsworth, and Erlanger; Hannon; Katz; Krislov; Mayhew; Pious; Pye; Rothstein; and Wexler.[34] Since my purpose is to examine litigant influence on the Supreme Court's agenda and decisions, I do not document the law reform successes and failures of LSP attorneys in lower courts and in legislatures, nor do I attempt to evaluate the implementation and impact of the LSP's Supreme Court cases beyond the subsequent development of the doctrines by the Court. Rather, I focus on how the Supreme Court responded to changing parameters of access to its docket.

While my examination of the LSP's participation in Supreme Court decision making is but a study of one example of litigant participation and influence, I believe that the Program's Supreme Court litigation also merits attention in its own right. First, the Program's provision of counsel to indigents has important normative implications. Since we often defend the Court's counter-majoritarian character as a salutary device for the protection of minority rights, it is important to examine empirically how the Court responds to various minorities, here the economically disadvantaged, in its decision-making processes. Does the Court provide an alternate, more receptive, forum where those disadvantaged in the political process can succeed, or is some measure of success in the political branches necessary to command judicial attention?

Furthermore, while participation and access issues have often been central to our understanding of the electorally accountable branches, they are not without consequence in the judicial branch. Given the Supreme Court's policy-making role, it is important to consider how the LSP's expansion of access

---

tional attributes associated with group litigation success. See Epstein, *Conservatives*, pp. 9–15 and sources cited therein on factors that lead to interest group success. Furthermore, numerous students of the Program have concluded that the LSP failed to do enough law reform or bring enough test cases. See, for example, Pious, "Policy"; Hannon, "Law Reform"; Handler et al., *Lawyers*, p. 64; Finman, "OEO Legal Services"; and Champagne, "Internal Operation." Perhaps even more important, many commentators have concluded that the Supreme Court was ultimately unresponsive to poverty claims. See Bennett, "The Burger Court"; Law, "Economic Justice"; Rosenblatt, "Legal Entitlements"; Gunther, *Cases*, 11th ed., pp. 566–68, 578–85, 665–66, 670–87, 787–99, 830–54.

[33] Johnson, *Justice and Reform*.

[34] Champagne, "Internal Operation"; Finman, "OEO Legal Services"; Handler et al., *Lawyers*; Hannon, "Law Reform"; Hannon, "Murphy Amendments"; Hannon, "Leadership Problem"; Katz, "Lawyers for the Poor"; Katz, *Poor People's Lawyers*; Krislov, "The OEO Lawyers Fail"; Mayhew, "Institutions of Representation"; Pious, "Congress"; Pious, "Policy"; Pye, "Role of Legal Services"; Rothstein, "Myth of Sisyphus"; Wexler, "Practicing Law."

to the Court affected the development of constitutional doctrine. If we can show that changes in who has access to the Court and changes in who participates in Supreme Court decision making affects the Court's "authoritative allocation of values"—its decisions about "who gets what, when, how"[35]— then the case for considering litigation as a form of political participation is strengthened.

Second, the LSP's litigation provides a unique opportunity to supplement our understanding of Supreme Court decision making. The current literature predominantly focuses on the justices, their values, and the dynamics of their decision-making processes. To the extent litigant influence has been assessed, it has largely been studied through examinations of the organization and strategy of interest groups that have pursued policy change through the courts.[36] However, these groups focus on representing interests rather than clients. In contrast, the LSP's Supreme Court litigation efforts were an extension of its individual client service and proceeded without many of the resources for success identified in the literature. The LSP's Supreme Court cases were the result of uncoordinated efforts by various local projects and individual attorney-client interactions, making the cases a random collection of poor people's problems. Despite this lack of strategy and this lack of the organizational attributes associated with group litigation success, the Program's attorneys, taken collectively, enjoyed success rates unrivaled by other groups that have been studied. This phenomena suggests a need to examine whether our current understanding of interest group litigation and judicial decision-making processes can explain how and why certain classes of litigant claims receive favorable treatment from the Court. This work is part of such an exploration.

Third, the continuing debate over the proper role of government-funded legal services for the poor pits individual client service against law reform and appellate advocacy, insisting that we must choose between the two.[37] My examination of the LSP's participation in the Supreme Court's docket suggests that this debate rests, at least in part, on a false dichotomy. The Program's appellate cases were primarily an extension of its casework for individual clients. LSP attorneys mixed the client server and reformer roles of attorneys and thereby provided a kind of "delegate" representation in the courts. I evaluate the LSP's performance in terms of its ability to convince the Court to review and accept its client's claims rather than in terms of its ability to achieve the specific policy reform goals often attributed to it.

Furthermore, the current debate fails to recognize appellate litigation as a legitimate form of political participation by individuals, rather than simply an

---

[35] Easton, *The Political System*, pp. 136–37; Lasswell, *Politics*.

[36] Two major exceptions to this categorization are Casper, *Lawyers Before the Warren Court*; and Grossman, "A Model for Judicial Policy Analysis."

[37] See especially Breger, "Legal Aid for the Poor"; and Failinger and May, "Litigating Against Poverty."

extension of lobbying activities by groups. Once we acknowledge the role of the courts in enforcing, implementing, and developing government policy in response to litigant demands, as demonstrated in LSP cases, I believe that access to the courts must be considered part of the franchise in a democratic regime if we are to live up to our promise of political equality. By viewing appellate advocacy as an integral part of its individual client service, the LSP represented a step forward in that direction. It expanded the poor's ability to participate in one arena of governmental decision making.

This book examines the participation of LSP attorneys and clients in the Supreme Court's decision-making processes, both as a petitioner and as a respondent. It seeks to assess the Court's response to these claims in the context of the current literature on Supreme Court decision making and interest group litigation. Organizationally, it follows the chronological sequence of the Court's decision process. (Methodological considerations are outlined in Appendix A.) Chapter 2 briefly recounts the development of the Legal Services Program, examining how and why the LSP, unlike its legal aid predecessors, came to adopt a view of the attorney's role that blended client service and reform. Chapter 3 examines the LSP's inability to adopt and implement a litigation strategy and the serendipitous nature of the decisions to appeal to the Supreme Court, demonstrating that the LSP's involvement in Supreme Court litigation did not fit the reformer model of interest group litigation. The resulting heterogeneous mix of LSP sponsored cases placed before the Court is dissected. These cases are a much more diverse lot than the term "poverty law" suggests. Chapter 4 assesses the Program's success in the case selection process and explores the utility of our current understanding of case selection in explaining the Court's willingness to review almost three-fourths of the 164 LSP sponsored appeals. Chapter 5 compares the Court's decisions on the merits in LSP cases to the Court's usual response to the cases it selects for review in terms of case and litigant attributes commonly associated with success. Judicial support for the LSP and agreement among the justices in these cases is examined. Continuing an argument begun in Chapter 4, the Program's success is explained as a confluence of litigant claims, available legal bases, and judicial values joined by a political climate attentive to poverty and equality issues. Chapter 6 evaluates the role of LSP sponsored cases in the development of constitutional doctrine. It both reconciles the LSP's success rates with the traditional accounts that characterize poverty law as a failure and demonstrates that the LSP's cases were important (though not as seminal as some had hoped) components in the Court's development of its due process and equal protection jurisprudence. Chapter 7, the conclusion, presents a final assessment of the LSP's influence in the processes of Supreme Court decision making and affirms the importance of considering litigants, and the institutions that shape the parameters of access to the Court, in explaining judicial decision making and its role in a democratic polity.

# CHAPTER TWO

# Philosophies of Legal Assistance and Access to the Courts

AMERICAN COURTS function simultaneously as both conflict resolvers and law developers.[1] This duality is paralleled by two attorney roles—client server and reformer. For both courts and attorneys, these dichotomies are actually ends of a continuum; the roles are intertwined, but one can be emphasized over the other. To sketch out the extremes, an attorney can focus on serving the immediate needs of the client outside the courtroom where there is virtually no opportunity to affect law development. Or, at the other end of the continuum, he or she can emphasize reform to such a degree that the titular client is merely a means to acquire standing to present arguments for legal change to judges. More commonly, the choice is whether to seek the short-term or long-term good for the client—for example, a relatively favorable early settlement or a judicial ruling that the client may find useful in future situations as well.[2]

The attorney's decision to emphasize one role over the other has an effect on who has access to the appellate courts and the composition of the courts' opportunities for decision. While conflict resolvers engage in appellate litigation when it is necessary to vindicate the client's immediate interest, reformers will put a premium on acquiring authoritative appellate court rulings.[3] Indeed, there is evidence that over half of the civil rights and civil liberties cases that the Supreme Court has decided were argued by attorneys who saw themselves as emphasizing the reformer role.[4] To continue the analogy to the legislative

[1] See Council on the Role of Courts, "What Courts Do and Do Not Do Effectively."

[2] Galanter, "Why the 'Haves,' " suggests that infrequent court users, and the attorneys who represent them, will focus on expedient resolutions of their conflicts while frequent court users, and the attorneys who represent them, will be more likely to "play for the rules." Furthermore, the infrequent court users tend to be economic 'have nots' while the frequent users tend to be 'haves.'

[3] In studying attorneys who argued civil rights and civil liberties cases before the Supreme Court between 1957 and 1966, Casper found that attorneys who viewed litigation as primarily a method of conflict resolution tended to see themselves as primarily representing their particular client. Attorneys who viewed litigation as a method of producing social change tended to see themselves as representing a group or democratic principles as well as their client. Casper, *Lawyers Before the Warren Court*, esp. pp. 78–87, 191–98.

[4] Casper found that of the eighty-two attorneys he interviewed who had argued civil rights and civil liberties cases before the Supreme Court between 1957 and 1966, 58 percent (48) viewed the law as a mechanism for maintaining a democratic political system and for promoting social change. Fifty-one percent (42) of them also believed that the bar should play an active role in

process, a focus on immediate client service is analogous to a Congressman's constituency service activity. As we move toward the reform end of the continuum, the focus on serving the client through advocating some legal reform is analogous to the "delegate" model of representation and the far end of the continuum corresponds to the "trustee" model.[5]

While traditionally the two attorney roles are combined, especially in elite private law practice, in situations of limited resources there is a certain tension between the two. When organizations providing legal representation believe that they have to choose to allocate their resources to either the immediate client server role or to the reformer role, the organizations' philosophies, which are determined by the political and legal climates in which they operate and their funding sources, will influence which role they choose to emphasize. The history of organizations providing civil legal assistance to the poor illustrates the tension between the two attorney roles and demonstrates the influence of political and legal climates and financial sponsors on resolution of the tension. More important for our purposes, this history demonstrates the implications of yielding to one role over the other for the poor's access to appellate courts and, thereby, for the range of opportunities for conflict resolution and law development presented to the Supreme Court.

In this chapter, we will briefly discuss the political and legal climates and financial factors that lead the LSP's predecessors, the early legal aid societies, to adopt a philosophy that focused on serving the immediate needs of their poor clients and the implications of this choice for the distribution of access to appellate courts for those disadvantaged by the de facto assistance of counsel requirement. Then, we will turn to the political and legal climates and financial factors that lead to the development of new philosophies about the delivery of legal assistance to the poor in the 1960s. We will see how these influenced the development of the federally financed Legal Services Program, resulting in a Program that mixed the roles of client server and reformer and expanded access to the appellate courts for those burdened by the assistance of counsel requirement. In later chapters, we will see that the same political and legal climates that precipitated a change in philosophies regarding the delivery of legal assistance to the poor also influenced the Court's receptivity to the claims the LSP presented. In the next chapter, we will contrast the LSP's

---

shaping society through litigation. Most of the other attorneys were involved in criminal justice litigation and were often appointed by a court to represent the defendant. They tended to appeal to the Supreme Court as a means of assisting their clients in avoiding the stringent penalties of the criminal law. Casper, *Lawyers Before the Warren Court*, esp. pp. 80–89, 99–107. Of course, as discussed in chapter 1, many of the civil rights and civil liberties cases decided by the Supreme Court have been brought by interest groups that approach a pure version of the reformer model.

[5] This is not to minimize the problems of lawyer dominance that occur in both attorney roles. See Handler, *Social Movements*; Rosenthal, *Lawyer and Client*; Olson, *Client and Lawyer*. However, similar problems are also present in representation in the legislative setting. See Pitkin, *The Concept of Representation*; Fenno, *Home Style*.

participation in Supreme Court litigation to that of interest groups which approach a pure version of the reformer role. There we will provide further evidence that the LSP's Supreme Court litigation was a product of its blending of the client server and reformer roles. As a result of the distinctive development of the LSP, the Program directly expanded the poor's access to the Supreme Court, presenting the Court with the litigation of, rather than for, the poor.

## LEGAL AID: THE FORERUNNER

### A Brief History

In 1965, when the Legal Services Program was established, legal aid societies had been providing legal assistance to the poor in civil matters for nearly a hundred years. The nation's first experiment with legal aid was an outgrowth of the Reconstruction era Freedman's Bureau. Between 1865 and 1868, the Bureau retained private attorneys in the District of Columbia and some southern states to represent poor blacks in criminal and civil cases. During the last quarter of the nineteenth century, numerous private legal aid societies with charitable goals developed. The first was Der Deutsche Rechtsschutz Verein, established by the German Society in New York City in 1876 to discourage exploitation of newly arrived German immigrants. It later became the Legal Aid Society of New York. In 1886, the Women's Club of Chicago established "The Protective Agency for Women and Children," a legal aid program designed to reduce the number of "seductions and debaucheries of young girls under guise of proferred employment." In 1888, the Chicago Ethical Cultural Society established the Bureau of Justice, "the first true legal aid society open to people of any nationality or gender."[6]

By 1919, the first thorough study of legal aid in America, Reginald Heber Smith's *Justice and the Poor*, could report that there were legal aid societies in forty-one cities. Nationwide, $181,408 was spent annually on legal aid. Sixty-two full-time legal aid attorneys and 113 part-time attorneys provided legal assistance to the poor. Legal aid organizations handled a total of 117,201 cases in 1917. Smith, considering the then current situation inadequate, called for more funding and the establishment of a national organization of legal aid offices.[7]

Smith's *Justice and the Poor* caused a great deal of controversy in the private bar. Certain bar leaders were stirred, most notably future Chief Justice of the United States Supreme Court, Charles Evans Hughes. Largely at Hughes' instigation, the entire sixth session of the Forty-third Annual Convention of the American Bar Association (1920) was devoted to a panel on legal aid. The

---

[6] Johnson, *Justice and Reform*, pp. 4–5; Westwood, "Getting Justice for the Freedman"; Maguire, *The Lance of Justice*.

[7] Smith, *Justice and the Poor*.

Special Committee on Legal Aid was created, and Hughes was named chairman. In 1921, it became the ABA Standing Committee on Legal Aid. Smith served as chairman until 1937. In 1923, the National Association of Legal Aid Organizations (later renamed the National Legal Aid and Defender Association) was established.[8]

Legal aid continued to grow in the 1920s, but then, as charitable contributions dried up during the Depression, legal aid entered a period of stagnation that lasted through the 1940s. In 1949, Britain's establishment of a government-financed legal aid system that compensated private attorneys for the legal services they provided to indigents created renewed interest in America's charitable legal aid organizations. Fearing that the United States might adopt the British model, resulting in "socialization of the legal profession," many formerly apathetic local bar associations established legal aid societies supported by charitable donations. In 1950, the American Bar Association (ABA), responding to the political fears of the era and stressing Association control, came out strongly against any government role in providing legal aid.[9] Throughout the 1950s, legal aid societies remained private charitable institutions.

### Limited Access: Legal Aid as Client Server

As America ushered in the decade that would see the launching of a War on Poverty and the establishment of federally funded legal services for the poor, Emery A. Brownell updated his comprehensive 1951 survey of the availability of legal assistance for indigents, *Legal Aid in the United States*. He reported that, as of 1 June 1960, there were 209 legal aid offices providing civil legal assistance to the poor, 132 of which were staffed by salaried attorneys.[10] Extrapolating from Brownell's figures, we can estimate that these 209 legal aid offices served almost half a million clients in 1959 at a cost of just over $4 million.[11]

---

[8] Johnson, *Justice and Reform*, pp. 3–8; and Handler et al., *Lawyers*, pp. 17–22.

[9] Johnson, *Justice and Reform*, pp. 3–19; Egerton and Goodhart, *Legal Aid*, pp. 6–9; Maguire, "Poverty and Civil Litigation"; Smith, "Introduction." By 1949 many other countries including Scotland, Northern Ireland, Canada, New Zealand, South Africa, Australia, Queensland, New South Wales, Victoria, Tasmania, Austria, Belgium, and Sweden also had statutorily mandated some form of civil legal aid for indigents. Abel has put forth an economic explanation of the emergence of state supported legal aid and legal services in advanced capitalist states. Abel, "Law Without Politics."

[10] Brownell, *Legal Aid*; Brownell, *Supplement*, p. 10.

[11] Brownell was only able to obtain civil caseload data from 137 of the 209 legal aid offices. He reports that these 137 offices handled 306,166 cases in 1959, or an average of 2,235 per office. Multiplication of the per office average by the actual number of offices yields an estimated caseload of 467,115. Similarly, Brownell was only able to obtain financial data from 135 offices. He reports that these 135 offices had a combined operating cost of $2,783,000, or an average of

Clearly, legal aid societies provided some with legal assistance they could not afford otherwise. But the scope of the legal aid societies' work was limited. In 1960, 39 million people were poor by government's official definition.[12] According to Brownell's findings, only about 1 percent of these 39 million people annually received civil legal assistance from the legal aid societies.[13] In the early 1960s, legal aid's budget represented less than two-tenths of 1 percent of the total expenditures for legal services in the United States.[14] Legal aid's reliance on local charitable funding also limited the nature of its work. Many legal aid societies would not provide representation in divorce, bankruptcy, workmen's compensation, tort, or wage and money claim cases.[15]

Even among those who were served by legal aid societies, few received legal representation in the courts. Legal aid societies chose to emphasize the immediate client server role, and they often lacked the financial resources to even pursue trial court litigation. Brownell wrote, "It is always the aim to avoid litigation whenever possible and Legal Aid offices are notably successful in this." In the 1950s, only 6 percent of legal aid's cases involved "court work."[16] While 6 percent is within the range of reported litigation rates among the general population who consult lawyers,[17] it appears that only another 13 to 18 percent of legal aid's clients received any other type of legal assistance from legal aid lawyers. A full 76 percent of legal aid's cases were closed after a single consultation and sometimes a referral to another lawyer or a social service agency.[18]

---

$20,615 per office. Multiplication of the per office average by the actual number of offices yields an estimated cost of $4,308,535. Brownell, *Supplement*, pp. 10, 33, and 46.

[12] Patterson, *America's Struggle*, p. 100.

[13] It is unlikely that only 1 percent of the poverty population had a legal problem each year. For example, an ABA national survey published in 1977 found that persons in the lowest quintile of family income (less than $6,296 in 1973) reported having 3.8 legal problems during their lifetime. The ABA estimate is probably low for three reasons: (1) respondents were asked whether they had had a series of specific legal problems; (2) responses were based on recollection; and (3) the survey only captured problems that had been labeled as legal problems by the respondent. Curran, *The Legal Needs of the Public*, pp. 57, 70, 162–63.

[14] Carlin and Howard, "Legal Representation," p. 410.

[15] In 1959, 55 percent of legal aid's funding came from United Funds and community chests. Another 12 percent came from bar associations, 7 percent from tax funds, and 5 percent from clients. The remaining 21 percent came from "capital funds, contributions from the general public and foundation grants." Brownell, *Supplement*, pp. 62–63. Brownell, *Legal Aid*, pp. 71–76; Carlin and Howard, "Legal Representation," pp. 410–16.

[16] Brownell, *Legal Aid*, p. 187; Brownell, *Supplement*, pp. 42, 49–53.

[17] See Galanter, "Landscape of Disputes," pp. 18–32 and sources cited therein.

[18] These figures are especially peculiar in light of the sources of legal aid cases. In 1959, 12 percent of legal aid's caseload consisted of referrals from courts and lawyers, 11 percent from social service agencies, and 3 percent from labor unions or employers. We would expect these referrers' characterization of the client's problem as a legal problem to be fairly accurate. Brownell, *Supplement*, pp. 38–42.

Although 6 percent of legal aid's clients did enjoy access to the civil trial courts, only a very few were able to pursue their claims in the appellate courts. Legal aid attorneys showed little interest in the reformer role and appellate litigation. Brownell's comprehensive survey of legal aid provides no record of appellate litigation. Indeed, the word "appeal" never appears except in a reprinting of the National Legal Aid and Defender Association's Standards, number 14 of which reads, "Every Legal Aid organization should: . . . Undertake appeals to right palpable miscarriages of justice or, when costs are available, to establish useful principles."[19] At most, legal aid attorneys filed only a "handful" of civil appeals over the course of nearly one hundred years. Most important, from the perspective of assessing how parameters of access affect judicial outcomes in the U.S. Supreme Court, legal aid societies apparently never appealed a single client's case to the Supreme Court.[20] Legal aid did little to expand access to the appellate courts by mitigating the effect of the de facto assistance of counsel requirement.

Perhaps the lack of legal aid appeals is not so surprising. During most of legal aid's history, there were not many examples of reform-oriented litigation for the disadvantaged that could have served to alert legal aid attorneys to the potential gains that could be derived from appellate challenges.[21] The Supreme Court had only just begun to evince some concern for disadvantaged minori-

---

[19] Brownell, *Legal Aid*, pp. 156–58. Brownell does provide a favorable account of several legal aid societies' promotion of reform through legislation. Brownell, *Legal Aid*, pp. 192–94.

[20] Johnson, *Justice and Reform*, pp. 13–14. Johnson reports, "It is difficult to establish this sort of negative fact conclusively. However, Philip Murphy, former deputy executive director of the NLADA [National Legal Aid and Defender Association] reported that no legal aid case had reached the U.S. Supreme Court and there appears to be no reference to such a case in the many histories and surveys of the legal aid movement. Moreover, the staff of the New York Legal Aid Society, the oldest and largest, reported that agency had not appealed to the Supreme Court at any time before 1966." Johnson, *Justice and Reform*, pp. 337–38 n.22. See also Rosenblatt, "Legal Entitlements"; Silver, "How to Handle a Welfare Case"; U.S. Congress, Senate, Committee on Labor and Public Welfare, *Legal Services Program of the Office of Economic Opportunity, Hearings before the Subcommittee on Employment, Manpower, and Poverty*. 91st Cong., 2d sess., October 1970; U.S. Congress, House, Committee on Health, Education, and Welfare, *Establishment of a Legal Services Corporation, Hearings before the Subcommittee on Education and Labor, on HR 3147, HR 3175, and HR 3409*. 93d Cong., 1st sess., February and March 1973; Hannon, "Leadership Problem"; Handler et al., *Lawyers*, p. 19; Note, "Neighborhood Law Offices." Casper, in his study of attorneys who argued civil liberties and civil rights cases before the Supreme Court between 1957 and 1966, reports that only one attorney was affiliated with a legal aid society and he argued a criminal justice appeal. Casper, *Lawyers Before the Warren Court*, pp. 89, 143.

[21] The NAACP LDF's efforts were not yet highly publicized. The American Liberty League did not provide a suitable model since it had convinced the Court to strike down legislation advantageous to workers. The National Consumers' League joined government in defending legislation; it did not seek reform through the courts. Even the academic community did not seem to recognize the importance and potential of group litigation for the disadvantaged until the 1950s. See Vose, "Litigation."

ties.[22] Further, the law was generally not seen as playing a role in the creation or maintenance of an economically disadvantaged class. In the popular mind, it was economic depressions or individual laziness that caused poverty, and it was economic growth and hard work that would raise people out of poverty.[23] The law itself treated the rich and poor equally. The administration of the legal system simply needed some fine tuning to extend equal justice to the indigent.

The philosophy of the legal aid societies came largely from bar leaders who "were shocked by the deprivation of due process caused by poverty," rather than being inclined to view the law itself as in need of reform.[24] As Reginald Heber Smith, the grandfather of legal aid, wrote: "The body of the substantive law, as a whole, is remarkably free from any taint of partiality. . . . [I]t is instantly apparent that the legal disabilities of the poor in nearly every instance result from defects in the machinery of the law and are not created by any discriminations of the substantive law against them."[25] If the law itself was fair, and it was simply the absence of legal counsel that made its operation unfair, then the poor did not need precedent-setting appellate court decisions; they just needed legal aid's preventative legal counseling, occasional settlements, and rare trial court appearances.[26]

## THE TRANSITION TO THE LEGAL SERVICES PROGRAM

In the early 1960s, others outside the legal aid movement and the organized bar began to question the substantive fairness of the laws governing the poor. As poverty was rediscovered and reexamined through new lenses, activists came to view destitution as anomalous and immoral in an affluent society that seemingly could afford to abolish poverty. They sought to reform the institutions that prevented a substantial proportion of the population from benefiting from the nation's economic progress.[27] The NAACP LDF's recent civil rights victories provided a vivid example of how appellate litigation could produce such social reform for disadvantaged groups.[28] The Supreme Court, in such widely publicized cases as Gideon v. Wainwright (1963), had begun to address poverty issues. Perhaps lawyers had a role to play in the new War on

[22] In retrospect, it is apparent that the Court had announced that it would turn its attention to "discrete and insular minorities" and Bill of Rights' guarantees in Justice Stone's famous 1938 Carolene footnote, but up through the mid-1950s the Court received only a few cases that raised these issues. Pacelle, "The Supreme Court and the Growth of Civil Liberties."

[23] Patterson, *America's Struggle*, esp. pp. 78–96.

[24] Johnson, *Justice and Reform*, pp. 12–13; Handler et al., *Lawyers*, pp. 19–22.

[25] Smith, *Justice and the Poor*, pp. 13–14, 15, quoted in Johnson, *Justice and Reform*, p. 13. See also Smith, "Introduction."

[26] See Brownell, *Legal Aid*, pp. 45–52, 179–88.

[27] Patterson, *America's Struggle*, pp. 99–114, esp. p. 113.

[28] Handler calls the NAACP LDF model "the single most important influence in the development of OEO Legal Services." Handler et al., *Lawyers*, pp. 22–29.

Poverty. Some thought so, and in 1965 the Office of Economic Opportunity launched the first nationwide, federally funded, legal assistance program for the poor—the Legal Services Program.

Earl Johnson, Jr., the Program's second director, has published an extensive and thorough account of the formation, establishment, and management of the national LSP, *Justice and Reform: The Formative Years of the American Legal Services Program*. The history he presents, briefly summarized here, provides a detailed account of the "personalities and forces, the decisions and negotiations" that resulted in a Legal Services Program that greatly expanded the poor's access to the civil courts.[29] The Program that developed was more aggressive than legal aid, yet it retained the societies' commitment to representing clients rather than adopting the interest group model of representing interests through litigation. The LSP mixed the client server and reformer roles. The Program was not specifically designed to pursue precedent-setting Supreme Court litigation, but by decreasing the burden of the de facto assistance of counsel requirement on the poor and by adopting a policy that encouraged appellate litigation, LSP attorneys ultimately represented a significant number of poor clients in Supreme Court litigation.

### New Forms and New Philosophies

As was the case with many of the Great Society Programs, the genesis of the LSP can be traced to experimental projects funded by the new foundation philanthropy of the late 1950s and early 1960s.[30] These new sources of funding, most notably the Ford Foundation's Grey Areas Program and the President's Committee on Juvenile Delinquency, which sponsored Mobilization for Youth (MYF) in New York City, allowed experimentation with new forms and philosophies of providing legal assistance to the poor. In New Haven and Washington, D.C., lawyers were added to the Ford Foundation's neighborhood social service centers. These centers sought to assist the "financially and educationally incapacitated citizen" by providing coordinated "social, economic, educational, and legal services for the individual family as a unit and for the neighborhood with high concentrations of families in crisis."[31] Lawyers involved in these centers quickly learned that aggressive client representation was not always possible when legal services were administratively combined with other social services. In New York, MYF took a different approach, creating a legal services unit in cooperation with Columbia University. The Director of the legal unit, Edward Sparer, with the assistance of social welfare planner Elizabeth Wickenden, focused on using test cases to achieve reform

[29] Johnson, *Justice and Reform*, p. xxx.

[30] Moynihan, *Maximum Feasible Misunderstanding*, pp. 21–101.

[31] Community Progress, Inc., *Proposal*, pp. 2–3, quoted in Johnson, *Justice and Reform*, p. 26.

in public housing, housing code enforcement, unemployment insurance, and welfare. Adopting the reformer model of interest group litigation dramatized by the NAACP LDF's success in Brown v. Board of Education, MYF referred clients with traditional or routine civil law problems to New York's Legal Aid Society.[32]

It was experience with these new legal assistance agencies, rather than with the legal aid societies, that provided the impetus for the establishment of the Office of Economic Opportunity's Legal Services Program. These new agencies conceived of legal services as part of a broad attack on poverty, not merely as a due process corrective in the administration of justice. As Johnson's history reveals, the crucial link between these experiments with legal services and the design of the War on Poverty was an early draft of a *Yale Law Journal* article by Edgar and Jean Cahn.[33]

The Cahns had been very involved in developing the first New Haven neighborhood multiservice center and Jean Cahn was one of the two lawyers employed by the center in 1963.[34] Drawing on this experience, their influential *Yale Law Journal* article called for the establishment of "university affiliated, neighborhood law firm[s] . . . [to] represent persons and interests in the [poverty] community with an eye towards making public officials, private service agencies, and local business interests more responsive to the needs and grievances of the neighborhood."[35] The Cahns viewed the provision of legal services to the poor as a method of "vesting in the citizenry the means and the effective power wherewith to criticize, to shape, and even to challenge the actions or proposed actions of officials," especially those government officials that would be fighting the new War on Poverty. Representation by counsel would provide the poor with a tool for the constructive exercise of political power in those areas that effect them most. In the Cahns' proposal, providing access to appellate courts was just one of a variety of suggested "means of revitalizing the democratic process by providing representation in those forums of decision making where legislators, elective and non-elective, and where judges, frocked and unfrocked, hand down the common law of the poor." The role of the indigent's lawyers described by the Cahns was very different from the placid approach of the legal aid attorney.[36] Attorneys would

[32] Johnson, *Justice and Reform*, pp. 22–25; Handler et al., *Lawyers*, p. 30.

[33] Johnson, *Justice and Reform*, pp. 21–35; Handler et al., *Lawyers*, pp. 29–31; Cahn and Cahn, "War on Poverty." Both Cahns were attorneys; Edgar Cahn also had a Ph.D. in political science.

[34] Johnson, *Justice and Reform*, pp. 22–23.

[35] Cahn and Cahn, "War on Poverty," p. 1334.

[36] Ibid., pp. 1330, 1334, 1344. In the summer of 1964, Edgar Cahn met with MYF director Edward Sparer, but in composing both the *Yale* article and the proposal for the Washington, D.C. Neighborhood Legal Services Project, Cahn rejected Sparer's "narrow" test case approach. Johnson, *Justice and Reform*, pp. 30–31.

aggressively serve their clients' short- and long-term interests by adopting the "delegate" reformer role in and out of court.

The Cahns' article did not call for a federally funded legal assistance program, but when the authors moved to Washington and began circulating a draft among friends and associates, the idea was adopted by a group of well-placed Washingtonians intrigued by the Cahns' proposal. Edgar Cahn secured a position as special assistant to Sargent Shriver who was heading the Presidential task force on poverty. Shortly after Shriver was named director of the new Office of Economic Opportunity late in the summer of 1964, Edgar Cahn convinced him to establish a special committee to consider the role of lawyers in the War on Poverty. This committee was composed largely of members of that early group that had coalesced around the Cahns' article.[37]

## Launching the LSP

On 12 November 1964, at an HEW conference on the new experimental legal assistance programs, Edgar Cahn announced that OEO had decided to establish a national legal services program to be developed and coordinated by Jean Cahn. However, Jean Cahn's tenure ended less than six months later when she resigned on 1 April 1965 because Shriver failed to assure her that she, rather than the Community Action Program (CAP) with OEO, would have final authority over legal services grants. With her went an institutionalized commitment to the development of neighborhood law offices as part of a series of coordinated social services designed to "rescue" families from poverty.[38]

The OEO's decision to launch a major federally funded Legal Services Program was made without consulting the National Legal Aid and Defender Association (NLADA), the national organization of legal aid societies that had been serving the poor for almost one hundred years. Indeed, the NLADA was so insulted by the criticism leveled against legal aid at the November HEW conference that the NLADA Executive Committee adopted a resolution opposing the "creation of separate, duplicating agencies to offer legal services under Economic Opportunity programs," suggesting that such agencies "will be more costly and less effective than will the proper use of existing facilities."[39] The NLADA was not being paranoid; those advocating an OEO legal assistance program repeatedly characterized legal aid as "deficient in manpower, qual-

[37] This early group of supporters included: Abram Chayes, a legal advisor at the State Department and Jean Cahn's supervisor at the time; Antonia Chayes, Abram's wife and an attorney; Adam Walinsky, a top speech writer and idea man for Robert Kennedy; Dr. Len Duhl, a psychiatrist at the National Institutes of Mental Health; and Gary Bellow, deputy director of Washington's public defenders' office. Johnson, *Justice and Reform*, pp. 40–43.

[38] Johnson, *Justice and Reform*, pp. 47, 65, 128.

[39] National Legal Aid and Defender Association, Executive Committee, *Resolution*, 16 December 1964, quoted in Johnson, *Justice and Reform*, p. 49.

ity, and philosophy.'' These advocates were committed to creating new institutions with new approaches to the delivery of legal services. They sought to bypass the legal aid societies and fund new agencies that would seek out the poor and their legal problems, reshape their legal and political relationships, and thereby increase their power and, perhaps, decrease their destitution.[40] The impetus for federally funded legal services came, not from the legal aid movement, but from these advocates. From their perspective, legal aid had already shown itself to be unable to address the problem of poverty in an affluent society.

The American Bar Association (ABA) was less insulted by these critiques of legal aid, although it had been a longtime supporter of the societies. According to Johnson, what did alarm the ABA was a November 1964 speech by Shriver that was interpreted as an indication that OEO intended to use laymen to deliver legal services to the poor. Concerned and curious about what OEO was contemplating, ABA leaders began to meet with Edgar and Jean Cahn late in 1964. By the time Jean Cahn resigned in April 1965, she had forged what would come to be a powerful alliance between the ABA and the new Legal Services Program. The inevitability of some kind of OEO legal assistance program and the visionary and skillful leadership of ABA President Lewis Powell, led to a unanimous ABA House of Delegates resolution endorsing the LSP in February 1965, despite the ABA's earlier opposition to government funding of legal services. The Cahns' desire to insure that the LSP would obtain autonomy within OEO and the need to enlist local bar association support for the neighborhood offices, both to preempt hostile actions from the bar itself and to serve as a shield from the community pressure that occasionally threatens attorneys' vigorous representation of their indigent clients interests, led the Cahns to cautiously negotiate with the ABA for its support. The ABA was promised a place on the LSP's permanent National Advisory Committee. As a result, the ABA obtained a voice in the development of the LSP and assurance that the Program would be under lawyer control. The LSP obtained a powerful source of support that could be called upon when disputes arose within OEO and when battles needed to be fought in Congress.[41]

One of the first decisions the ABA participated in was the selection of a Legal Services director to replace Jean Cahn. ABA President Lewis Powell brought the NLADA's leadership into the process. Indeed, it was the NLADA's Washington counsel, Howard Westwood, who nominated the man who became the first official director of the LSP on 24 September 1965, Clinton Bamberger. Bamberger had virtually no experience with either legal aid or the experimental legal services agencies that had provided models for the proponents of the LSP. As a 39-year-old trial attorney with Baltimore's largest firm, Piper and Mar-

---

[40] Johnson, *Justice and Reform*, pp. 45–52.
[41] Ibid., pp. 42–64.

bury, he arrived without a commitment to either perspective. With Jean Cahn relegated to mere membership in the National Advisory Committee and the ABA having extracted few substantive promises about the structure and goals of the LSP, development of the Program and its mission was largely left to Bamberger.[42]

Like Bamberger, the national LSP staff he recruited had little experience with legal aid or with the new reform-oriented legal services projects. The one exception was Earl Johnson, Jr., whom Bamberger selected as deputy director and who would become the LSP's second director in the summer of 1966 when Bamberger resigned to run for Maryland Attorney General. At the time of his appointment to the LSP, Johnson was deputy director of one of the experimental legal services agencies, the Washington Neighborhood Legal Services Project, but, like Bamberger, his appointment was also endorsed by NLADA's Washington counsel, Howard Westwood.[43] By and large, the LSP's national staff was drawn from elite private practice or government; they had few strongly held beliefs about the role of lawyers serving the poor. They brought with them both a traditional conception of the elite lawyer's role in representing well-paying clients and a sensitivity to federally funded agencies' need to cultivate political support.

When Bamberger accepted the directorship of the LSP, it had yet to fund its first local LSP project. Within weeks, Bamberger and Johnson began drafting criteria for awarding LSP grants that would be published in 1966 as *Guidelines for a Legal Services Program*. These guidelines were the major policy statement of the LSP and as such, they were subject to approval by the National Advisory Committee. This committee did have substantial experience with the competing philosophies of legal assistance. It included NLADA leaders, Jean Cahn and others associated with the neighborhood lawyer experiments, and ABA leaders.[44] Just before publication of the *Guidelines*, a provision was added that stated:

> Advocacy of appropriate reforms in statutes, regulations, and administrative practices is a part of the traditional role of the lawyer and should be among the services afforded by the program. This may include judicial challenge to particular practices and regulations, research into conflicting or discriminatory applications of laws or administrative rules, and proposals for administrative and legislative changes.[45]

The appropriateness of appellate advocacy was noted, but it was not highlighted. Reform was simply acknowledged as part of the traditional attorney

---

[42] Westwood had earlier been involved in developing the Washington, D.C. Neighborhood Law Office Program, Johnson, *Justice and Reform*, pp. 67–70, 94.

[43] Johnson, *Justice and Reform*, pp. 72, 94, 98.

[44] Ibid., pp. 106–7.

[45] *Guidelines for Legal Services Programs* (1966), pp. 21, 23, quoted in Johnson, *Justice and Reform*, p. 116.

role. As the final revision was circulated to the National Advisory Committee, Johnson reports that no one objected to this addition.[46]

Realizing the fickleness of political support and monetary commitments, Bamberger sought to create a full-fledged, functioning, LSP as rapidly as possible. Johnson's account reveals that this meant issuing grants to local LSP projects across the nation before the Program's own philosophy and goals were completely developed. Lacking the hostility to legal aid that characterized some of the early proponents of an OEO legal assistance program, Bamberger tried to convince the existing legal aid societies to commit to reform goals and apply for LSP grants. In addressing the 1965 NLADA convention, Bamberger explained, "The role of [the] OEO program is to provide the means within the democratic process for the law and lawyers to release the bonds which imprison people in poverty, to marshal the forces of law to combat the causes and effects of poverty."[47] Bamberger also sought the support of local bar associations. Under the LSP *Guidelines* and congressional statute, local bar associations were required to participate in the drafting of LSP grant applications and serve on the local projects' board of directors along with other lawyers, middle class laymen, and representatives of the poverty community.[48]

Conversions and compromises were achieved. By 30 June 1967, the LSP had issued over $40 million in grants to three hundred agencies in over 210 communities. Virtually all of the grants were made before the national LSP had resolved the questions of *how* lawyers were supposed to combat poverty, through the client server or reformer role. Moreover, despite all the early criticism of legal aid, nearly 40 percent of the LSP grants went to modified legal aid societies. Few additional LSP projects would be funded after 1967 as OEO saw its popularity wane and its budget syphoned off to the Vietnam War effort.[49]

The new legal services proponents had not succeeded in implementing the Cahns' neighborhood law office proposal, but their advocacy had disrupted the status quo and challenged the bar and legal aid to reexamine and revise their view of legal services for the poor. And, the infusion of federal funds greatly increased the resources committed to legal assistance. In 1959, roughly $4 million had been spent on funding 209 civil legal aid offices whose 292 full- and part-time salaried attorneys provided services to almost half a million clients.[50] In fiscal year 1971, the LSP spent $61.2 million on funding 265 Legal Services projects with 934 offices. These projects em-

[46] Johnson, *Justice and Reform*, pp. 105–16. See also Pye, "Role of Legal Services."

[47] Bamberger, "Address to NLADA Annual Meeting," pp. 17–22, quoted in Johnson, *Justice and Reform*, p. 75

[48] Johnson, *Justice and Reform*, pp. 79–82.

[49] Ibid., pp. 70–102, 126ff.

[50] Brownell, *Supplement*, pp. 10, 33, 46.

ployed over 2,500 full-time staff attorneys who handled over one million cases annually.[51]

The structure and size of these 265 local Legal Services projects varied a great deal. They all retained full-time staff attorneys and were overseen by a board of directors which had "control over hiring, establishing eligibility requirements and general operating policies."[52] These boards consisted of representatives of the poor, middle class laymen representing concerned community groups, members of the local bar, and other attorneys.[53] Most projects had multiple offices located in poor neighborhoods. A few projects, as in Chicago, designated a particular office to focus on reform and appellate litigation.[54] Later, as the Program developed, it funded a dozen national "back-up centers" that provided research, training, and support to local project attorneys. Occasionally these centers filed cases themselves, but the centers were not directly involved in client service.[55] As Johnson describes the results of the first wave of funding that ended in 1967, "the median agency fit the following profile: an annual budget of $177,000, three neighborhood offices, a staff of seven attorneys, three clerical personnel and one community worker."[56]

To a large extent, during the first year and a half, the LSP operated within the standard OEO rhetoric of decentralization and local control.[57] The *Guidelines* allowed a wide variety of activities and insisted that "[p]olicy for the [local] legal assistance program must be formulated with the participation of the 'residents of the areas and members of the groups served' . . . [by] an autonomous policy-making board separate from the governing body of the community action agency."[58] In other words, at the local level, the boards were in charge. Johnson reports that policy making by the national LSP was incremental and cumulative, made in response to specific issues as they arose. No single method or goal was imposed on LSP grantees; consequently, many of them "set out to accomplish a vast assortment of goals and to cure legal aid of an almost inexhaustible accumulation of real and imagined deficiencies."[59]

---

[51] U.S., The Office of Economic Opportunity, "The Legal Services Program," 1971.

[52] Champagne, "Internal Operation," p. 656.

[53] Nationwide, 55 percent of the board members were attorneys. Johnson, *Justice and Reform*, p. 100.

[54] Katz, *Poor People's Lawyers*, p. 67.

[55] Johnson, *Justice and Reform*, pp. 181–82. The role of these centers in Supreme Court litigation will be discussed more fully in chapter 3 when we examine how closely the LSP fit the pure reformer role.

[56] Johnson, *Justice and Reform*, pp. 99–100. See also Note, "Neighborhood Law Offices."

[57] Krislov, "The OEO Lawyers Fail"; Hannon, "Law Reform"; Hannon, "Murphy Amendments"; Johnson, "Refutation"; Johnson, *Justice and Reform*, pp. 104–26, 173–76; Cahn and Cahn, "What Price Justice; Note, "Beyond the Neighborhood Office."

[58] *Guidelines for Legal Services Programs*, p. 11, quoted in Johnson, *Justice and Reform*, pp. 321–22. See also Hannon, "Law Reform," and "Leadership Problem."

[59] Johnson, *Justice and Reform*, pp. 116–27.

*Selecting and Implementing a Role*

The evaluations of local programs that began in July 1966 revealed the price of the national Program's ambiguity about goals and convinced LSP leaders that a national priority had to be set. Local offices were inundated with clients requesting traditional casework help, forcing attorneys to abdicate a role in promoting fundamental social and economic reform. There was no agreement on how LSP attorneys should go about reducing poverty. The crisis of "too many clients and too many goals," led LSP leaders to fear that the Program was in danger of becoming just a larger version of legal aid, providing due process justice to the poor without increasing the substantive justice of the legal system. As OEO Director Sargent Shriver wrote, "Equal justice cannot be accomplished by solving the problems of the poor on a case-by-case basis. There are too many problems, too few attorneys, and too many cases in which there is no solution given the present structure of the law, a structure which to a large extent the poor had absolutely no hand in building."[60]

Four different strategies vied for the allegiance of LSP leaders in the winter of 1967. Then director of the LSP, Earl Johnson,[61] outlined them as follows:

1. Social rescue—participation in coordinated social services designed to "rescue" low-income family units from poverty.
2. Economic development—the creation and operation of credit unions, laundromats, co-op grocery stores, housing projects, and other business enterprises designed to bring more money into the low-income community.
3. Community organization—a concerted drive to organize poor people into groups that could exert pressure in the political and private economic spheres.
4. Law reform—test cases, legislative advocacy and other techniques directed toward causing changes in the laws and practices which formed the social and economic structure of poverty.[62]

Johnson reports that the three criteria used by the LSP leadership led to the selection of law reform as the Program's top priority. The first criterion was "the comparative effectiveness of each strategy in providing benefits to the largest number of low-income people." The primary concern was serving the "greatest number of people"; the "greatness" of the "good" provided seemed less important. Perhaps more significant, exactly what constituted

[60] Ibid., p. 127. Shriver, "Law Reform." See also Note, "Neighborhood Law Offices."

[61] Bamberger had resigned 28 June 1966 to run for Attorney General in Maryland. On 29 June Johnson was named acting director, and on 2 October 1966 he was named permanent director. Johnson, *Justice and Reform*, pp. 94–99.

[62] Johnson, *Justice and Reform*, pp. 128–32. Johnson also discusses the merits and demerits of each of these four options. The first was basically the Cahns' "civilian perspective" prescription. Cahn and Cahn, "War on Poverty." The LSP primarily focused on test cases and appellate advocacy rather than legislative lobbying. See Hazard, "Law Reforming"; Johnson, *Justice and Reform*, pp. 185–234.

"benefits to . . . low income people" was not specified. This question was never resolved. As a result, the LSP attorneys who took cases to the Supreme Court simultaneously pursued diverse "goods." The second criterion was "the relevance of a lawyer's special skills and training." With their elite private practice experience, the LSP's leaders were familiar and comfortable with client service that included law reform. Appellate advocacy had "deep roots in the ideals of the legal profession." The leaders saw law reform as the best strategy for LSP attorneys because it "fully employ[ed] the lawyer's skills and training," not because it would necessarily be the most effective method of reducing poverty. The third criterion was "political feasibility." Political compromise played an important role in establishing law reform as the LSP's policy priority. The LSP's priorities had to be acceptable to the Program's diverse coalition of supporters, particularly the legal aid proponents and the veterans of the neighborhood lawyer experiments. Appellate advocacy was one part of the lawyer's traditional role that combined service and reform.[63]

Law reform was formally announced as the Program's "priority management goal" on 17 March 1967. A great effort was made to assure legal aid forces that LSP was "not suddenly abandoning their [legal aid's] primary goal of extending due process justice to the multitude." But, with the limited managerial powers of a federal grant-making agency, the LSP urged local projects and attorneys to seek change in the laws that deprived the poor of substantive justice as well.[64]

The national LSP used five tactics to promote law reform activity among local LSP attorneys. First, the national LSP, with the assistance of the leaders of the national bar, campaigned to persuade local attorneys and directors of the importance and appropriateness of appellate advocacy. Second, annual evaluations of local programs were used to "reorient" programs that were not involved in law reform. Grant termination was threatened as the ultimate sanction.[65] Third, the national LSP engaged in various activities designed to en-

· [63] Johnson, *Justice and Reform*, pp. 128–31. LSP attorneys probably did perceive litigation as the best way to secure the rights of the poor. See Scheingold, *The Politics of Rights*, esp. pp. 170–219; Handler et al., *Lawyers*, p. 5; Brill, "Uses and Abuses." Cf. Wexler, "Practicing Law."

[64] Johnson, *Justice and Reform*, pp. 131–32, 163–67. See Hannon, "Law Reform"; Hannon, "Leadership Problem."

[65] These annual evaluations were conducted by three-person teams who spent three days in each community investigating the local legal services projects. Former LSP director Johnson reports that they interviewed "staff and board members, local judges and lawyers, CAA personnel, representatives of the client community and anyone else who might provide information about the agency and its activities." Usually these teams prepared a report for the national LSP staff, and usually the staff sent the project an evaluation letter. Johnson concludes, "Not the evaluation itself, but the follow-up stage was critical: a firm recommendation for change, delivered orally or in an official letter, coupled with a threat of grant termination, then a series of personal negotiations by an OEO staff member, and a final settlement between the Legal Services office and the agency board. Although it was a time-consuming process, it usually worked relatively well, and,

courage local LSP attorneys to pursue law reform regardless of the predisposi- tions of their local boards and directors.[66] Fourth, the LSP established the Reginald Heber Smith Fellowship Program that recruited high-caliber legal talent, provided training in poverty law, and sent its fellows on year-long in- ternships with local projects where their "mission was to undertake activities calculated to have a broad effect on the problems of poverty."[67] And finally, the national Program funded a dozen national back-up centers specializing in specific areas of the law modeled on the Columbia Center for Social Welfare Policy and Law that Edward Sparer had originally established with MYF fund- ing. These centers furnished training and research materials to local attorneys. Back-up center attorneys sometimes acted as co-counsel with local attorneys or took a case over completely. They could also initiate a suit when they be- lieved it would be a significant test case.[68] But, as we will see, at the Supreme

---

as a result, almost a dozen weak directors were replaced between January 1, 1967 and July 1, 1968. Restrictive policies discouraging law reform were abolished in a score of agencies, and other significant modifications were made in several others." According to Johnson, because the national LSP was reluctant to deprive the locality's poor of their "sole source of legal help," the grant termination option was "little more than a bluff." However, the Program did reallocate funds, decreasing the budgets of agencies receiving unfavorable evaluations and increasing the budgets of those who received favorable evaluations. Johnson, *Justice and Reform*, pp. 173–84.

In contrast, Finman reports that the LSP's evaluators were insufficiently attentive to the project promoters' ideology, which he found to be the most significant factor determining a project's law reform activity. Finman, "OEO Legal Services Programs," pp. 1079–84. The LSP also funded two outside evaluations of local projects in 1970. One was conducted by the Auerbach Corpora- tion, the other by the John D. Kettle Corporation. The results of these two studies are summarized in Champagne, "Internal Operation."

[66] These activities included publication of a newsletter that provided attorneys involved in law reform successes with national publicity; establishment of a national clearinghouse of legal mem- oranda and pleadings in law reform cases and publishing a monthly summary of these in the Program's journal, *Clearinghouse Review*; creation of a national training program; information dispersion and research by the back-up centers; and establishment of a Project Advisory Group that gave some local attorneys a voice in national policy making. Johnson, *Justice and Reform*, pp. 176–77. Finman recounts the experiences of several law-reform-oriented attorneys who worked for local projects that were hostile to reform. (Usually projects only recruited staff with compatible perspectives.) Some, recognizing that reform activity would bring them into sharp conflict with the project's hierarchy, spoke of the importance of reform but failed to pursue it. Others, with national help, tried anyway. Finman says of one: "In effect, her contact with the national office provided her with an alternate source of approval and support. Had there been no intervention from the national office, however, it seems likely that LSP-D's [the local project's] ideology would have continued to inhibit her actions." However, he adds in a footnote: "Even the national office's intervention may not have completely overcome the inhibiting effect of LSP- D's ideology. After the evaluators from the national office had visited City D, our attorney still was anxious to keep the board of directors ignorant of her work with tenants' organizations, and this suggests that program ideology may still have been at work." Finman, "OEO Legal Ser- vices," pp. 1062–71.

[67] Johnson, *Justice and Reform*, p. 179.

[68] The LSP back-up centers included the social welfare policy center at Columbia University that had originally been an MYF project; a housing law center at the University of California,

Court level, these centers were less involved in case sponsorship than is commonly supposed.

Despite these tactics, numerous scholars who studied the LSP while it was in operation concluded that the national Program essentially failed in its attempt to engage local projects in law reform activities. Pious puts it most strongly: "The performance of local projects funded by the LSP did *not* match the policies enunciated at the national level by LSP officials or supported by bar leaders."[69] Krislov attributes the lack of widespread law-reform activity to the continuing conflict between those who advocated the traditional legal-aid approach and those who "wanted to generate the 'test cases' required to attack broad institutional practices."[70] Hannon suggests that some of the local antipathy toward law reform was generated by the LSP's switch from stressing creative proposals emphasizing local control to heavy-handed demands that projects engage in law reform. He asserts that LSP's methods in promoting law reform, more than animosity toward law reform itself, created local opposition.[71] Handler, Hollingsworth, and Erlanger found that 60 percent of the local LSP attorneys reported outside pressure to do less law reform. However, they also found that the average "law reform time" reported for offices increased slightly between 1967 and 1972, from 21 to 25 percent.[72] Finman concluded that the ideology of project promoters was the most important factor in determining the level of activity directed at social change.[73] Champagne found that the attitudes of the local project directors and the staff attorneys also affected program activity. Only 14 percent of the local LSP projects were rated as having substantial law reform activity and 23 percent were judged to have none.[74] Another estimate of local projects' adherence to the national goal of law reform can be gained by counting the number of local projects that were involved in significant appellate cases. Johnson's survey revealed that only forty-seven local projects had more than ten cases reported in the Program's

---

Berkeley; a consumer law center at Boston University Law School; a juvenile law center at St. Louis University Law School; an employment law center in New York; an education law center at Harvard Law School; a health law center at U.C.L.A. Law School; and an elderly law center at the University of Southern California Law School. Johnson, *Justice and Reform*, pp. 180–84; Note, "Beyond the Neighborhood Office."

[69] Pious, "Policy."

[70] Krislov, "OEO Lawyers Fail," p. 218.

[71] Hannon, "Law Reform"; Hannon, "Leadership Problem."

[72] Similarly, the average reported time each lawyer spent on law reform was 25 percent in 1967 and 31 percent in 1972. LSP projects were not using time-reporting systems comparable to those used in private practice for billing. Handler says, "The line between law reform and service work is not distinct; moreover, our data rely on classification by the respondents themselves. . . . In fact, we cannot say how much law reform is going on in Legal Services." Handler et al., *Lawyers*, pp. 54–55, 64. See also Cahn and Cahn, "Power."

[73] Finman, "OEO Legal Services."

[74] Champagne, "Internal Operation." Champagne's data were taken from studies done for the LSP by the Auerbach Corporation and the John D. Kettle Corporation.

monthly journal that included summaries of appellate litigation by LSP attorneys, *Clearinghouse Review*.[75]

All these accounts of the LSP projects' reform activities have one implicit or explicit theme in common. There was great diversity in the various projects' commitment to and involvement in law reform. Different projects and different attorneys balanced the client server and reformer roles differently. Critics of the national Program's ability to implement its law reform priority rightly suggest that local LSP projects could have been more active in law reform. Nonetheless, the LSP engaged in substantially more reform activity, particularly through appellate advocacy, than the legal aid days had seen.[76]

### *Expanded Access: Client Server and Reformer*

LSP projects did significantly increase the poor's access to legal services and the civil courts. Primarily, the LSP provided counsel to litigants who were too poor to retain private attorneys. Independent evaluations of the local projects' handling of routine service cases rated the LSP's performance superior to legal aid's and at least equal to private attorneys' serving paying clients.[77] LSP attorneys were willing, some even anxious, to go to court, thus decreasing the barrier that the de facto assistance of counsel requirement imposes on the poor. By the 1970s, LSP attorneys were litigating 17 to 28 percent of the roughly one million cases they handled each year. And, Johnson estimates that LSP attorneys across the country filed between one thousand and three thousand appeals each year.[78] During the Program's nine-year tenure (1965–1974), 164 of these

[75] Johnson surveyed the September 1967 through October 1972 issues of *Clearinghouse Review* (with the exceptions of April, August, September, October, November, and December, 1969; October and December, 1970; March, July, and October, 1971). Johnson, *Justice and Reform*, p. 296. However, Johnson's data are curious. He claims that, "fully 279 of the 320 Legal Services agencies have had cases reported in the *Clearinghouse Review*." Johnson, *Justice and Reform*, p. 192. The Office of Economic Opportunity's Annual Reports list only 260 Programs with 850 neighborhood offices in 1967–68; 268, with 934 offices in 1969–70; and 265, with 934 offices in 1971. U.S. Office of Economic Opportunity, "The Legal Services Program," 1968, 1969, 1970, and 1971. The list of LSP funded projects acquired from the Legal Services Corporation archives and used to establish LSP participation at the Supreme Court level listed 265 projects (see Appendix A). This 260 to 265 figure is found in many other published sources. Perhaps the discrepancy can be explained. In surveying *Clearinghouse Review* for Supreme Court appeals, I found that the *Review* sometimes included cases that were poverty related, even though they were sponsored by an organization that did not receive LSP funding. (I did not include those cases in my data base.) If this explains Johnson's figures, it means he was "over-counting"; hence, he over-estimates the number of projects engaged in significant litigation. On the other hand, perhaps he was counting offices rather than projects. If that is the case, then his count indicates that only about 30 percent of the offices were engaged in law reform.

[76] Johnson outlines the major success of the LSP's law reform efforts at all levels. Johnson, *Justice and Reform*, pp. 187–234. A more detailed account can be gleaned from the "Poverty Law Developments" section of each issue of *Clearinghouse Review*.

[77] Johnson, *Justice and Reform*, pp. 189–90.

[78] Johnson reports a 17 percent litigation rate in 1971. Johnson, *Justice and Reform*, p. 189. In

LSP sponsored cases reached the Supreme Court's jurisdiction agenda, changing the parameters of access to that institution. The Court accepted 119 of these cases for review. The poor participated in Supreme Court decision making in record numbers. Aside from federal and state governments, the LSP argued more cases before the Supreme Court than any other group during this era. The LSP produced a significant change in who had access to the U.S. Supreme Court.

The LSP also realized that the poor are among those who, for a variety of sociological and psychological reasons, are least likely to perceive the law and lawyers as accessible and appropriate for the resolution of their disputes.[79] To attempt to reach these groups, the 265 LSP projects established 850 storefront offices in poor neighborhoods and LSP attorneys kept evening and weekend hours. Some LSP projects also engaged in community legal education and encouraged referrals from other social service agencies.[80] Apparently these measures did increase the number of clients with lower incomes and less education served by the LSP compared to those served by the legal aid societies that were generally located near private firms. Statistics collected in 1969 revealed that 21 percent of the LSP's clients found the office through publicity, 20 percent were directed there by another poverty or social agency, and 7 percent were referred by another client. Forty-four percent of the LSP's clients had never, for any reason, consulted an attorney before.[81] Although the LSP did little to disrupt cultural normative systems that discourage litigation between status equals, it did seem to increase feelings of political efficacy among the poor. Armed with a tool of the government—lawyers—the poor began to believe that they could fight city hall. The lawyers' translation of the poor's problems into legal issues engendered beliefs in "rights" rather than pleas for charity.[82]

More than the legal aid societies, the LSP was willing to represent politically unpopular clients with politically unpopular claims. Largely freed from reliance on local charitable funding and having secured independence from local community action agencies, local LSP projects were able to challenge the ac-

---

comparing LSP funded and non-LSP funded legal assistance programs based on data from 1 January through 30 June 1969, Stiegler reports that LSP-funded projects disposed of 18 percent of their cases through "court action," while the other programs only litigated 8 percent of their cases. Stiegler, "All for the Sake of Statistics," p. 104. In reviewing "seven standard [LSP] Program grantees' operations," the GAO reported a 28 percent litigation rate during the 1971 program year. U.S., Comptroller General, "Report to Congress: The Legal Services Program—Accomplishments Of and Problems Faced By Its Grantees, B-130515," pp. 10–20.

[79] Campbell and Talarico, "Access to Legal Services." See also Mayhew, "Institutions of Representation"; Abel, "Law Without Politics," pp. 550–56, 622–25; Hannon, "Law Reform."

[80] Johnson, *Justice and Reform*, p. 188; Hannon, "Leadership Problem"; Pye, "Role of Legal Services."

[81] Fisher and Ivie, *Franchising Justice*, quoted in Abel, "Law Without Politics," p. 551; Stiegler, "All for the Sake of Statistics."

[82] Wexler, "Practicing Law"; Scheingold, *Politics of Rights*, p. 183. See also Piven and Cloward, *Regulating the Poor*, pp. 285–340; Sullivan, "Law Reform and the Legal Services Crisis."

tions of politically powerful groups, including government agencies.[83] Generally, LSP projects did not employ the subject matter restrictions that had characterized the legal aid societies.[84] However, beginning in 1967, statutory amendments designed to limit the politically controversial activities of LSP attorneys were introduced in Congress. The most notorious of these was introduced by Republican Senator George Murphy of California. The Murphy Amendments, which the Senate repeatedly rejected, provided that "no project under such program may grant assistance to bring any action against any public agency of the United States, any State, or any political subdivision thereof."[85] The Economic Opportunity Amendments of 1967 did include a ban on criminal representation.[86] The LSP was also frequently subjected to political attacks from governors who attempted to veto LSP grants to projects in California, Arizona, Connecticut, Florida, Louisiana, Missouri, and North Dakota, and from the OEO Community Action Program that sought to control the LSP and limit its ability to sue local community action agencies.[87]

As early as 1971, these political attacks led to the development of proposals for a new Legal Services Corporation insulated from politics. The Legal Services Corporation Act that was finally signed into law on 25 July 1974 moved legal services from the executive branch to an independent corporation, but it also included political restrictions. Legal Services Corporation attorneys were prohibited from representing clients in "actions involving collateral attack on criminal convictions, juveniles in certain circumstances, desegregation of elementary or secondary schools, nontherapeutic abortions, selective services violations, or desertion." More generally, appellate advocacy was no longer emphasized.[88] The Corporation was less able to overcome the barriers the de facto assistance of counsel requirement places on the poor's participation in appellate litigation.

## CONCLUSIONS

Unlike the old legal aid societies that had been serving the poor for nearly one hundred years, the Legal Services Program that was created in 1965 mixed the

[83] Under statute, local LSP projects did have to secure 20 percent of their funding from non-LSP sources, often local private sources. George reports that some of these local funding sources sought to limit the LSP's activities. He notes, "United Fund's support of LSP was withdrawn in St. Louis, Missouri; Albuquerque, New Mexico; and Oklahoma City, Oklahoma, as a result of suits against local government agencies that were heavy contributors to the United Fund." George, "Development," p. 688.

[84] Johnson, *Justice and Reform*, p. 188.

[85] U.S. Congress, House, Committee on Education and Labor, *Hearings on H.R. 8311*, p. 2130, quoted in Pious, "Congress," p. 427.

[86] Pious, "Congress," p. 430.

[87] George, "Development," pp. 683–90.

[88] Ibid., pp. 683–86, 690, 698, 707–8.

client server and the reformer roles. For both legal aid and the LSP, the attorney roles they emphasized were a function of the eras in which they developed and operated. Their choices had different implications for the extension of access to the appellate courts to those burdened by the de facto assistance of counsel requirement.

Legal aid operated in a political climate largely unaware of, or indifferent to, the role of government rules in perpetuating and exacerbating the plight of the poor. The legal environment was largely devoid of models of successful appellate litigation on behalf of the poor. Reliance on local charitable funding made the societies cautious and the paucity of funds often prevented even trial court litigation. Accordingly, the legal aid societies chose to focus on immediate client service through extending the rudiments of formal due process to the poor. Legal aid leaders believed that the law itself was fair; they simply sought to perfect its administration by providing legal assistance to the poor.

As America rediscovered poverty in the 1960s and activists became concerned with the anomaly of poverty in an affluent society, the politics of providing legal assistance to the poor changed. Equally important, the recent drama of the NAACP LDF's victory in Brown v. Board of Education provided a model for reform litigation on behalf of disadvantaged groups. Foundation philanthropy provided resources for experiments with new forms and philosophies of legal assistance. The status quo was disturbed and the architects of the War on Poverty were persuaded to add a legal services component to the Office of Economic Opportunity. Political compromises led to the selection of an LSP director and staff inexperienced with either legal aid or the new reform-oriented legal assistance projects. Rather, the LSP's leadership was schooled in elite private law practice and bureaucratic politics. They understood the importance of getting the Program "up and running" as quickly as possible and they embraced a traditional view of the elite lawyer's role that saw law reform as an extension of client service. As the Program set priorities for the local projects, it sought to encourage LSP attorneys to engage in vigorous advocacy for their clients that would, at times, extend into the appellate courts and include arguments for legal change. The various local projects and attorneys mixed the roles of client server and reformer differently; nonetheless, the national Program continued to remind local attorneys not to abandon the reformer role.

Of course, the LSP did not, and could not, remove all the barriers to the courts that result from the de facto assistance of counsel requirement. It did try to reach out to those members of the poverty community who for a variety of sociological and psychological reasons were unlikely to view their problems as legal problems. Initially, it was quite willing to represent politically unpopular clients and claims but, as the Program met with success, some congressmen and state governors tried to restrict this activity. Ultimately, the LSP was replaced by the Legal Services Corporation which, though designed to be

more insulated from such political attacks, was burdened with numerous statutory restrictions on the types of cases it could take. While the LSP had encouraged appellate advocacy as a part of a proper blending of the client server
and reformer roles and thereby greatly increasing the poor's access to appellate
courts, the new Corporation reverted to an emphasis on individual client service.

The LSP's expansion of the poor's access to the appellate courts resulted in
Program attorneys representing poor clients in 164 cases appealed to the U.S.
Supreme Court. As we will see in the next chapter, this Supreme Court litigation was the product of the Program's blending of the client service and
reform roles, providing ''delegate'' representation in the Court. It was not the
product of the kind of ''trustee'' representation interest groups provide when
they emphasize achieving policy goals through reform litigation. The distinctive development and operation of the LSP produced a Program that presented
the Supreme Court with opportunities to decide the cases of, rather than for,
the poor.

# CHAPTER THREE

# Appealing to the Supreme Court

OVER the last four decades, the Supreme Court's agenda has increasingly been dominated by civil liberties and civil rights issues; more specifically, by the claims of the politically disadvantaged.[1] Overwhelmingly, the litigants in these cases were among those burdened by the de facto assistance of counsel requirement. Few had the personal resources to mount exhaustive appellate litigation culminating in the Supreme Court on their own and, indeed, most of them did not. Frequently, as noted earlier, these litigants were represented by interest group attorneys who had adopted something approaching a pure version of the reformer role. These groups were pursuing policy goals through litigation and they husbanded their limited resources by primarily representing clients whose cases provided an opportunity to argue for the legal change their group sought. Moreover, prior to the establishment of the LSP, none of these groups focused on poverty per se. Interest groups' expansion of the poor's access to the Supreme Court was largely incidental to their pursuance of policy reform in other areas.

As the national LSP promoted appellate advocacy as a Program priority and as local attorneys began to meet with appellate success, it was sometimes assumed that the LSP had a specific set of policy goals that it was pursuing through a litigation strategy comparable to that of interest groups which focus on reform. It did not. If it had, then only those poor with cases that fit into a legal strategy developed by LSP leaders would have been represented in the appellate courts. Others, notwithstanding the utility of appellate litigation for vindication of their own interests, would not have had access to appellate review culminating in the Supreme Court. On the other hand, without a strategy guiding its litigation, we would expect LSP attorneys, like private counsel, to be less successful in the Supreme Court than interest groups that have adopted the reformer role.

As we saw in chapter 2, the legal and political climate surrounding the establishment and development of the LSP resulted in an organizational philosophy based on a traditional model of elite law practice that blends the client server and reformer attorney roles. In this chapter, we will focus on the Program's Supreme Court litigation, demonstrating that it was not the product of an interest group–type litigation strategy; rather, it was an outgrowth of the Program's blending of the client server and reformer roles. The decentralized

[1] Pacelle, "The Supreme Court and the Growth of Civil Liberties."

structure of a federal grant-making agency and the autonomy demanded by local LSP attorneys prevented even those few litigation strategies that were developed by Program leaders from being implemented. We will examine the factors that led LSP attorneys to appeal their clients' cases to the Supreme Court and dissect the resulting heterogeneity of the LSP's Supreme Court docket. The implications of the Program's lack of a litigation strategy for "citizen participation," both in the Program and in the Supreme Court, sheds light on the character of the access the LSP provided the poor and the range of opportunities for decision the LSP provided the Court.

## LITIGATION STRATEGIES

Although attorneys may use the term "strategy" to refer to the "tactics" used in a particular case, here "litigation strategy" refers to a planned effort to influence the course of judicial policy development to achieve a particular policy goal. The NAACP Legal Defense Fund's (LDF) twenty-year attack on segregation in education is the prototypical litigation strategy.[2] Wasby has defined "litigation strategy" as including:

> which goals to seek or what institutional targets to attack and then in what cases to become involved . . . [it subsumes] matters such as why cases are or are not initiated and then why they are or are not appealed, and questions such as: What types of cases are brought at the trial level with the intent to appeal them to the Supreme Court? Why are cases not pursued beyond the trial court?[3]

The extensive literature on interest group litigation rarely explicitly mentions "policy goals" or "litigation strategies" as factors critical to success, although it does occasionally mention the importance of being able to choose which cases to bring and when, and then retaining control over them. Rather, "policy goals" and "litigation strategies" are implicit in the very definition of interest group litigation; it is these elements that distinguish interest group litigation from other types of private representation in the courts. The literature instead tends to emphasize the organizational resources necessary to effectively implement a successful Supreme Court litigation strategy: (1) substan-

---

[2] See Kluger, *Simple Justice*. Handler says that "this [NAACP LDF's] model of class action law reform strategy became the single most important influence in the development of OEO Legal Services. . . . It became the popular standard for measuring the quantity and effectiveness of other legal rights activities." Handler et al., *Lawyers*, p. 23. See also Greenberg, "Litigation for Social Change," p. 331. Few other groups have fully lived up to this model. See Halpern, "ACLU Chapters"; Sorauf, *Wall*; Wasby, "Interest Groups in Court"; Wasby, "Planned Litigation"; Wasby, "Civil Rights Litigation"; Manwaring, *Render Unto Caesar*; O'Connor, *Women's Organizations*; Vose, *Caucasians Only*.

[3] Wasby, "Interest Groups in Court," p. 256. Sorauf has noted that a litigation strategy does not necessarily imply the existence of a "strategy of strategies, an overall priority of concerns." Sorauf, *Wall*, p. 129.

tial financial ability to engage in appellate litigation; (2) support of the Solicitor General as sponsor or amici; (3) longevity to allow "chipping away at (or building up) precedent over time"; (4) expert legal staff committed to the group's goals; (5) ability to generate extra-legal publicity for the group's legal arguments, particularly in law reviews; and (6) cooperation with like-minded groups so that cases and briefs can be coordinated.[4] Almost all of these resources presuppose that the group's engagement in appellate litigation is part of a litigation strategy, not "just" an extension of individual client service.

The effective development and implementation of a litigation strategy requires a great deal of centralization and coordination among the group's attorneys. Even then, such strategies are difficult to realize. Clients drop out; settlement offers are too good to refuse; courts reach the "wrong" decision; litigation sponsored by other groups preempts the strategic case.[5] Still, groups attempting to influence the course of public policy through litigation develop such strategies and do their best to implement them. Devoted to the reformer role, they seek to achieve policy change through legal change. These strategies largely dictate which clients and cases a group will represent in the appellate courts.[6] In this respect, interest group litigation strategies shape the parameters of access to the courts for litigants who are burdened by the de facto assistance of counsel requirement.

## Litigating Without a Strategy

Unlike many successful interest groups, the LSP did not have a single overriding policy goal or litigation plan to achieve it.[7] The national Program had

---

[4] I have adopted Epstein's, *Conservatives*, pp. 12–13, cataloguing of these resources, rewording some of them based on my own reading of the literature she cites.

[5] Wasby, "Planned Litigation"; and Wasby, "Civil Rights Litigation."

[6] See especially Kluger, *Simple Justice*; Halpern, "ACLU Chapters"; Sorauf, *Wall*; Vose, *Caucasians Only*. I am not claiming that interest groups never provide representation in cases that are not part of a planned litigation strategy. Rather, I am suggesting that litigation-oriented interest groups do not see individual client service, such as the LSP spent most of its time on, as one of their primary functions. When groups do provide such client service, it is analogous to a private law firm's *pro bono publico* work. For example, the NAACP Legal Defense and Education Fund handled many of the sit-in cases because it was the "only legal apparatus readily available to handle the mass arrests," but it was ill-equipped to do so. Hahn, "The NAACP Legal Defense and Education Fund," pp. 387ff, esp. p. 399. See also Halpern, "ACLU Chapters."

[7] Of course, not all interest groups litigating in a particular policy area always agree on their goals and strategies. Certainly a number of civil rights groups during the 1960s became disenchanted with the efficacy of appellate advocacy as a stimulus for social and economic change, but the NAACP LDF continued to pursue a litigation strategy, while other groups adopted different approaches. Hahn, "NAACP Legal Defense and Education Fund," p. 395. When conflict over goals and strategies began plaguing women's rights groups, many of them splintered into separate groups. O'Connor, *Women's Organizations*, pp. 93–134. Different religious and civil liberties groups simultaneously pursued different goals and strategies in church and state litigation. Sorauf, *Wall*, esp. pp. 91–129.

adopted appellate advocacy as a Program priority because it accommodated its diverse coalition of supporters by blending service and reform, not because it seemed to be the best way to achieve the Program's policy goals. Indeed, there was never much consensus on what the Program's goals were. The LSP never developed a litigation strategy analogous to the NAACP LDF prototype, although the LDF provided the model for other groups and the LDF's successes were "the popular standard for measuring the quality and effectiveness" of group litigation.[8] There were two primary reasons for the LSP's failure to approximate the LDF model of planned litigation.

First, the Program's organizational structure and its commitment to both individual client service and reform did not permit a unified strategy. Compared to other interest groups whose appellate advocacy has created new areas of constitutional adjudication such as separation of church and state or women's rights, the LSP was extremely decentralized. The national Program was making grants to 265 local projects. As is characteristic of federal grantees, the local LSP projects operated with substantial autonomy. They varied greatly in their commitment to the Program's law reform goal and, other than through *Clearinghouse Review* (a monthly LSP journal), there was little communication between projects about their appellate litigation.[9] The Program's 164 sponsored cases and its amicus curiae filings in twenty-four other cases were brought to the Court by attorneys from 116 of the 265 local projects. Only about half of these 116 projects participated in more than one case and only about a quarter participated in more than two.

In even sharper contrast to litigation-oriented interest groups, the LSP devoted the overwhelming bulk of its resources to individual client service rather than to explicitly law reform litigation. A 1971 OEO report on the LSP indicated that only about 10 percent of the Program's caseload was "directed activity affecting broad segments of the poverty community through group representation or legislation."[10] During the Program's nine-year tenure, it handled over six million cases and litigated over one million.[11]

Over 2,500 attorneys were in the field handling cases for individual clients. The local LSP projects and staff attorneys decided which clients to represent and which cases to take to court. The national LSP could not superimpose a

<hr>

[8] Handler et al., *Lawyers*, p. 23.

[9] Champagne, "Internal Operation"; Finman, "OEO Legal Services"; Handler et al., *Lawyers*, p. 64; Hannon, "Law Reform"; Pious, "Policy"; Johnson, *Justice and Reform*, pp. 163–84, 320n.82; Katz, *Poor People's Lawyers*. The fact that the LSP never compiled a list of all the Supreme Court appeals its attorneys were engaged in is indicative of the Program's lack of a coordinated litigation plan.

[10] U.S. Office of Economic Opportunity, "The Legal Services Program," 1971, p. 33.

[11] Estimated from caseload figures in U.S. Office of Economic Opportunity, "The Legal Services Program," 1966–72, and LSP litigation rates, reported in U.S. Comptroller General, "Report to Congress: The Legal Services Program—Accomplishments Of and Problems Faced By Its Grantees, B-130515"; and Stiegler, "All for the Sake of Statistics."

coordinated litigation strategy on the mass of casework being done by local attorneys across the nation. Unlike interest groups who have local affiliated attorneys, the LSP had no centralized structure that screened complaints and decided which ones would become LSP cases at the trial or appellate level.[12] Bound by statute to the ABA's Code of Professional Responsibility that prohibited interference in the individual attorney-client relationship once established, the national Program could not control the timing, subject, or arguments of the cases local attorneys chose to appeal. As one national LSP attorney observed: "It was up to the local attorney. The national Program could not tell him he could not appeal—it could not interfere with the attorney-client relationship as protected by the [ABA] Code of Professional Responsibility."[13] The appeal decision was very much the local attorney's decision. The underlying tension between the attorney's desire to help his client and the Program's desire to help its clientele was resolved in favor of the local staff attorney.

Not only did the ABA Code of Professional Responsibility provide ethical and legal imperatives that discouraged the implementation of an appellate advocacy plan, the professional autonomy demanded by the local attorneys provided bureaucratic imperatives in the same direction. One attorney involved in law reform said: "There never was, and maybe couldn't have been, a tight national litigation strategy. It would have been resisted by lawyers with egos and those who did not want law reform activity going on." The following story told by an LSP attorney illustrates the problems the Program faced in trying to coordinate appellate litigation:

> One attorney who was on staff at the first law reform unit had spent four years at the Justice Department before joining the LSP. There, approval had to be gained from the Solicitor General before appeals were taken. He tried to develop a system-wide procedure for the Program's appellate litigation. Under his proposal a back-up center attorney could appeal a case if the local staff attorney declined to file an appeal. If the local attorney did decide to appeal the case, he would have to follow certain centralized procedures. The local attorneys were outraged by this proposal. Their reaction was "who the hell do you think you are, telling me how to manage my case." All hell broke loose. As a result, the proposal was not instituted.

The LSP could not institute an NAACP LDF–type strategy because organizationally the two programs were radically different.[14] The NAACP LDF was not involved in casework, and, in the era that set the prototype, decisions on appeals were made by a small centralized cadre of attorneys.[15]

[12] On the ACLU's screening procedures, see Halpern, "ACLU Chapters."

[13] Unless otherwise noted, all quotations from LSP attorneys come from the author's interviews. See Appendix A.

[14] On the importance of organizational factors in influencing the development of litigation strategies, see Wasby, "Civil Rights Litigation"; Wasby, "Planned Litigation"; Wasby, "Interest Groups in Court."

[15] See Kluger, *Simple Justice*; Rabin, "Lawyers for Social Change," pp. 214–24.

Second, the LSP was unable to approximate the LDF model of planned litigation because the problem under attack, poverty, did not allow for a unified strategy. Poverty consists of a whole panoply of social and economic causes and conditions. As one LSP attorney said, "Poverty is a more complex and diverse situation than that faced by the NAACP. Planning had to be done by subject area." It is not that racial discrimination was a less pervasive problem than poverty; rather, it is that the NAACP LDF's original strategy that set the prototype was designed to establish a single principle: "separate is inherently unequal." Once established in education, the same argument could be made in other areas such as public accommodations, housing, and transportation. In contrast, LSP attorneys did not focus on creating a single legal principle designed to significantly alter the legal structure of poverty in the United States.[16]

To the extent that there was a policy goal implicit in the LSP's emphasis on appellate advocacy, it was alleviating poverty in the United States.[17] One attorney commented, "A good deal of the litigation had the goal of redistributing income and power." Although the rhetoric of the War on Poverty focused on the elimination of poverty, the limited powers of the judiciary made this an inherently unattainable goal for the LSP. Judges, having neither the sword nor the purse, cannot single-handedly create or redistribute public and private wealth.[18] Furthermore, such a goal lacks the specificity necessary to construct a litigation strategy. LSP attorneys appealed cases to the Supreme Court involving twenty-five subjects. Their arguments were based on a variety of different constitutional provisions. There were statutory claims as well. As one attorney commented, "In the beginning all the areas of poverty law were so unlitigated that any [legal] theory that was developed provoked a multitude of litigation. It was just too good an opportunity to pass up."

Not only were the problems of the poor not amenable to solution by widespread adoption of a single principle, the problems and causes were not always

[16] Obviously, challenging racial discrimination involves more complex strategies today. See Wasby, "Civil Rights Litigation." The NAACP LDF also had the advantage of dealing with race which has the "imprimature of history" on its side. Furthermore, the LDF was presenting questions of legal status that courts are accustomed to adjudicating. "[I]n the welfare rights cases there may be less inclination to decide favorably issues of distributive or social justice." Greenberg, "Litigation for Social Change," pp. 332–33.

[17] See Johnson, *Justice and Reform*, pp. 192–94. Katz writes, "Legal Services formally was an arm of the antipoverty program, but its mission never was to alter social-class relations. For one thing, the antipoverty program as a whole was not that radical. Even on a rhetorical level, the antipoverty banner was a classic liberal compromise. At first glance, the 'war' certainly appeared resolute, but the failure to specify the enemy signaled political bad faith. It was a call for radical improvement in the status of the poor without a simultaneous commitment to reduce the superior status of the well-to-do." Katz, *Poor People's Lawyers*, p. 91.

[18] See Hazard, "Social Justice"; Hazard, "Law Reforming"; "Developments," *Harvard Law Review*; Gunther, "Foreword"; Kurland, "1971 Term"; Sosin, "Legal Rights and Welfare Change"; Mead, "Comment."

readily apparent. The LSP, like many of the War on Poverty programs, did not have a clear theory of the causes of poverty. In the early 1960s scholars began addressing the interaction between poverty and the legal order and the constitutional issues arising out of the administration of the welfare system. Indeed, some of the research that was published in this area was sponsored and funded by the LSP. Still, to a large extent, the LSP did not have an NAACP LDF–type litigation strategy because the LSP did not begin with a clear notion of the complex interaction between poverty and the legal order. It had not specified its goals. As one attorney said, "There was a general recognition that institutional change was needed, rather than a recognition that specific changes A, B, and C were needed." The emerging research suggested justiciable issues and innovative legal arguments to be used in appeals, but primarily the LSP attorneys learned what needed to be litigated from the clients who came through their offices. An LSP attorney commented: "I fought with my supervisor when he wanted me to dream up eighteen cases to litigate. It couldn't be done. I found out what to litigate by looking at the stream of cases that came in. I looked at what the clients came in with. I still believe that is the only way you can do it, but it takes more time and effort that way." The specific case strategies that were developed resulted from interaction with the poor. As another attorney reported:

Some notions about what to do came from people who had been in the welfare area for some time. Some came from thirty clients coming in with the same or a similar problem. Take residency requirements—non-lawyers involved with welfare for years had seen it as a problem. It is hard to divorce casework and law reform. For example, Sparer, the architect of the welfare strategy, had spent two years on the firing line with Mobilization for Youth—he had worked with the problems.

When asked about the goals of the LSP's Supreme Court litigation, one back-up center attorney said, "If you're asking if the program had a monolithic litigation strategy—no—not except to win, to help poor people." Another staff attorney commented: "The 'client-model' predominated. The broad interest group theory that did exist was to maximize benefits and institute procedural requirements. Most of the Supreme Court cases were a result of serendipity—accident. They were a reflection of policy goals, but not a result of them." Former LSP director, Earl Johnson, Jr., wrote:

In describing the social and economic impact of cases taken by poverty lawyers, I do not mean to suggest that these attorneys deliberately set out to achieve such results. Undoubtedly, the vast majority of cases were brought or defended by counsel bent only on serving a specific client and his or her goals. Even where a test case was filed or a legislative measure advocated, the long-run impact on the overall poverty community was only vaguely perceived.[19]

[19] Johnson, *Justice and Reform*, p. 195.

It was through the patterns the lawyers saw in their series of individual cases that they discovered what problems the poor repeatedly face that could be diminished by Supreme Court rulings. The reform LSP attorneys sought was an extension of their client service. In this respect, the LSP more closely resembled a specialized private law firm than a litigation-oriented interest group.

On the other hand, like some interest groups, the LSP had the advantage of having a number of clients with similar problems so that the local attorneys could sometimes pick the "best" case to appeal. Since the LSP was operating nationwide, its attorneys could bring essentially the same case in a number of jurisdictions, thereby possibly creating conflicts that would presumably increase the likelihood of Supreme Court review. But these advantages accrued to LSP litigation more through coincidence than design. According to project attorneys, few cases were begun with an eye on the Supreme Court. Client service preceded the appellate initiative.[20] Finman's study of local LSP projects found that "the programs that accomplished the most when working on behalf of individual clients were also the ones most involved in promoting law reform." The important point is that the poor brought their problems to the LSP attorneys; the LSP attorneys did not define the problem and then search for a client.[21] The LSP did not have an NAACP LDF–type litigation strategy that set the parameters of access to the Court for the poor.

## The Back-Up Centers and Local Attorneys

To the extent that the national Program did engage in litigation planning, it developed separate plans for a variety of issues. The national LSP funded twelve back-up centers, each of which focused on a specific area such as housing or mental health. As a staff attorney noted: "The setting up of law reform units [back-up centers] was a recognition of the need for a strategy. It is important that they were specialized by issue areas. This was done pursuant to a perceived need to specialize in the development of strategy." Some LSP back-up centers had issue-specific goals and some focused on reforming state laws. One national staff member described the variation: "For example, in the welfare area there was a plan headed by Edward Sparer. In housing law the Berkeley center had an overall plan—one of their goals was to get an implied warranty of habitability adopted in as many states as possible. State and

[20] Ibid.

[21] Finman, "OEO Legal Services," p. 1008. In 1967, Ortique, President of the National Bar Association, testified that "one of the tremendous advantages of this Program [LSP, is that] the people in the ghetto feel that this is their institution. This gives them a bit of law on their side." U.S. Congress, Senate, Committee on Labor and Public Welfare, *Examination of the War on Poverty, Hearings before the Subcommittee on Employment, Manpower, and Poverty on S. 1545, Part 8*, 90th Cong., 1st sess., June 1967, p. 2376. See U.S. Congress, House, Committee on Health, Education, and Welfare, *Establishment of a Legal Services Corporation, Hearings before the Subcommittee on Education and Labor*, 93d Cong., 1st sess., February and March 1973, pp. 54–80, for a discussion of whether LSP attorneys sought out clients for test cases.

metropolitan back-up centers had plans for litigation relevant to that state.'' Many of the back-up centers focused on a full panoply of law reform activities directed at the state and local level rather than at the federal courts.[22] Generally, the back-up centers were not pursuing clear, preordained goals through a litigation plan directed toward the Supreme Court.

The actual working relationship between back-up centers and the attorneys employed by the local LSP projects almost makes the question of the centers' litigation strategy irrelevant. The back-up centers' role as an institutional home for research, information, and guidance eclipsed their role as actual litigation planners. Local attorneys controlled the decision to appeal. Project attorneys were free to pursue a case without contacting a back-up center or in direct opposition to the center's advice. Some lawyers preferred to retain complete control over their cases while others anxiously sought the expertise of center attorneys. The scope of the back-up center's role was controlled by the local attorney. The final decision on whether or not to appeal a case lay with the local attorney who was representing the client. The comments of two LSP attorneys illustrate the varying relationships between centers and local attorneys:

> Local attorneys received from back-up centers both a little encouragement on what kinds of cases to appeal and a little discouragement on what kinds of cases to appeal—usually at the request of local attorneys—but local attorneys could go off on their own.

> Technically the back-up centers had no control over local attorney's decision to appeal. In reality, it varied. We [back-up center staff] worked with some attorneys a lot and they would let us have a substantial role and inexperienced attorneys who needed our expertise would let us play a major role. Plenty of lawyers never talked to us—they just went on their way. Several times we advised against appeal and people did it anyway.

The back-up centers, striving for the ''big picture,'' tried to fit individual cases into a larger design. Center attorneys, many of whom had graduated in the top of their law school classes, certainly had ideas about what litigation should go to the Court. Sometimes they ''put out the word that they wanted to litigate X.'' They participated in a number of the major LSP Supreme Court cases, but they did not have control over the LSP's Supreme Court docket. Decisions on what cases to appeal were largely discrete and insular. In practice, the Program's lawyers focused more on individual cases and clients than on larger goals. Back-up centers supplemented this perspective but they did not replace it. As one back-up center attorney said: ''When the center was representing the client, the first consideration was the client. When we were

---

[22] See Sullivan's description of the Housing and Economic Development Law Project, in which he argues that these activities are comparable to the services private attorneys provide to their clients. Sullivan, ''Law Reform and the Legal Services Crisis.''

not the client's primary counsel, we asked the question, 'How will this affect all poor people?' We gave serious attention to whether we wanted to make it the law of the land. Decisions were made on a case-by-case basis.''

At the Supreme Court level, the back-up centers were less involved in case sponsorship than is commonly supposed. The LSP back-up centers served as counsel or cocounsel in only thirty-three of the 164 LSP sponsored Supreme Court appeals.[23] Back-up centers formally participated, as counsel or amicus, in only about a quarter of the LSP's Supreme Court docket, although they undoubtedly provided informal assistance in a number of other cases.

### Sparer's Welfare Strategy

Only the LSP's Center on Social Welfare Policy and Law at Columbia University, headed by Edward Sparer, had a Supreme Court–oriented litigation plan.[24] The Center had originally been funded by Mobilization for Youth and it was one of the new models of legal assistance that led to the development of the LSP. The other LSP back-up centers were patterned after the Columbia Center but none of them became as involved in developing a Supreme Court litigation strategy. As a congressional staffer involved in LSP oversight reported:

> Only in the welfare area did LSP consciously model themselves on the NAACP. That came out of the Columbia Center. Only in the welfare area was there a litigation strategy. In other areas everything was much more diffuse. Ed Sparer was the brain behind the Columbia welfare strategy. The other attorneys sat around the feet of Ed Sparer. Sparer was the only one with a real sense of strategy.

Sparer sought to "transform the widely held notion of welfare as a privilege into a right." He had diagnosed the welfare system as requiring "militant advocacy" in two general areas. These were: "(1) issues concerning the civil liberties denied those of welfare client status; and (2) legal issues stemming from the granting, denial, or disregard of eligibility and particular forms of assistance."[25] His strategy was to challenge, through adjudication, four major defects in the American welfare system:

> (1) the innumerable tests for aid and exclusions from aid, most of which were unrelated to need; (2) procedures which reduced the welfare recipient to a "client," stripped of constitutional and other rights assumed by other citizens and forced into dependency upon the welfare agency's whim; (3) the state and local character of the

---

[23] As we will see, the Supreme Court agreed to review 76 percent (25) of these thirty-three cases, compared to the 72 percent (118) review rate for all LSP sponsored cases. The LSP won 68 percent (17) of these twenty-five cases, compared to a 62 percent (74) overall win rate.

[24] See Note, "Beyond the Neighborhood Office," pp. 756–60; Greenberg, "Litigation for Social Change," pp. 335–40.

[25] Greenberg, "Litigation for Social Change," p. 336; Sparer, "The Role of the Welfare Client's Lawyer," p. 366.

welfare system, which, among other things, is responsible for the numerous welfare "residence" rules for the continuing major reliance on state and local funding; and (4) the inadequate and often shockingly low amount of the money grant.[26]

His ultimate goal was to convince the Supreme Court to "read a 'right to life' into the equal protection clause of the fourteenth amendment that would guarantee an adequate minimum payment for every needy individual in society."[27]

Sparer's strategy coincided with and followed doctrinal developments in nonpoverty areas. The Supreme Court's increasing attention to procedural due process claims and its flirtation with a rejection of the right-privilege distinction opened the door to advocacy for procedural protections in the administration of public welfare. The Court's expanding interpretation of the equal protection clause provided LSP attorneys with a constitutional basis for challenges to rules that treat the poor, or subgroups within the poverty community, differently.[28] Indeed, had the Court not already begun enforcing due process provisions in the criminal justice system and condemning violations of the equal protection clause in the treatment of racial groups, Sparer's strategy, if even conceived, would have been implausible.

Many of Sparer's critiques of the welfare system were ultimately addressed in LSP Supreme Court cases.[29] These cases were only partly a result of Sparer's strategy and the Columbia Center's work; most of them were brought "out-of-order" and without the direct assistance of the Columbia Center. The de-

[26] Sparer, "The Right to Welfare," p. 66.

[27] Krislov, "OEO Lawyers Fail," p. 223. Piven and Cloward and the National Welfare Rights Organization advocated a "flood-the-system" litigation plan. The idea was to bring thousands of welfare cases in order to overwhelm the system until it broke down completely, forcing the legislature to enact fundamental changes. This did not appear to be Sparer's approach while he was at the LSP, but the two strategies are not mutually exclusive. Cloward and Piven, "A Strategy to End Poverty."

[28] See Gunther, *Cases*, 10th ed., pp. 646–49, 670–72; Tribe, *American Constitutional Law*, pp. 501–15; Sherbert v. Verner (1963); Reich, "New Property"; Van Alstyne, "The Demise of the Right-Privilege Distinction"; Gunther, "Foreword"; but later see Van Alstyne, "Cracks in 'The New Property.'"

[29] In *King v. Smith* (1968), the Court struck down the "man-in-the-house" regulation (see also *Lewis v. Martin* [1969]); in *Goldberg v. Kelly* (1970), the Court required a hearing before termination of welfare benefits (see also *Wheeler v. Montgomery* [1970]); in *Shapiro v. Thompson* (1969), the Court struck down one year residency requirements (see also *Pease v. Hansen* [1971]); in *Graham v. Richardson* (1971), the Court struck down provisions denying welfare benefits to resident aliens who had not resided in the U.S. for a specified number of years; in *Department of Agriculture v. Moreno* (1973), the Court struck down the denial of food stamps to households whose members are not all related to each other; in *Lascaris v. Shirley* (1975), the Court ruled that AFDC recipients could not be compelled to cooperate in paternity or support actions against absent parents (see also *Shapiro v. Doe* [1970]); in *Rosando v. Wyman* (1970) the Court struck down a statute that eliminated special needs grants from welfare benefits; in *Shea v. Vialpando* (1974) the Court invalidated a regulation fixing standard allowances for certain work expenses to be deducted from income in determining eligibility for AFDC, but not allowing deduction for expenses exceeding standard; and in *Towsend v. Swank* (1971) the Court struck down regulations excluding 18- through 20-year-old college students from AFDC benefits.

centralized nature of the LSP and the autonomy of the local attorneys impinged on the Center's planning efforts.

The story of some of the LSP's major welfare cases illustrates the inability of the Columbia Center to implement Sparer's plan. The Center had targeted the maximum family-grant regulation for early Supreme Court adjudication of Sparer's equal protection arguments. Instead, *King v. Smith* (1968), challenging "man-in-the-house" rules, reached the Court first. It was decided on narrow statutory grounds even though LSP attorneys had made an equal protection argument. When a challenge to the maximum grant rule finally reached the Court in 1970, the Court upheld it in *Dandridge v. Williams*, failing to declare wealth a "suspect class" that would trigger heightened scrutiny under the equal protection clause. An interviewer of Sparer reports that:

> Sparer, the author of the original blueprint, feels even today [1973] that if the *Dandridge* case had reached the Court first, it would have been won, but there was no way of getting it there when he wanted to. Moreover, he feels that a case from Maryland was a relatively bad case to bring up because the maximum grant was a relatively high $250 per month. A far better case would have been one from Mississippi where the grant was only $108 and the state was well known as racist. But the Maryland case was brought by lawyers who appeared to want nothing to do with the Center and after they had won in the trial court, the decision to go on to the Supreme Court of the United States was in the hands of Maryland, not the plaintiffs.[30]

*Dandridge* was a major loss for the LSP. Had the Court accepted the LSP's argument that there was a constitutional "right to the necessities of life," *Dandridge* would have been a powerful precedent, inviting equal protection challenges to a broad array of disadvantages that the poor suffer. Instead, Justice Stewart's majority opinion scolded, "The Constitution does not empower this Court to second guess state officials charged with the difficult responsibility of allocating limited public welfare funds among the myriad of potential recipients."

Unlike Sparer, who believed *Dandridge* could have been won if it had come up earlier, Krislov attributes the Program's failure in *Dandridge* to its premature appearance before the Court. He argues that it was not the "casework versus test cases" tension or lack of acceptance of the law reform goal that cost the Program *Dandridge*; rather, it was the speed of the attack. In 1973, he wrote:

> In the end, however, it was not these problems which caused the ultimate failure of the OEO effort; but rather, it was the problem of time. There was not enough time for the necessary analysis, criticism and refinement of the "right to life" doctrine. There

---

[30] Greenberg, "Litigation for Social Change," p. 338. Greenberg interviewed Sparer on 16 September 1973. Other scholars' accounts of interviews with Sparer are relied on here because his death in 1982 prevented an interview by the author.

was not enough time to permit a judicial acceptance of a new constitutional doctrine nor was there time to obscure the fine line between judicial and legislative rulemaking authority. The OEO lawyers overenthusiastically used rather than totally misused that process. Their espousal of a strategy, their tactics and their sense of what was achievable in a short period of time all appear faulty. A more cautious approach, a more limited set of expectations and above all a patience might achieve much of what was originally aspired. There is no reason to believe that the ultimate goal cannot be achieved with realistic aims and expectations.[31]

Krislov's essential argument is that the LSP's reform efforts were too much too soon. It is impossible to know whether Sparer or Krislov has best identified the reasons for the Program's failure in *Dandridge*; what is clear, is that the appearance of *Dandridge* on the Court's calender in 1970 was not the result of an LSP litigation strategy.

The Center was equally unable to control the timing of litigation that resulted in a major LSP victory. The Center was "caught off guard" as local project attorneys brought innumerable cases challenging welfare residency requirements. One of them, *Shapiro v. Thompson*, reached the Court in 1969 against the wishes of the Center, "which had projected that these kinds of issues should come up later."[32] Many years later, one of the Center's attorneys commented on the Center's role in *Shapiro*:

> Welfare residency cases were not high on the priority list of the [Columbia] national back-up center because it did not feel that it had a very good chance of winning. Not because they [Center attorneys] didn't think it was a serious problem, but because they wanted some victories for precedent value before they raised that issue. But the local attorneys felt differently and they had clients. The back-up center got into the case long before it went to the Supreme Court, but the back-up center was pulled into it kicking and screaming.

Another attorney's final verdict on the Center was: "The Columbia Center's effort backfired. There were constant tensions—struggles between local agencies where the cases began and Columbia who would take them over when they got to the Supreme Court." Hence, Sparer and the Columbia Center provided much of the intellectual groundwork for the LSP's welfare cases and technical assistance to some of the attorneys involved in these cases. But the Center did not and could not orchestrate a litigation campaign.[33]

[31] Krislov, "OEO Lawyers Fail," p. 245. Of course, at the time Krislov was writing, the bench had a much different ideological composition than it does today.

[32] Greenberg suggests that "Legal Services neighborhood offices probably stimulated so many residency restriction cases because the issues were easily understood without mastery of the technical complexities of welfare law. The higher volume occurred even though the welfare testing memoranda [of the Columbia Center] discouraged early litigation of *Shapiro* issues because of their complexity and adverse precedent." Greenberg, "Litigation for Social Change," p. 337.

[33] Greenberg writes, "Litigation was not executed as their [Columbia Center's] original mem-

*Factors That Influenced the Decision to Appeal*

Although local LSP attorneys made the decision to appeal to the Supreme Court on a case-by-case basis, sometimes with guidance from the back-up centers, there were certain common factors in the decision-making process. Rathjen, studying appeal decision-making processes generally, has found that, regardless of the "legal value perspective" of the attorney, "far and away the single most important consideration [in the decision to appeal] . . . involved the lawyer's estimate of securing a favorable outcome from the Supreme Court."[34] Regardless of whether attorneys focus on client service or reform, there is little reason to appeal if defeat seems certain. The importance of securing a victory is reflected in some of the factors that influenced the LSP's appeal decisions. It is significant that the Program's appeals grew out of individual client service; the decision on whether or not to use a case as a vehicle for policy reform was almost always made after the case had been through the trial courts. LSP attorneys report that very few cases were "filed specifically with an eye on the Supreme Court."[35]

Often, as we would expect, the first factor in the decision to appeal was the perceived receptivity of the Court, in terms of both the current state of doctrine and the justices' manifest value preferences. In the Program's early days, some LSP attorneys were concerned about securing victories for precedential value. The Columbia Center felt that challenges to the welfare system should follow a sequential order. A favorable precedent, once established, encouraged LSP attorneys to appeal cases in which they could invoke a similar argument. When the Court rejected a line of reasoning, many LSP attorneys avoided appealing similar cases. One attorney described an example of this process:

> From *King v. Smith* until 1972, LSP lawyers were big on using the *King* rationale; then the Court decided *New York State Department of Social Services v. Dublino*. It refused to strike down restrictive work requirements. The Court decided a case the

---

orandum suggested because other lawyers had their own ideas of how and when to proceed, cases tended to arise where poverty lawyers were." Greenberg, "Litigation for Social Change," p. 340.

[34] Rathjen, "Lawyers and the Appellate Choice." On the other hand, O'Connor reports that not all interest group litigation has "obtain[ing] policy objectives through favorable judicial determinations" as its goal. Particularly for groups engaged in "publicity-oriented litigation," the likelihood of gaining favorable decision may not be controlling. O'Connor, *Women's Organizations'*, esp. pp. 2–5.

[35] Available evidence suggests that LSP attorneys were not appealing a disproportionate number of cases to the U.S. Supreme Court. It has been estimated that the LSP appealed one thousand to three thousand cases a year, or nine thousand to twenty-seven thousand during its nine-year tenure; hence, the 164 Supreme Court appeals represent 0.6 to 1.8 percent of the Program's cases decided by appellate courts. In contrast, 20.3 percent of all cases decided by the Second, Fifth, and D.C. Courts of Appeals were appealed to the U.S. Supreme Court in 1965–67. Howard, *Courts of Appeals*, p. 68.

other way. It had a chilling effect on attorneys bringing cases using the *King* line of argument. The Court, for political reasons, could not bring itself to say states couldn't try to make people work. *Dandridge* stopped the constitutional equal protection argument.

The LSP attorneys report that their decision to appeal was affected not only by actual changes in Court rulings, but also by changes in Court personnel, as the Nixon appointees assumed the bench:

[In the] early seventies we perceived the Supreme Court as hostile. The change in the Supreme Court put a damper on the LSP's litigation. There was a sense in the Warren Court era that you could point to the Court; that the Court would bail you out.

Change in the Court made the LSP more reluctant to appeal—even if they lost below. They did not want to risk losing for everybody in the country instead of just one jurisdiction.

During the Burger Court era we set out to get to the Court less frequently, although we were less afraid of statutory claims.

Certainly, the ideological composition of the Court affected LSP attorneys' perception of their chance of success, but LSP attorneys actually appealed more cases after 1971, when there were four Nixon appointees on the bench, than they did before 1971. Of the 108 cases in which the LSP represented the appellant or petitioner, 59 percent (64) were decided or denied review between 1972 and the end of the 1974 October Term.[36] Furthermore, as we will see, the Program won the same ratio of cases after 1971 as before.

A second factor that sometimes influenced the appeal decision was the suitability of the case for policy development. Back-up center attorneys were more likely to encourage an appeal if the case presented a good fact situation. An attorney described the considerations in one of the more carefully planned LSP cases:

*King v. Smith* was the first welfare case to ever go to the Supreme Court. We thought it through very carefully and at every stage. We were concerned to take the most sympathetic case. We thought through what jurisdiction we wanted to bring it in.

[36] These patterns of increasing numbers of Supreme Court appeals may be explained by the development of doctrine by the Program's early litigation and the organizational maturation we would expect. Indeed, Hannon suggests that the LSP did not really encourage law reform until 1969. Hannon, "The Leadership Problem." But see Johnson, "Refutation." Perhaps LSP attorneys would have appealed even more cases had they not interpreted the Burger Court as hostile to the poor. However, there is much debate over how much of a shift to conservatism there really was in the early and mid-seventies as the Burger Court took the bench. See especially Howard, "Is the Burger Court a Nixon Court?"; Blasi, *The Burger Court*. A similar pattern emerges for the fifty-six cases in which the LSP represented the appellee or respondent, with 64 percent (36) being decided or denied review in the later period. Hence, 61 percent (100) of the LSP sponsored cases were decided or denied review after 1971 when the four Nixon appointees were sitting.

We consciously selected a deep South state and a woman who did not have a man living with her, but had only had sexual intercourse a few times. We first took a case that would appeal at a gut level—one that was easy to be outraged at.

The attorney of record, Martin Garbus, also describes the factors operating in the decision to use the case as a vehicle for reform:

From Alabama's point of view, Mrs. Smith's case was the worst possible one to litigate. Alabama seemed to have no proof of any wrongdoing by Mrs. Smith or of support being given by any substitute father. . . . Our decision to litigate was dictated in part by the "erosion theory of litigation": take the worst example of a practice or rule, the gross or excessive form in the most highly suspect social setting, and challenge it.[37]

Although back-up centers looked for cases with "good" fact patterns, local attorneys who appealed cases were not always so sensitive. For example, the factual record in *Wyman v. James*, upholding New York's welfare home visitation regulations, was unsympathetic enough to be noted by Justice Blackmun in a footnote to his opinion:

The record is revealing as to Mrs. James' failure ever really to satisfy the requirements for eligibility; as to constant and repeated demands; as to attitude toward the case-worker; as to reluctance to cooperate; as to evasiveness; as to occasional belligerency. There are indications that all was not always well with the infant Maurice (skull fracture, a dent in the head, a possible rat bite). The picture is a sad and unhappy one.

A related consideration was maximization of the breadth of the decision. One attorney described how he combined several cases so that the Court would have to reach the constitutional issue:

I held off the Connecticut case to let [another LSP case] catch up. The Connecticut case could have been decided more narrowly. The Connecticut statute was weird. It had a lot of technicalities. And my ego was involved. I could argue it better than the Connecticut attorneys. I filed a motion with the Supreme Court to keep them from hearing the Connecticut case until [another LSP case] was ready.[38]

The position of other actors in the poverty field was also considered. For example, the Department of Health, Education, and Welfare (HEW) occasionally filed amicus curiae briefs in welfare cases. One attorney reported that the back-up centers discouraged an LSP appeal if HEW was planning to file a brief in opposition because this would increase the LSP's chance of losing. In many instances, HEW knew that the state was not acting in accord with HEW regu-

---

[37] Garbus, "Mrs. Sylvester Smith," pp. 149–52, quoted in Greenberg, "Litigation for Social Change," p. 368.

[38] Three cases were heard together and the LSP won.

lations but, for a variety of reasons, it had not applied the ultimate sanction of terminating HEW funds to the state. HEW's disapproval of state regulations encouraged LSP attorneys to challenge these practices. For example, according to the attorney in *King v. Smith*:

> The Department of Health, Education, and Welfare had told Alabama to change the [man-in-the-house] regulation, but it continued to give Alabama funds to carry out the AFDC program despite the defects in the state law. To have cut the program off would have been a greater tragedy, HEW reasoned, for then no federal aid would go to any Alabama children. HEW's past criticism of the Alabama program meant it did not feel forced to oppose us in a legal challenge. In fact, we hoped HEW might even support our arguments.[39]

Thus, even though there was no grand litigation strategy, tactical considerations did figure into some of the appeal decisions.

A third factor that influenced the decision to appeal was motivations peculiar to the local attorney involved in the case. The Program's combining of casework and law reform affected these motivations. Some attorneys appealed to the Supreme Court out of a commitment to their client, irrespective of the suitability of the case for policy making or the case's place in a larger litigation design. One attorney, committed to law reform, remarked: "I respected Sparer a great deal, but I would like to think that I would appeal a case if the client wanted to, even if Sparer said no in terms of national strategy."

Perhaps most significant, appellate advocacy, in and of itself, was important to some LSP attorneys. It was a way to give meaning to the seemingly routine client service that consumed most of the lawyers' time. Katz's sociological study of Chicago's legal aid and legal services organizations reveals that while "lawyers [had come] . . . to Legal Aid out of a common perception of marginal market position," and were socialized into a "complacent perspective on the requirements of equal justice for the poor," "in socioeconomic status and educational background the new poverty [LSP] lawyers represented a cross-section of the young bar," bringing with them a "historically novel diversity of altruistic, political, and activist themes into the institution."[40] Katz demonstrates that while "there was no simple, positive, direct relationship between the strength of the sixties movements for social change and the aggressiveness with which [LSP] lawyers for the poor interpreted the requirements of equal justice," LSP attorneys did search for "involvement" and personal fulfillment in their work in ways legal aid attorneys had not. Katz writes, "Legal Services lawyers have shared an emphasis on 'involvement' that sharply distinguishes them from those at Legal Aid. . . . [Legal Services]

[39] Garbus, "Mrs. Sylvester Smith," pp. 149–52, quoted in Greenberg, "Litigation for Social Change," p. 368.

[40] Katz, *Poor People's Lawyers*, pp. 51, 52, 71.

lawyers have gravitated toward reform activities as a necessary means to making work stay attractive, not necessarily as a preconceived goal or overriding career motive."[41]

Appellate advocacy was one way LSP attorneys could "transform the social structure of [their] everyday work world . . . [it could] remove each of the limitations imposed by the proximate social environment on the development of cumulative meaning in everyday work."[42] Katz reports that, in attempting to add significance to their work, "the common methodology is to redefine an individual client's problem as it has been narrowly defined by an adversary so that it impinges upon greater interests. These strategies raise the stakes for Legal Services practice, with the result that work experience literally becomes more challenging."[43]

More generally, participation in appellate litigation provided LSP attorneys the opportunity for unusually rapid career development and enhancement of professional prestige, despite the low status generally associated with working for an indigent clientele.[44] They had an incentive to search for appealable cases as they handled their routine daily case load. In contrast to the everyday, low-status casework, law reform provided LSP attorneys with "more responsibility for matters of greater public controversy, with less internal constraint, in higher courts and at a younger age, than [enjoyed by] their peers elsewhere."[45] Even in elite private practice where the client server and reformer roles mix, junior lawyers are rarely allowed to handle the client's ap-

---

[41] Ibid., pp. 10, 50–64, 71, 90–104, 105–6. In examining the development of legal assistance in Chicago, Katz found that "separated by widely divergent personal backgrounds, lawyers came to Legal Aid [before 1965] out of a common perception of marginal market position. . . . Lawyers joining the staff did not initially understand Legal Aid work in the rhetoric of altruism. An appreciation of a Legal Aid job as a step up in occupational mobility does not equip one to feel comfortable in it. By adopting 'reasonableness' as a work ethic, Legal Aid lawyers translate the procedural, day-in-court jurisprudence into a means for personally accepting everyday professional and moral limitations." In contrast, "the overwhelming majority of [Legal Services] entrants [after 1965] have come with the demand—extraordinary in the history of this institution although not among young professionals generally—that the workplace continuously engage them in order to retain them. . . . It is primarily through the pursuit of involvement that Legal Services lawyers have made themselves vehicles for reforming the structure of poverty." Katz, *Poor People's Lawyers*, pp. 52, 56, 105. Erlanger found that the background characteristics of LSP lawyers were not very different from those of the bar as a whole, though considerably more impressive than legal aid's. He suggests that the "radical" nature of LSP (i.e., aggressive appellate advocacy) was due to the expanded opportunities to pursue clients' interests the LSP offered lawyers. Erlanger has debunked the "new breed of activist lawyers with elite credentials myth." Erlanger, "Lawyers and Neighborhood Legal Services."

[42] Katz, *Poor People's Lawyers*, pp. 107–8.

[43] Ibid., p. 107.

[44] Prior to the establishment of the LSP, legal aid positions were viewed as low-status jobs and as a last resort for many young graduates entering the job market. See Auerbach, *Unequal Justice*; Katz, *Poor People's Lawyers*, pp. 51–64; Rothstein, "Myth of Sisyphus," pp. 504–6.

[45] Katz, *Poor People's Lawyers*, p. 110.

pellate work. As one LSP attorney reminisced, "It was an ego trip. My wife kept a scrapbook of my newspaper clippings." The need for "involvement" through reform litigation was so strong that individual attorneys fought to retain control over their "significant" cases.[46] Such cases generated publicity for the attorney. Indeed, the LSP cultivated in-house publicity for these attorneys as one way of motivating them to engage in law reform. Another attorney reported: "Attorneys appealed to the Supreme Court as a personal ego stroke. The incredibly high visibility was job compensation." Some LSP attorneys appealed cases to give meaning to the drudgery and frustration of their day-to-day practice.

Ironically, some of the same attorney-related factors that prevented the LSP from implementing a coordinated litigation strategy also motivated individual LSP attorneys to appeal to the Supreme Court. The autonomy that attorneys demanded was an important component in both phenomena.

### Representing the Appellee/Respondent

Not only was the LSP unable to guide and control the cases that Program attorneys chose to appeal to the U.S. Supreme Court, but the LSP attorneys' lower court victories also allowed the opposing parties in these cases to control the decision to appeal to the High Court.[47] In 34 percent (56) of the 164 Supreme Court cases sponsored by the LSP, Program attorneys, who had won below, represented the appellee or respondent at the Supreme Court level.

While the LSP had virtually no opportunity to influence its opponents' decisions on what to appeal and these cases were not the product of an LSP litigation strategy, the poor's participation in Supreme Court decision making in these cases was also a result of the LSP's expansion of the poor's access to the courts. The LSP's blending of client service and reform made its attorneys willing to engage in litigation on behalf of their poor clients, a prerequisite to Supreme Court action. If LSP attorneys had not gone to trial and mounted lower court appeals, the LSP's opponents would have had few occasions to appeal to the Supreme Court. The LSP's advocacy forced those involved in poverty policy to take cognizance of the legal and constitutional issues that had so often been ignored when dealing with the poor. As the LSP provided counsel to millions of poor people, the LSP's opponents could not ignore the "adverse" precedents the LSP's representation of the poor was creating; they had to challenge them or honor them. Furthermore, the LSP's decentralized system of representation meant that in these cases the poor appellee or respondent enjoyed the benefit of counsel familiar with the case from its inception

[46] Ibid., pp. 109–13.

[47] Interest groups that are pursuing a litigation strategy also find this to be an impediment to effective control over the course of litigation that affects their policy goals. See Wasby, "Planned Litigation."

and experienced with the legal problems of the poor. This was particularly important since the petitioners in these fifty-six cases were overwhelmingly state and local governments (84 percent [47]) who could deploy considerable resources to defend their rules and statutes.[48]

While most appellate courts usually uphold the court below, in the Supreme Court the defensive posture is an unfavorable one since the Supreme Court generally reverses two-thirds of the decisions it reviews.[49] Nonetheless, some of the LSP attorneys welcomed the opportunity to try to convince the Supreme Court to nationalize their lower court victories, particularly before the Nixon appointees joined the Court. As one attorney noted: "During the Warren Court era, if the LSP won below and the other side appealed, there were mixed feelings about going up to the Supreme Court. We did not mind going up as much. It was a chance to make national law. During the Burger Court era the LSP did not want to go up. The risk of losing everything was too great."

And, strangely, the LSP did end up on the defensive in a smaller proportion of its cases after 1971. Whereas the LSP had represented the respondent in 45 percent (20) of the sixty-four cases it sponsored that were decided or denied review up through 1971, the LSP was only cast in the defensive posture in 36 percent (36) of the one hundred cases it sponsored that were decided or denied review during 1972 through the end of the 1974 October Term.

Appeals by the LSP's opponents, no less than appeals by the LSP, presented the Supreme Court with new and different opportunities for decision and, whether on the defensive or offensive, LSP attorneys provided the poor with a voice in Supreme Court decision making.

## THE HETEROGENEITY OF THE LSP'S DOCKET

The LSP's inability to implement a litigation strategy, or control which of its lower court victories were appealed, resulted in an uncoordinated, heterogeneous LSP Supreme Court docket that reflected the concerns of individual clients as translated into legal controversies by their local LSP attorneys and by the lower courts.[50] There is a great diversity in the cases the LSP sponsored in the Supreme Court, reflecting the diverse concerns of the Program's clients.

A breakdown of the 164 LSP sponsored cases by subject shows that the LSP presented the Court with opportunities for decision in a wide array of areas (see table 3-1). Transfer program cases account for 37 percent (60) of the LSP's Supreme Court docket—by far the largest single slice. No other group of cases consumed more than 15 percent of the docket. At first glance, this seems to

---

[48] The remaining 16 percent consisted of seven cases filed by the federal government, which has even greater resources than the states to devote to litigation, and two cases filed by private organizations.

[49] See Howard, *Courts of Appeals*, pp. 40, 58.

[50] Of course, there is always some "slippage" in this translation process. See esp. Handler, *Social Movements*; Olson, *Clients and Lawyers*; Rosenthal, *Lawyer and Client*.

TABLE 3-1
The LSP's Supreme Court Docket by Subject, 1966–1974 Terms

| Subject | LSP Appellant/ Petitioner (n) | Appellee/ Respondent (n) | Total (n) | Percentage of LSP Docket (%) |
|---|---|---|---|---|
| Transfer Programs | 26 | 34 | 60 | 37% |
| Welfare | 20 | 26 | 46 | |
| Social Security | 3 | 3 | 6 | |
| Unemployment Comp. | 2 | 4 | 6 | |
| Food Programs | 0 | 1 | 1 | |
| Workman's Comp. | 1 | 0 | 1 | |
| Criminal Justice | 18 | 5 | 23 | 14 |
| Criminal | 9 | 3 | 12 | |
| Juvenile | 7 | 1 | 8 | |
| Prisons | 2 | 1 | 3 | |
| Shelter | 17 | 2 | 19 | 12 |
| Housing | 13 | 2 | 15 | |
| Public Utilities | 4 | 0 | 4 | |
| Personal Well-Being | 9 | 10 | 19 | 12 |
| Domestic Relations | 1 | 0 | 1 | |
| Health | 1 | 2 | 3 | |
| Mental Health | 0 | 2 | 2 | |
| Education | 4 | 6 | 10 | |
| Licenses | 3 | 0 | 3 | |
| Financial Relationships | 15 | 2 | 17 | 10 |
| Employment | 3 | 1 | 4 | |
| Consumer | 9 | 1 | 10 | |
| Bankruptcy | 3 | 0 | 3 | |
| Legal Procedure | 13 | 1 | 14 | 9 |
| Civil Procedure | 6 | 0 | 1 | |
| Legal Services | 1 | 0 | 2 | |
| I.F.P. Procedures | 6 | 1 | 7 | |
| Political Rights | 6 | 1 | 7 | 4 |
| Voting Rights | 3 | 1 | 4 | |
| Civil Rights | 2 | 0 | 2 | |
| Demonstrations | 1 | 0 | 1 | |
| Indian Rights | 4 | 1 | 5 | 3 |
| Totals | 108 | 56 | 164 | 101%[a] |

[a] Percentage in excess of 100 due to rounding error.

*Note*: *Clearinghouse Review's* subject categorizations were adopted here.

confirm the notion that poverty law is welfare law. On closer examination, the failure of other subjects to exceed 15 percent seems to be a function of the specificity of the classifications and the diversity of the Program's litigation. Poverty law cannot simply be equated with welfare law. Over 60 percent of the LSP's cases did not involve redistributive programs. The poor have legal problems beyond extracting benefits from government. The breadth of the subjects addressed in LSP cases is a reflection of the clients' voice in directing LSP litigation. The preeminence of the Columbia Center on Social Welfare Policy and Law suggests that had the LSP been able to implement a litigation strategy, it is likely that there would have been an even stronger emphasis on redistributive programs in the LSP's docket. Instead, the inability of the Center to direct LSP litigation is further evidenced by the diversity of the Program's cases. Ironically, despite the Columbia Center's desire to implement a litigation strategy designed to reform welfare, the LSP was the appellant/petitioner in only 43 percent (26) of the sixty transfer program cases that the LSP sponsored, and, indeed, of the Program's fifty-six defensive postures, 61 percent (34) were in transfer program cases.[51] In only one other group of cases, those involving personal well-being, did the Program find itself defending lower court victories more often than it was asking for a reversal.

Not only did the LSP's cases encompass a wide variety of subjects, but they also presented the Court with a wide variety of legal issues. In 82 percent (134) of the cases, Legal Services attorneys made a constitutional argument (see table 3-2). While the equal protection and due process clauses were, by far, the most frequently invoked constitutional provisions, both to secure and overturn lower court decisions, Program attorneys also pursued claims based on various Bill of Rights guarantees. Furthermore, as we will see in examining the doctrinal importance of the Court's plenary decisions in these cases, LSP lawyers invoked the equal protection and due process clauses in arguing for a variety of different legal rights for their poor clients. The Program's Supreme Court docket did not consist of multiple cases designed to convince the Court to adopt a single constitutional principle.

The LSP presented the Court with legal challenges from across the nation. Legal Services Program attorneys from 116 of the 265 local projects participated in the Program's Supreme Court docket. The LSP's 164 cases were appealed from twenty different states, the District of Columbia, and from all the Courts of Appeals except the Sixth Circuit.[52] The Program's cases came dis-

[51] There are several possible explanations for this phenomena. First, the lower courts may have been more inclined to rule in favor of the poor in welfare cases than in other areas, particularly after the Supreme Court had upheld their claims in some significant early cases such as *King v. Smith, Goldberg v. Kelly*, and *Shapiro v. Thompson*. Second, in welfare cases the opposing party is generally a governmental unit. Government has the funds to appeal cases and in welfare cases it often had financial incentives to do so.

[52] Of the fifty-two cases that were appealed from state courts, the single largest group consisted of eleven cases from California, followed by five cases from New York. Of the forty-two cases

TABLE 3-2

The LSP's Supreme Court Docket by Constitutional Issue, 1966–1974 Terms

| Constitutional Issue | LSP | | Total (n) | Percentage of LSP Docket (%) |
| --- | --- | --- | --- | --- |
| | Appellant/ Petitioner (n) | Appellee/ Respondent (n) | | |
| Equal Protection, 5th and 14th Amendments | 42 | 23 | 65 | 40% |
| Due Process, 5th and 14th Amendments[a] | 29 | 17 | 46 | 28 |
| First Amendment | 4 | 0 | 4 | 2 |
| Criminal Procedure Amendments | 5 | 2 | 7 | 4 |
| Right to Access to the Courts | 8 | 1 | 9 | 6 |
| Other | 2 | 1 | 3 | 2 |
| None | 18 | 12 | 30 | 18 |
| Totals | 108 | 56 | 164 | 100% (N = 164) |

[a] Use of the Fourteenth amendment for incorporation purposes alone was not included in the due process category; rather, such cases were coded based on the claimed Bill of Rights guarantee.

proportionately from the federal courts with 43 percent (70) being direct appeals from three-judge district courts (see table 3-3).[53] Only 32 percent of the Program's Supreme Court cases were appealed from state courts, though state laws were at issue in 72 percent (118) of the LSP's cases and local rules or private practices were challenged in another 7 percent (12) and 6 percent (9) of the cases, respectively. Furthermore, state and local governments were the LSP's opponents in 74 percent (121) of the Program's 164 sponsored cases. The LSP was using the federal courts to force state and local governments to honor federal statutes and the U.S. Constitution in their interaction with the poor.

While in the single most common type of LSP case, the LSP sought to con-

that came from the Courts of Appeals, ten came from the Second Circuit; seven from the Ninth Circuit; six from the Fifth Circuit; five from the Seventh Circuit; three each from the Third, Eighth, and D.C. Circuits; two each from the Fourth and Tenth Circuits; and one from the First Circuit.

[53] Overall, 68 percent (112) of the LSP's appeals and petitions were from federal courts. The advantages of pressing the poor's claims in federal courts rather than state courts are outlined in Note, "Federal Judicial Review of State Welfare Practices"; see Redlich, "The Act of Welfare Advocacy," pp. 85–89.

TABLE 3-3
The LSP's Supreme Court Docket by Source, 1966–1974 Terms

| Source | LSP | | Total (n) |
|---|---|---|---|
| | Appellant/ Petitioner (n) | Appellee/ Respondent (n) | |
| U.S. Courts of Appeals | 27%  (29) | 23%  (13) | 26%  (42) |
| 3-Judge U.S. District Courts | 30  (32) | 68  (38) | 43  (70) |
| State Courts | 44  (47) | 9  (5) | 32  (52) |
| Total | 101%ᵃ(108) | 100%  (56) | 101%ᵃ(164) |

ᵃ Percentage in excess of 100 due to rounding error.

vince the Court to uphold, on equal protection grounds, a three-judge district court's overturning of a state welfare rule, more cases in fact deviate, in one respect or another, from this prototype than conform to it. Because the LSP let its Supreme Court docket grow out of its client service, and because it served diverse clients that had only their indigence as a common bond, the Program presented the Supreme Court with a heterogeneous collection of the legal problems faced by the poor.

### AMICUS CURIAE PARTICIPATION

In addition to sponsoring 164 cases before the U.S. Supreme Court, the LSP, like other litigation-oriented interest groups, also represented the poor as "friends of the court" by filing seventy amicus curiae briefs in fifty-nine cases during the 1966 through 1974 Terms.[54] These seventy briefs represent 12 percent of all amicus briefs filed during this period.[55] Amicus briefs were one way the LSP back-up centers lent their specialized expertise to the cases brought by local LSP projects. Fifty-six percent (39) of the seventy LSP amicus briefs were filed by the back-up centers. In thirty-five of the fifty-nine cases in which the LSP filed amicus briefs, LSP attorneys were also serving as counsel

[54] Indeed, the filing of amicus curiae briefs is the most common way groups participate in Supreme Court decision making. In studying the 1969 through 1980 Terms, O'Connor and Epstein report that liberal groups simply filed amicus briefs in 61 percent (414) of the cases in which they participated and conservative groups simply filed amicus briefs in 97 percent (254) of the cases in which they participated. O'Connor and Epstein, "The Rise of Conservative Interest Group Litigation," p. 482.

[55] There was a total of 603 requests to file amicus curiae briefs granted between 1966 and 1974. Bradley and Gardner, "Underdogs, Upperdogs and the Use of the Amicus Brief," p. 91. By way of comparison, between 1920 and 1973, the ACLU filed 178 amicus briefs—more than any other group, including the U.S. Solicitor General, who filed 161. Puro, "The United States as Amicus Curiae," p. 223.

in the case. In the remaining twenty-four cases, the LSP participated only by filing amicus curiae briefs.[56]

Scholars have disagreed about the influence of amicus curiae briefs on Supreme Court decision making, but there is an increasing recognition that amicus briefs do play an important role.[57] Barker has outlined five functions that such briefs perform for the Court. They (1) add factual data often necessary for rational decision making; (2) focus attention on the broad issues involved, allowing the Court to view the controversy in a similar perspective to other decision makers; (3) illuminate the inability or unwillingness of other governmental institutions to deal with pressing issues; (4) allow the weighing of ''political'' information in a judicial way; and (5) permit identification of potential supporters and opponents of a particular course of decision.[58] Most interest groups consider amicus briefs to be an important part of their litigation strategies[59] and the Court does seem to give them some consideration. O'Connor and Epstein found that between 1969 and 1981, amicus briefs were cited by majority, concurring, or dissenting opinions in 18 percent of the cases where at least one amicus brief was filed.[60]

Although it is not possible to separate and measure the influence of the LSP's amicus briefs on the Court's decisions, it is important to recognize that the LSP participated in Supreme Court decision making as a friend of the Court as well as through sponsorship. The LSP's twenty-four amicus cases represent a 15 percent addition to its participation in the Supreme Court docket.

A description of the LSP's twenty-four amicus cases is outlined in table 3-4. The LSP generally filed in support of the appellant/petitioner. Criminal cases

[56] The disadvantaged litigants in these twenty-four cases were represented by private counsel (50 percent [12]), other interest groups such as the NAACP LDF or ACLU (29 percent [7]), or counsel appointed by the Court (21 percent [5]).

[57] In 1963 Krislov found that the Court viewed amicus filers ''as a potential litigant in future cases, as an ally of one of the parties, or as the representative of an interest not otherwise represented.'' Krislov, ''The Amicus Curiae Brief.'' In 1966 Hakman argued, contrary to the conventional wisdom, that ''organized interest groups appear to play a relatively minor role in Supreme Court decision-making.'' Hakman, ''Lobbying the Supreme Court''; Hakman, ''The Supreme Court's Political Environment.'' However, in 1967 Barker maintained that amicus briefs perform important functions for the Court and alter the nature of the adjudicatory process: ''Just as group participation injects a more popular and majoritarian characteristic into the legislative process, it does the same for the judicial process.'' Barker, ''Third Parties.'' In 1981, O'Connor and Epstein wrote, ''Whether or not Hakman was correct in disparaging the 'folklore' of studies of judicial interest group activity, the same conclusion could not be drawn today.'' They found that amicus briefs were submitted in 53.4 percent of the noncommercial cases before the Court between 1970 and 1980. (Between 1953 and 1966 amicus briefs had been submitted in 23.8 percent of the noncommercial cases.) O'Connor and Epstein, ''Amicus Curiae.'' See also McIntosh, ''Supreme Court Impact on Third Parties''; McIntosh and Parker, ''Amici Curiae in the Court of Appeals.''

[58] Barker, ''Third Parties,'' pp. 54–60.

[59] O'Connor and Epstein, ''Amicus Curiae,'' p. 313. See also Epstein, *Conservatives*.

[60] O'Connor and Epstein, ''Court Rules and Workload,'' p. 42.

TABLE 3-4

An Outline of the LSP's Amicus Curiae Participation, 1966–1974 Terms

| | Percentage of LSP Amicus Cases (n) |
|---|---|
| Side of Participation | |
| Appellant/Petitioner | 83%(20) |
| Appellee/Respondent | 17   (4) |
| Total | 100%(24) |
| Subject | |
| Criminal Justice | 63%(15) |
| Personal Well-Being | 33   (8) |
| Legal Procedure | 4   (1) |
| Total | 100%(24) |
| Constitutional Issue | |
| Equal Protection, 5th and 14th Amendments | 29%   (7) |
| Due Process, 5th and 14th Amendments | 29   (7) |
| First Amendment | 8   (2) |
| Criminal Justice | 21   (5) |
| Other | 8   (2) |
| None | 4   (1) |
| Total | 99%[a](24) |
| Target | |
| Federal | 8%  (2) |
| State | 92  (22) |
| Total | 100%(24) |
| Source | |
| Federal Courts of Appeals | 33%  (8) |
| 3-Judge U.S. District Courts | 21   (5) |
| State Courts | 46   (11) |
| Total | 100%(24) |

[a] Percentage less than 100 due to rounding error.

predominated (63 percent [15]).[61] Like LSP sponsored cases, the principal target of LSP amicus cases was state legislation and practices (92 percent [22]); however, a greater proportion of the amicus cases came from the state courts (46 percent [11]). On the whole, there are no substantial differences between those cases in which the LSP only filed an amicus brief and those that it sponsored. Both groups are a heterogeneous lot suggesting that neither LSP spon-

[61] This is probably related to the statutory restrictions on LSP sponsorship of criminal cases enacted in 1967. *Economic Opportunity Act, Amendments of 1967*, H.R. Rep. No. 012, 90th Cong., 1st sess. (1967).

sorship nor amicus filing was guided by a litigation strategy. The Program's involvement in client service and appellate case sponsorship alerted LSP attorneys to the diversity of the legal issues affecting the poor.

## ATTORNEY, CLIENT, AND "CITIZEN PARTICIPATION"

It is clear that LSP attorneys' participation in Supreme Court litigation was not the product of an orchestrated litigation strategy analogous to those adopted by interest groups pursuing legal change through the courts. Individual LSP lawyers and clients made the decisions about which cases to pursue in the appellate courts and appeal to the Supreme Court. More by default than by design, the LSP's blending of client service and reform allowed for an unusual degree of "citizen participation" in the shaping of its Supreme Court docket, though this "citizen participation" was not accomplished through the procedures the architects of the Great Society had prescribed.

Like many other Great Society programs, by statute, "citizen participation" in LSP decision making was supposed to be achieved through the representation of the poverty community on the local projects' boards of directors.[62] The *Guidelines for Legal Services Programs*, issued in 1966, required local projects to involve the poor in the formulation and operation of the project.[63] Most boards of directors also included lawyers (some of whom represented the local bar), and middle-class laymen (some of whom represented other groups concerned with poverty).[64] There has been some question about the effective-

[62] *The Economic Opportunity Act, United States Code*, Title 42, Sec. 202(a)(3).

[63] The *Guidelines* read, "We must involve the impoverished people themselves in the formulation and operation of programs to alleviate poverty. The poor will not only be helped but must help themselves. The [Economic Opportunity] Act requires that programs for legal assistance, like all components of community action programs, be developed, conducted and administered 'with the maximum feasible participation of the residents of the areas and members of the groups served.' Policy for legal assistance programs must be formulated with the participation of the 'residents of the areas and members of the groups served.'. . . The poor must be represented on the board or policy-making committee of the program to provide legal services, just as they are represented on the policy-making body of the community action agency. The board members who represent the poor need not be poor themselves. However, if they are not 'residents of the areas and members of the groups served' then they must be truly representative of those residents and groups. This essential quality may be assured by truly democratic selection by the poor. There should neither be a requirement that the residents of the area must select lawyers nor any other arbitrary restriction. OEO does not require a fixed proportion of the people to be served or their representatives on the policy-making board. . . . The representation of the people to be served should be sufficient to assure that the concerns of people in poverty will be articulated and considered. Additional effective participation of the residents of the areas may be provided by advisory councils already existing under community action agency sponsorship or such councils formed for this specific purpose." *Guidelines for Legal Services Programs*, 1966, quoted in Johnson, *Justice and Reform*, pp. 321–22. For a discussion of the controversy surrounding adoption of this section of the *Guidelines*, see Johnson, *Justice and Reform*, pp. 108–12.

[64] Johnson, *Justice and Reform*, p. 100.

ness of the poor's participation in board decision making given the potential for dominance by the well-educated professionals with whom they shared power. Champagne reports:

> The Kettle data suggest that while the bar may control the local agency, poverty community representatives do have a voice in the operation of the projects. The board members overwhelmingly tended to believe that poverty representatives participate in discussions and have significant influence over policy outcomes, though participation by poor people and controversial case activity are not strongly related.[65]

On the other hand, Abel argues that the poor and their representatives were dominated by other board members, "who [were] more articulate, better educated, of higher status, and often legal professionals." Furthermore, he asserts that "many of the boards mandated by law [were] paper institutions."[66]

But, to evaluate "citizen participation" in the LSP based only on the effectiveness of the poor's participation on the local boards of directors, as prescribed by OEO, is to ignore the other avenues of participation that were unique to the LSP. Because the "service deliverers" were attorneys, they could limit the boards' influence by invoking the ABA Code of Professional Responsibility to protect their autonomy in the attorney-client relationship and to defend vigorous representation of the client. The LSP attorneys may have been better able to deal with the tension between the professionals and the clientele "citizen participation" produced in most OEO programs, since in litigation the attorney and client form an organic unit. The attorney-client relationship provided a crucial mechanism by which the "citizens," the poor clients, could control the Program's activities. At least in court, LSP attorneys had no voice without a willing client at their side. While LSP clients could not force attorneys to pursue their cases, they provided the attorneys with the pool of opportunities for litigation and they could refuse to participate in appellate challenges, leaving the attorneys powerless to act.[67] The adjudicatory policy-making process, which requires real cases and controversies, keeps the policymakers (i.e., lawyers and judges), tied to the "citizen" or client.

The Program's blending of client service and reform and its decentralized structure kept it from picking and choosing which clients to represent in the appellate courts based on preordained policy goals. Had the LSP operated more like an interest group, the boards of directors' role in defining and approving a litigation strategy would have allowed the boards to set the parameters of access to LSP representation before the Court. Of course, the LSP was not immune to the lawyer dominance problems generally found in litigation set-

---

[65] Champagne, "Internal Operation."

[66] Abel, "Law Without Politics," p. 523. See also Pious, "Policy"; Hannon, "Law Reform"; Finman, "OEO Legal Services." For a general review of the "citizen participation" component of the Great Society programs, see Moynihan, *Maximum Feasible Misunderstanding*.

[67] See Katz, *Poor People's Lawyers*, pp. 105–22.

tings.[68] And, some of the LSP's clientele may have preferred less emphasis on appellate advocacy.[69] Nonetheless, the structure of the adjudicatory process and the LSP's immersion in case service allowed a unique brand of individual "citizen participation" even when the OEO mechanisms failed. This "citizen participation" extended beyond the Legal Services projects into the courts, enfranchising poor individuals in one of the nation's major governing institutions. The poor retained *some* control over the Program's appellate advocacy; *some* poor people were allowed access to the appellate courts, including the Supreme Court; and at least *some* of the poor benefited from the Program's litigation. The LSP did not simply litigate for the poor; it directly expanded poor litigants' access to the U.S. Supreme Court's decision processes.

This is not to trivialize the effect of the apparent failure of the poor to control the boards of directors that oversaw local projects. The Program's appellate docket may have developed quite differently if the OEO statutory structure for "citizen participation" had been effective. Able tells us:

> When clients act collectively to shape a legal [services] program that they control . . . they express priorities very different from the subject matter distribution in most legal [services] offices. . . . [T]he local advisory council in an Oregon Legal Services office stressed housing, health, government benefits, community education, and senior citizen rights. . . . When asked what they would like a legal services office to do, clients of another program emphasized housing, health, family problems, and unemployment, *even though these were not the problems they actually took to the office.*[70]

However, this discongruity does not necessarily mean that LSP projects were unresponsive to the poor's needs as they defined them. Rather, it may simply show that interests are defined differently when they are articulated in the abstract by representative institutions than when they are expressed through participatory structures that directly allow individual client requests to set the agenda.[71]

---

[68] See Cain, "The General Practice Lawyer and the Client"; Olson, *Clients and Lawyers*; Handler, *Social Movements*; Rosenthal, *Lawyer and Client*.

[69] See Wexler, "Practicing Law."

[70] Emphasis added. Abel explains this discongruity as resulting from the role of existing law in shaping clients' beliefs about what problems are amenable to a legal solution. Abel also notes, "But, even when lawyers establish their own guidelines they may ignore these preferences. One LSC program declared an interest in education, employment, and police misconduct but did virtually no work in these areas. It is extremely difficult, of course, both morally and practically, to close the doors of a legal aid program and to turn people away because they have the wrong problem." Abel, "Law Without Politics," pp. 567–69 and n.577. In another article that presents a more favorable evaluation of the importance of Legal Services' litigation and the courts' declarations of rights in these cases, Abel discusses the problem of artificially defining "the poor" as a group that requires a single set of reforms in the law given the incredible heterogeneity in any population we might reasonably label as "the poor." Abel, "Informalism," p. 376.

[71] See Barber, *Strong Democracy*.

The cases the LSP presented to the Supreme Court were, undoubtedly, not a perfect reflection of the problems that the poor believed to be most pressing.[72] This goal proves quite ephemeral with such a heterogeneous group as "the poor." Nonetheless, the LSP did allow the poor to direct their own participation in Supreme Court decision making to a much greater extent than they had been able to in the past. The LSP was not a participation panacea, but the Program's clientele, in its capacity as clients, had more direct influence on the LSP's Supreme Court docket than the purported beneficiaries of interest group litigation commonly do. The LSP's lack of preordained policy goals and strategies, its decentralized structure and attorney autonomy, allowed the Program to present the Supreme Court with a random collection of the legal controversies important to the litigants it represented.

## CONCLUSIONS

By blending client service and reform, the LSP provided one category of people burdened by the de facto assistance of counsel requirement, the poor, with access to the Supreme Court's decision-making processes. The Program's philosophy, its inability to come to a consensus on goals, its decentralized structure, and its acquiescence to local staff attorneys' demands for autonomy and "involvement" in their work, prevented the LSP from implementing an NAACP LDF–type litigation strategy. Although the Columbia Center on Social Welfare Policy and Law tried to develop a litigation plan to reform the welfare system, it lacked the control over Program attorneys necessary to implement such a strategy. In the end, less than half of the LSP's Supreme Court docket consisted of challenges to the laws governing transfer programs. Instead, unlike interest groups, local LSP attorneys provided their clients with a kind of "delegate" representation in the courts. Decisions about what cases to litigate and appeal were made by local attorneys in consultation with their clients. Clients were accepted because they met the income criteria of the Program, not because their cases fit a litigation strategy. Appellate challenges were serendipitous outgrowths of client service. In this way, there was considerable "citizen participation" in the setting of the LSP's Supreme Court docket.

As a result, the LSP presented the Supreme Court with a heterogeneous collection of its clients' problems. In cases involving transfer programs, the criminal justice system, shelter, personal well-being, legal procedures, financial relationships, political rights, and Native American Indian rights, LSP attorneys mounted challenges to state and federal laws using arguments based on the equal protection and due process clauses, as well as a variety of statutory and Bill of Rights provisions. There was great diversity in both the cases in

---

[72] Of course, the LSP's clients did not constitute a "perfect sample" of the poor. On the possible biases introduced by selective use of lawyers by the poor, see esp. Campbell and Talarico, "Access to Legal Services."

which LSP attorneys sought to overturn lower court decisions and those in which they sought to nationalize favorable lower court decisions.

By blending the client server and reformer roles, LSP attorneys changed the Supreme Court's jurisdictional agenda by presenting it with new and different opportunities for decision in the cases of some of those previously barred from participation in Supreme Court decision making by the de facto assistance of counsel requirement.

# CHAPTER FOUR

# Getting on the Court's Decision Agenda

ALTHOUGH the Supreme Court has a limited ability to shape the parameters of litigant access to its own jurisdictional docket, the Court has enormous discretion in choosing which cases to place on its decision agenda.[1] Between 1966 and 1974, the Court only reviewed about 10 percent of the over thirty thousand cases brought before it. The Court responded to less than 5 percent of all petitions with a written opinion.[2] Most of the opportunities for decision that litigants present to the Court are never fulfilled. This makes the Court's "decision-to-decide" a crucial part of its policy-making process. Case selection decisions are the filter through which litigant claims must pass to reach the Court's decision agenda.

Obviously, the mere fact that Legal Services lawyers and their opponents petitioned the Supreme Court was no guarantee that the justices would address the concerns of the poor. Access to the Court's jurisdictional agenda does not insure access to its decision agenda. The Court could have easily denied all 164 requests for review in LSP sponsored cases. Had the acceptance rate in LSP sponsored cases merely corresponded to general review rates in certiorari and appeal cases, the Court would have only decided about sixty-four LSP cases, giving plenary consideration to twenty-four.[3]

In fact, the LSP fared remarkably well in the Court's case selection process. The Court accepted 118 LSP cases, giving eighty plenary consideration. The LSP's 64 percent (68) acceptance rate as a petitioner is second only to that of the Solicitor General, who is commonly regarded as the most successful liti-

---

[1] But see Baum, "The Judicial Gatekeeping Function," on courts' "gatekeeping" powers beyond case selection.

[2] These figures include cases coming to the Court on appeal and as a petition for a writ of certiorari. References to petitions for writs of certiorari as distinct from appeals will be referred to explicitly. Unless otherwise noted, all data in this chapter on the Court's business were compiled from "The Supreme Court, 1966–1974 Terms: The Statistics."

[3] These figures are based on the Court's different acceptance rates for certiorari and appeal cases during this time period compiled from "The Supreme Court, 1966–1974 Terms: The Statistics"; "Supreme Court," *ABAJ*; Stern and Gressman, *Supreme Court Practice*, p. 151. The fourth edition of Stern and Gressman's book is used here since it was the edition in circulation during the LSP's tenure. The predictions are fifty-eight appeals (41 percent) and six certiorari petitions (9 percent) granted review, with only eighteen appeals (22 percent) and four certiorari petitions (7 percent) given plenary consideration.

gant before the Court.[4] Scholars who have discussed case selection with various justices and clerks report that the Court itself is not aware that anyone, or group, has rivaled the success of the Solicitor General in the case selection process.[5] Indeed, since the organizational affiliation of counsel was not listed on the briefs filed with the Court, it is unlikely that the justices were aware which petitions were LSP sponsored cases, though they were clearly aware that the LSP was representing poor litigants in appellate challenges.[6] The LSP's review rate also noticeably exceeds the NAACP LDF's 56 percent (9) acceptance rate in petitions sponsored between 1947 and 1957, even though the NAACP LDF is commonly considered to be the most successful interest group representing those burdened by the de facto assistance of counsel requirement.[7] The LSP's opponents were even more successful than the LSP in gaining review, enjoying an 89 percent (50) review rate. The LSP's arguments against review failed, but, as suggested earlier, often the Program was not strongly opposed to Supreme Court review which might result in nationalization of a lower court victory. The Court's acceptance of petitions from both the LSP and its opponents suggests that the Court was very interested in the issues raised in these cases.

The Supreme Court's review of 72 percent (118) of the cases sponsored by the LSP demonstrates that agenda setting in the Court is truly a process in which both litigants and the justices play significant roles. Contrary to common assumptions that all conceivably review-worthy issues are present in the enormous volume of petitions the Court receives—leaving judicial values free to play the leading role in the Court's agenda-setting decisions—limitations on access to the Court presented by the de facto assistance of counsel requirement keeps certain issues off the judicial agenda. The LSP's representation of those burdened by the de facto assistance of counsel requirement was the essential prerequisite to the justices' decision to turn their attention to the civil claims of the poor in the late 1960s and early 1970s. The LSP's expansion of access

[4] The Solicitor General represents the federal government in all cases to which it is a party before the Supreme Court and he decides which of the government's lower court defeats will be appealed to the High Court. See Provine, *Case Selection*, pp. 86–92; Scigliano, *The Supreme Court and the Presidency*, pp. 174–75; Stern and Gressman, *Supreme Court Practice*, p. 151; Caplan, "The Tenth Justice."

[5] O'Brien, Interview; Perry, Interview. O'Brien worked with Chief Justice Burger's Administrative Assistant, Marc Cannon, as a Judicial Fellow during the early 1980s. See O'Brien, *Storm Center*. Perry has interviewed a number of Supreme Court justices and their clerks in connection with his research on the Court's case selection process. See Perry, "Deciding to Decide."

[6] Indeed, seven of the justices had endorsed the creation of the LSP. Justice Goldberg wrote letters to President Johnson and Sargent Shriver urging that a "Justice for the Poor" section be included in the OEO legislation. That section became the LSP. In 1965, then ABA President, Lewis Powell, was instrumental in gaining ABA support for the LSP. Johnson, *Justice and Reform*, pp. 49–64. See also Brennan, "Address."

[7] Provine, *Case Selection*, p. 201. See Appendix C for other interest group's review rates.

to the Court's jurisdictional docket ultimately changed the range of issues present on the Court's decision docket.

In this chapter, we will see that the review rate in LSP cases is indeed extraordinary. Our traditional understandings of the Court's case selection process and interest group advantages do not seem to predict or explain the Program's success. Rather, we will turn to judicial role conceptions and see that the justices allowed the political climate of the era to shape their perceptions of the importance, and relative safety, of addressing the legal claims of the poor.

## REVIEWING PETITIONS FOR WRITS OF CERTIORARI AND APPEALS

The LSP sponsored cases, like most cases, reached the Supreme Court's docket through two jurisdictional routes, as either petitions for writs of certiorari or on appeal. The 1925 Judiciary Act gave the Supreme Court complete discretion over whether or not to review certiorari cases, while technically (though not in practice), review of appeals is mandatory.[8] Traditionally, the percentage of cases reviewed that come to the Court as a petition for a writ of certiorari is much lower than the percentage of cases reviewed that come on appeal. Hence, we would expect the review rate in LSP certiorari cases to be lower than the review rate in LSP appeals and, if most of the Program's cases came up on appeal, the LSP's seemingly high review rate may be explained.

Generally, over 90 percent of the cases brought to the Court come as petitions for a writ of certiorari and only about 5 to 10 percent of them receive the four votes to review needed to grant the petition.[9] In contrast, while only 44 percent (71) of the 164 LSP sponsored cases came to the Court as petitions for a writ of certiorari, a surprising 53 percent (37) of them were granted review. This is at least five times the normal rate of review for certiorari petitions. Furthermore, 38 percent (27) of the Program's certiorari cases were granted plenary review.

Until very recently, about 10 percent of all cases filed with the Court each year came up under the Court's appeal jurisdiction. During the era in which the LSP was litigating, the Judiciary Act allowed litigants a right of appeal to the Supreme Court from three-judge U.S. district court judgments in "suits to restrain the enforcement of state and federal statutes upon grounds of unconstitutionality . . . and also suits to enjoin . . . the enforcement of orders of the Interstate Commerce Commission."[10] Congress also determined that "cases in which federal or state laws have been held unconstitutional, . . . cases in which state courts have rejected contentions that state laws violate the

[8] See also Stern and Gressman, *Supreme Court Practice*, pp. 147–49.

[9] Federal Judicial Center, *Caseload*, p. 615.

[10] "Three-judge district courts, with direct appeals to the Supreme Court, are also provided for in the Voting Rights Act of 1965 . . . and in the Civil Rights Act of 1964." Stern and Gressman, *Supreme Court Practice*, pp. 48–49.

federal Constitution, antitrust equity suits brought by the Government, . . . and certain types of criminal appeals'' would come to the Court by way of appeal.[11] Of the 164 cases the LSP sponsored before the Court, 56 percent (92) came to the Court on appeal, and 75 percent (69) of those came from three-judge district courts.[12] Largely because there was a direct right of appeal to the Supreme Court from these three-judge courts, the LSP's Supreme Court docket did contain a disproportionate percentage of appeals.

Although review of cases that come up on appeal is, by congressional statute, mandatory, the Supreme Court has found ways to avoid plenary, or full, review of these cases. Generally, close to half of all appeals are dismissed for lack of a ''substantial federal question.'' In 1972, the Freund Commission reported that ''the discretionary-mandatory distinction between certiorari and appeal has largely been eroded. The concept that all appeals are argued while most certiorari cases are disposed of summarily has not been true for many years.''[13] Stern and Gressman add ''the jurisdictional statement [in appeals cases] now performs a function similar to that of the petition for certiorari. Its purpose is to induce the Court not to dispose of the case summarily.''[14] Provine found that the Court employs the same considerations in selecting appeal and certiorari cases for review.[15] Consequently, case selection decisions on appeals are rarely studied separately from decisions on certiorari cases.

Given that Congress defined the Court's appeal jurisdiction based on a priori notions of what kinds of cases would be most important for the Supreme Court to review, it is not surprising that the Court does indeed review a substantially higher proportion of appeal cases than certiorari cases. Between 1960 and 1971, plenary review rates in appeal cases ranged from 12 percent in the 1966 Term to 23 percent in the 1964 Term.[16] Appeals that, in the view of four members of the Court, lacked substantiality were either dismissed or summarily decided.[17] For example, in the 1967 Term the Court acted on 197 appeals, dismissing 45 percent (89), summarily deciding 33 percent (65), and

[11] Stern and Gressman, *Supreme Court Practice*, pp. 193–94. Since the era of the LSP's litigation, Congress, at the request of the Court, has substantially narrowed the Court's appeal jurisdiction. In 1976, Congress dramatically limited the jurisdiction of three-judge district court panels. In 1988, Congress eliminated almost all categories of appeal. See Title 28, *United States Code*.

[12] See Note, ''Federal Judicial Review of State Welfare Practices,'' for a discussion of the advantages of challenging welfare practices in three-judge district courts. Apparently in the welfare area, the Columbia Center director, Edward Sparer, advocated the filing of cases, whenever possible, in three-judge district courts because of the speedy right of review in the U.S. Supreme Court. See Greenberg, ''Litigation for Social Change,'' p. 336. Indeed, of the sixty-two cases brought to the Court involving transfer programs, 76 percent (47) came to the Court on appeal.

[13] Federal Judicial Center, *Caseload*.

[14] Stern and Gressman, *Supreme Court Practice*, p. 195.

[15] Provine, *Case Selection*, see especially pp. 13–22; Perry, ''Deciding to Decide,'' pp. 36–37, 58, 146–47; Stern and Gressman, *Supreme Court Practice*, p. 199.

[16] Gressman, ''Requiem,'' p. 1329; Federal Judicial Center, *Caseload*, p. 596.

[17] See Provine, *Case Selection*, pp. 13–17; Gressman, ''Requiem''; Casper and Posner, ''A Study of the Supreme Court's Caseload''; Griswold, ''Rationing Justice.''

giving full consideration to 22 percent (43).[18] As in the certiorari cases, the LSP enjoyed higher review rates in its appeal cases than do most litigants. The Court only dismissed 12 percent (11) of the Program's appeal cases and it gave plenary review to 57 percent (52) of the cases, more than twice the percentage of all appeal cases given full treatment in any Term between 1960 and 1971.

The unusual frequency of appeal jurisdiction in LSP sponsored cases does not explain the Program's extraordinary review rate. Both the LSP's rate of review in certiorari cases and its rate of plenary review in appeals cases substantially exceed the usual rates created by the Court's case selection decisions. Instead, we must turn to the factors that are said to influence litigant success and the Court's decisions about which cases to review regardless of whether they come to the Court as a petition for a writ of certiorari or on appeal.[19]

## PREDICTING AND ASSESSING THE LSP's REVIEW RATE

During the era in which the LSP was litigating, the Court's only published set of standards for its review decisions was the nonbinding Rule 19 of the Supreme Court's Revised Rules. Rule 19 is vague and general, pointing basically to conflicts among lower courts or with Supreme Court precedents and to "important" federal questions.[20] In recounting these standards, Stern and Gressman's quintessential guidebook to Supreme Court practice hastens to add that, "it must be emphasized, however, that the presence in a case of any one or any combination of these factors is not a guarantee that certiorari will be granted. Nor is the apparent absence of such factors a guarantee that certiorari will be denied. Certiorari is a discretionary jurisdiction, one that can be invoked or withheld for any reason that the Court sees fit."[21] The Court seldom

[18] Stern and Gressman, *Supreme Court Practice*, p. 148.

[19] Unless otherwise noted, appeal and certiorari cases will be analyzed together in this chapter. In analyzing the two classes of cases separately, no important differences in the Court's response were found. See Lawrence, "The Poor in Court," pp. 341–52.

[20] Rule 19 sets out "the character of reasons which will be considered in the case selection process." They are: "(a) where a state court has decided a federal question of substance not theretofore determined by this court, or has decided it in a way probably not in accord with applicable decisions of this court, and (b) where a court of appeals has rendered a decision in conflict with the decision of another court of appeals on the same matter; or has decided an important state or territorial question in a way in conflict with applicable state or territorial law; or has decided an important question of federal law which has not been, but should be, settled by this court; or has decided a federal question in a way in conflict with applicable decisions of this court; or has so far departed from the accepted and usual course of judicial proceedings, or so far sanctioned such a departure by a lower court, as to call for an exercise of this court's power of supervision." Supreme Court, *Revised Rules*, Appendix (1967). Rule 19 was in effect during the course of the LSP's Supreme Court litigation. In 1980, the Supreme Court's Rules were revised and Rule 19 was modified slightly and renamed Rule 17.

[21] Stern and Gressman, *Supreme Court Practice*, p. 153.

articulates meaningful reasons for granting or denying review in particular cases despite some of the justices' repeated claims that most cases filed with them are "frivolous" and clearly not "cert. worthy."[22] For example, in studying the 1947–1958 Terms, Tanenhaus found that in a sample of three thousand denied petitions, the Court only explained its reasons for denying the petition in forty cases. Among the cases granted review during the 1956–1958 Terms, the Court cited Rule 19 standards in only 47 percent of the cases and in over half of those cases it simply cited the "importance" of the issue presented.[23] Rule 19, and the Court, did not provide the LSP with much guidance about what cases to bring and they do not provide us with many clues as to why the Court accepted so many LSP cases. Rather, the LSP, like other attorneys and scholars, was left on its own to discern the unwritten criteria that guide the Court's case selection decisions.

## The Advantages of the "Repeat-Player"

Generally, group litigants fare better in the Court's case selection process than ordinary individual litigants. Based on a sample of paid petitions from the 1976–1980 Terms, Perry reports that organized groups enjoyed a 10 percent review rate while individuals only achieved a 3 percent rate.[24] As we have seen, the NAACP LDF, the prototypical group litigant, enjoyed 56 percent (9) acceptance rate in the petitions it filed between 1947 and 1956.[25]

Adopting Galanter's terminology, interest groups are "repeat-players" before the Court[26] and two characteristics of their operation give them an advantage in the Court's case selection process, resulting in higher review rates. First, given that much of their litigation is directed toward the High Court, attorneys working for interest groups tend to have more experience and expertise in Supreme Court litigation than those retained by an individual, or "one-shotter," who may appear before the Court maybe once or twice in their ca-

---

[22] Perry, "Deciding to Decide," pp. 254–59; Provine, *Case Selection*, pp. 42–43; Stern and Gressman, *Supreme Court Practice*, pp. 149–54.

[23] Tanenhaus et al., "Cue Theory," pp. 132–33.

[24] In Perry's sample, all of the federal government's petitions were granted; 12 percent of state governments' and 14 percent of corporations' petitions were granted. Perry, "Deciding to Decide," pp. 352, 380.

[25] Provine, *Case Selection*, p. 201.

[26] Galanter defines the "ideal" repeat-player as "a unit which has had and anticipates repeated litigation, which has low stakes in the outcome of any one case, and which has the resources to pursue its long-run interests." One-shotters are defined as "a unit whose claims are too large (relative to his size) or too small (relative to the cost of remedies) to be managed routinely and rationally." Galanter's list of advantages the repeat-player enjoys includes: (1) ability to structure the transaction; (2) specialized expertise, economies of scale; (3) ability to develop long-term strategies; (4) ability to play for rules; (5) bargaining credibility; and (6) ability to invest in penetration. Galanter, "Why the 'Haves,' " pp. 97–98, 125. Provine has applied Galanter's analysis to the case selection process. Provine, *Case Selection*, pp. 86–92.

reers. Indeed, Provine suggests that "differences that exist in the petitioning expertise of litigants" is one of the two primary factors that account for "differences in the success rate of litigants in gaining review."[27] Repeat-players' experience with Supreme Court litigation makes them better able to discern the unwritten criteria that guide the Court's decision making and to ascertain what issues the Court, or particular justices, are especially interested in.[28] And, because groups are able to pick and choose which cases they will sponsor, they are freed from client pressure to appeal cases that their experience indicates the Court is unlikely to review. It is this kind of experience and control that is often cited as one of the explanations for the most frequent litigator's success, the Solicitor General.[29]

Second, the very fact that interest groups are pursuing a litigation strategy means that they are bringing cases that have some public importance and that have been carefully screened by the group for technical defects and other problems that would be likely to preclude review. In contrast, generally, the individual litigant's stake in his or her particular case is high, thus providing a strong incentive to appeal, even though the issue may not be of general importance and the case may have technical problems. Usually, individuals give little attention to the broader policy implications of their cases, if any. They are one-shotters playing for broke.[30]

Galanter's repeat-player/one-shotter typology refers primarily to attributes of the litigants rather than of the attorneys who represent them, but Galanter points out that the organization and quality of counsel can imbue the infrequent litigant with some of the repeat-player's advantages.[31] This is particularly true in interest group litigation since the group is a repeat-player and the one-shotter client is provided counsel only because the case fits the group's litigation strategy. Although the LSP enjoyed a higher acceptance rate than has been reported for any other group, it was not a true repeat-player and it did not share many of the operational characteristics that give groups their advantage in the case selection process. On the other hand, the LSP did not suffer all the disadvantages that plague one-shotters either. The LSP falls in the middle of a repeat-player/one-shotter continuum.

For example, typically, the one-shotter is represented by the "lower echelons" of the legal profession in terms of socio-economic origins and education. Legal Services attorneys did not conform to this stereotype. Both Katz and Handler have found that the socio-economic background of LSP attorneys

[27] The other is "the conception the justices hold of the proper work of the Court." We will address this factor later. Provine, *Case Selection*, p. 86.

[28] See Perry, "Deciding to Decide," pp. 243–46.

[29] Provine, *Case Selection*, pp. 87–92. See also Caplan, "The Tenth Justice" (10 August), pp. 32–41.

[30] Galanter, "Why the 'Haves,' " pp. 97–98.

[31] Ibid., pp. 114–19.

matched that of the bar as a whole, though LSP attorneys were somewhat better educated. In the higher quality LSP projects, presumably those more engaged in law reform and appellate advocacy, 56 percent of the attorneys had attended major law schools.[32] The LSP attorneys petitioning the Court may have been more skilled than the average member of the bar, although there is no reason to suspect that LSP attorneys and briefs were of a higher quality than those of their opponents. Indeed, given that governmental units were the predominant opponent, the expectation would be reversed. Few LSP attorneys had enough experience in Supreme Court litigation to allow them to discern the Court's unwritten case selection criteria. The Program's 164 Supreme Court cases came from 116 different local LSP projects. While, presumably, the back-up center attorneys were somewhat more skilled at case preparation and occasionally an LSP case was cosponsored by a more experienced group such as the NAACP LDF, the ACLU, or the federal government, the review rate of 74 percent (51) in the sixty-nine cases cosponsored by a back-up center or interest group is not significantly higher than the 72 percent (68) review rate in the ninety-five cases petitioned by a local LSP attorney alone.[33]

The LSP's place in the War on Poverty and the resources and emphasis it gave to law reform did remove some of the other handicaps that one-shotter attorneys usually suffer. The LSP's neighborhood offices and their responsiveness to referrals from other social service agencies overcame the problem of mobilizing a clientele. The Program's duality of roles—client service and reform—showed the repeating character of the problems and encouraged big solutions rather than mass processing.[34] Program attorneys could demonstrate to the Court that their cases would have a broad impact. Back-up centers generated and dispersed expertise. LSP attorneys became specialists in poverty law. The Program's ideology of serving a group of people while serving a series of individual clients moved it toward the repeat-player end of the continuum.[35]

[32] Katz, "Lawyers for the Poor," p. 276. Forty-two percent of all the LSP attorneys went to a major national or regional law school, whereas only 37 percent of the bar as a whole attended such schools. Handler et al., *Lawyers*, pp. 143–47. Coding cases based on litigant, rather than attorney, status, Ulmer reports that "underdogs" had a lower review rate than "upperdogs" during both the Warren and Burger Court eras. Ulmer, "Selecting Cases."

[33] Yule's Q = +.06. Furthermore, we would expect the back-up centers and other groups to only pick the most "review likely" cases to become involved in. (Yule's Q is a statistical measurement of association for dichotomized dependent variables that takes into consideration the fact that the marginals for the dependent variable are fixed by the method of research. It is used here because the data represent a universe rather than a sample. Q = 0.0 when the variables are completely independent, and Q = 1.0 [positive or negative] when they are perfectly associated. See Blalock, *Social Statistics*, pp. 306–7.)

[34] Compare Galanter, "Why the 'Haves,' " pp. 116–17.

[35] Rothstein characterizes the LSP as giving the poor all the repeat-player advantages. However, Rothstein's assessment may have been overly optimistic and, at least at the Supreme Court level, he overestimates the degree to which the LSP was a repeat-player. Rothstein, "The Myth of Sis-

Even so, the LSP was not a true repeat-player. The Program's immersion in client service, out of which its test cases grew, kept the attorney tied to one-shotter clients. It was not picking and choosing its cases based on a litigation strategy as do repeat-player groups like the NAACP LDF and the ACLU. Optimizing choices were prevented; it would have been unethical for an LSP attorney "to play his series of OSs [one-shotters] as if they constituted a single RP [repeat-player],"[36] and the autonomy local attorneys demanded kept the national Program from attempting to do so. The LSP fell far short of achieving the organizational characteristics we associate with success in the case selection process, yet this did not prove to be the disadvantage we would expect.

### Correlates with Review: Cue Theory

Students of the Court have also tried to discern the justices' unwritten review criteria by seeking to identify the case attributes that correlate with a decision to grant review. Noting that Rule 19 is a rather unsatisfactory explanation of the Court's exercise of its certiorari jurisdiction, Tanenhaus hypothesized that given the enormous volume of certiorari petitions and the justices' repeated claims that more than half of the petitions are frivolous, the justices must employ "cues" to distinguish between those cases that deserve serious consideration in the case selection process and those that do not. According to this theory, cases with such cues will be reviewed at a higher rate than cases without such cues, which will generally be routinely denied. Tanenhaus found that three cues were significantly associated with review grants: Solicitor General favors review; dissension, or disagreement among the judges in the court or courts below; and presence of a civil liberties issue. While the review rates varied by the particular cue present, in cases with at least one cue, Tanenhaus reports a review rate of 28 percent, whereas it was only 7 percent in cases without any of the cues.[37] Tanenhaus' cue theory has become a leading explanation of the Court's case selection decisions although a number of scholars have presented convincing critiques of it, particularly based on the actual records of "special listed cases" and certiorari votes contained in the Burton papers.[38]

Scholars who have sought to refine Tanenhaus' cue theory have differed on

---

yphus." As discussed in chapter 3, the decisions to go to the Supreme Court were discrete and insular as was the handling of the cases at that level. Katz's description of legal services practice in Chicago corresponds more to Galanter's image of the one-shotter than Rothstein's rose-colored view of LSP projects as repeat-players. Katz, "Lawyers for the Poor."

[36] Galanter, "Why the 'Haves,' " p. 117.

[37] Tanenhaus also tested presence of an economic issue as a cue, but he did not find it to be significantly correlated with review. Tanenhaus et al., "Cue Theory," pp. 136–41.

[38] Provine, Case Selection, pp. 77–83; Ulmer, "The Decision to Grant or Deny." See also Perry, "Deciding to Decide," pp. 330–68; Teger and Kosinski, "Cue Theory: A Reconsideration."

exactly how the various cues should be defined and coded. Although it is generally agreed that the Solicitor General's opposition is a deterrent to review, the Solicitor General's official status as respondent does not always indicate that he opposes review; indeed, the Solicitor General's success before the court is partially explained by his willingness to occasionally "confess error" and urge the Court to reverse a lower court victory for the government.[39] Tanenhaus included instances where the federal government clearly indicated that it favored review even when the Solicitor General was not formally the petitioner, but Teger and Kosinski apparently did not.[40] Ulmer has substituted "conflict," either between Courts of Appeals or between lower court decisions and Supreme Court precedents for the dissension cue.[41] Teger and Kosinski abandoned the dissension cue completely because the frequency of unreported lower court decisions made unbiased data collection too difficult.[42]

Perhaps most significant, Teger and Kosinski redefined Tanenhaus' civil liberties cue to include issues that have only recently gained salience in the Court's docket. Using cases decided in the 1975 Term, almost twenty years later than Tanenhaus' sample, they confirmed the importance of the civil liberties cue by substantially redefining it to include nonracial equal protection claims, government benefit claims, and noncriminal due process claims.[43] The breakdown of LSP cases by subject and constitutional issues presented in tables 4-1 and 4-2 suggests that virtually all of the LSP's cases fall into the categories Teger and Kosinski's added to Tanenhaus' definition of the civil liberties cue. Furthermore, as we will see later, it was the opportunities for decision that the LSP presented to the Court that were partly responsible for the development of

[39] Tanenhaus et al., "Cue Theory," p. 137; Caplan, "The Tenth Justice" (10 August), pp. 38–39; Scigliano, *The Supreme Court and the Presidency*, p. 165. The Solicitor General also frequently files amicus curiae briefs on certiorari when the federal government is not a party to the case. Between 1959 and 1982, the Solicitor General filed amicus briefs in support of the petitioner in 337 cases, 82 percent (276) of which were accepted for review. He filed in support of the respondent in 358 cases, 49 percent (177) of which were reviewed, suggesting that the mere filing of an amicus brief by the Solicitor General serves as a "cue" that the case is important. Salokar, "Solicitor General," p. 32.

[40] Tanenhaus et al., "Cue Theory," p. 137; Teger and Kosinski, "Cue Theory: A Reconsideration," pp. 838–40.

[41] Ulmer, "Certiorari Decisions: Conflict."

[42] Teger and Kosinski, "Cue Theory: A Reconsideration," p. 838.

[43] Teger and Kosinski, "Cue Theory: A Reconsideration." In studying the 1950–59 Terms, Tanenhaus classified "benefit and welfare legislation" as an economic cue along with "labor, regulation of economic life, and financial interest of the federal government." He describes the "benefit and welfare legislation" category as including "civil service rights, wage statutes, the Federal Employers Liability Act, seamen and longshoremen welfare legislation, servicemen's benefits, workmen's compensation, social security legislation, tort claims, agricultural benefit regulations, and unemployment insurance." He found that "the likelihood of review when only an economic issue is present is not much greater than when no cue at all is involved." Tanenhaus et al., "Cue Theory," pp. 139–40.

TABLE 4-1
Review Rates in LSP Sponsored Cases by Subject, 1966–1974 Terms

| | LSP | | |
| Subject | Appellant/ Petitioner (n) | Appellee/ Respondent (n) | All Cases (n) |
|---|---|---|---|
| Transfer Programs | 85%(22) | 100%(34) | 93% (56) |
| Criminal Justice | 50 (9) | 8 (4) | 57 (13) |
| Shelter | 47 (8) | 50 (1) | 47 (9) |
| Personal Well-Being | 44 (4) | 60 (6) | 53 (10) |
| Financial Relationships | 60 (9) | 100 (2) | 65 (1) |
| Legal Procedures | 77 (10) | 100 (1) | 79 (11) |
| Political Rights[a] | 40 (2) | 100 (1) | 50 (3) |
| Indian Rights | 100 (4) | 100 (1) | 100 (5) |
| All Cases | 64%(68) | 89%(50) | 72%(118) |

[a] In addition, one application for an injunction was heard.

constitutional doctrine in these areas, suggesting that perhaps it was the LSP's litigation that allowed these to become salient issues for the Court in the 1970s.

In order to avoid the debates on how to define the cues, and to provide cue theory with its best opportunity to explain the seemingly extraordinary review rates in LSP cases, it is assumed that all LSP cases contained civil liberties and dissension cues. Also, the Solicitor General is considered to have favored review in all of the twenty-two LSP cases he participated in, even though officially he was the respondent in thirteen of them. These assumptions clearly overestimate the number of cued cases in the LSP's docket and therefore *should* result in *lower* review rates than cue theory predicts.

In Tanenhaus' study, the cue most strongly associated with review was support of the Solicitor General. Tanenhaus found that "when the federal government favored review and no other cue was involved the writ [of certiorari] was issued 47.1 percent of the time." When combined with other cues, Tanenhaus' predicted review rates in cases where the Solicitor General favors review range from 45 to 80 percent. In cases where the Solicitor General does not actively favor review, Tanenhaus predicts a 7 to 43 percent review rate depending on the presence of other cues.[44] Teger and Kosinski also found the

[44] Tanenhaus et al., "Cue Theory," pp. 138, 143. Many others have also found that the Court is more likely to review cases petitioned by the Solicitor General. See Provine, *Case Selection,*

TABLE 4-2

Review Rates in LSP Sponsored Cases by Constitutional Issue, 1966–1974 Terms

| Constitutional Issue | LSP | | |
| | Appellant/ Petitioner (n) | Appellee/ Respondent (n) | Total (n) |
| --- | --- | --- | --- |
| Equal Protection, 5th and 14th Amendments | 71%[a](29) | 91%(21) | 78%  (50) |
| Due Process, 5th and 14th Amendments | 66    (19) | 88    (15) | 74    (34) |
| First Amendment | 25    (1) | —    (0) | 25    (1) |
| Criminal Procedure Amendments | 60    (3) | 100    (2) | 71    (5) |
| Right to Access to the Courts | 50    (4) | 100    (1) | 56    (5) |
| Other | 50    (1) | 100    (1) | 67    (2) |
| None | 61    (11) | 83    (10) | 70    (21) |
| All Cases | 63% (68) | 89%(50) | 72%(118) |

[a] In addition, one application for an injunction was heard.

Solicitor General's support to be the most powerful predictor of review, reporting a 78 percent review rate in cases where the only cue was federal government as petitioning party, a 55 percent review rate when the federal government cue was combined with civil liberties and/or economic issue cues, and an 18 percent review rate among all cases that had at least one of the three cues.[45]

The Solicitor General only participated in twenty-two of the LSP's 164 cases, 91 percent (20) of which were reviewed. Among certiorari cases, LSP enjoyed a 75 percent (6) review rate when the Solicitor General was a participant, which falls between Tanenhaus' predicted review rates for cases that contain all three of his cues and for cases with only the Solicitor General and civil liberties cues (see table 4-3). Given the generous assumptions made about LSP cases and the small number of cases in the category, the LSP did very well.[46] In the sixty-three petitions for certiorari that proceeded without the

pp. 42, 87–92; Salokar, "Solicitor General," pp. 27–32; Scigliano, *The Supreme Court and the Presidency*, pp. 174–79; Stern and Gressman, *Supreme Court Practice*, p. 151.

[45] Teger and Kosinski, "Cue Theory: A Reconsideration," pp. 839–40.

[46] Of the eight certiorari cases in which the Solicitor General participated, he was the respondent in five, two of which were denied review. All three of his petitions (one with the LSP) were granted review. Of the fourteen appeal cases in which the Solicitor General participated, he was the appellee in eight cases (one with the LSP), and the appellant in six cases. All fourteen of the appeals were reviewed.

TABLE 4-3

Review Rates in LSP Sponsored Cases Compared to Tanenhaus' Predicted Rates, 1966–1974 Terms

| Cues | | | Tanenhaus'[a] Predicted percentage of Writs of Cert. to be Granted | Actual | | |
|---|---|---|---|---|---|---|
| | | | | Review Rates in LSP Sponsored Cases | | |
| Party | Civil Liberties | Dissension | | Cert. (n) | Appeal (n) | All (n) |
| + | + | + | 80% | 75% (6) | 100%(14) | 91% (20) |
| + | + | 0 | 70 | | | |
| + | 0 | + | 56 | | | |
| + | 0 | 0 | 45 | | | |
| 0 | + | + | 43 | 49 (31) | 86 (67) | 70 (98) |
| 0 | + | 0 | 32 | | | |
| 0 | 0 | + | 18 | | | |
| 0 | 0 | 0 | 7 | | | |
| All Cases (N = 163)[b] | | | | 52%(37) | 88%(81) | 72%(118) |

0 = Absence of a cue in all cases in set.

+ = Presence of a cue in all cases in set.

[a] Adapted from Tanenhaus et al., "Cue Theory," p. 143.

[b] In addition, one application for an injunction was reviewed.

participation of the Solicitor General, the LSP enjoyed a 49 percent (31) review rate exceeding Tanenhaus' predictions of 7 to 43 percent, depending upon the presence of civil liberties and dissension cues. The review rates for both appeal cases that proceeded with (100 percent [14] of the fourteen cases) and without (86 percent [67] of the seventy-eight cases) the Solicitor General's participation substantially exceeded Tanenhaus' predictions for certiorari cases even though it is believed that the same considerations guide the review decision in appeal and certiorari cases.[47]

Returning to Rule 19, Ulmer has used "conflict," either between Courts of Appeals or between lower courts and Supreme Court precedents, as a cue instead of dissension. He refers to these as violations of the "uniformity principle" of federal law that the Supreme Court, as head of the federal judicial

[47] Indeed, as Provine notes, it is unclear whether Tanenhaus examined only certiorari petitions or included appeals as well. In testing cue theory using Justice Burton's records of which cases were "special listed," Provine included both appeals and certiorari petitions. Provine, *Case Selection*, pp. 79–80.

system, has a special obligation to address.[48] Attorneys also generally interpret Rule 19 as referring to these kinds of conflicts rather than to dissension as Tanenhaus defined it,[49] but this makes attempts to correlate the presence of such conflicts with case selection decisions difficult since, hoping to provoke review, lawyers strive to cite conflicts in their briefs.[50] In studying case selection during the Warren and Burger Court eras, Ulmer found that only 18 percent of the conflicts claimed by attorneys in their petitions were "genuine," but the genuine conflicts did correlate with review.[51]

Given the dearth of poverty-related Supreme Court litigation before 1966 and the breadth of the LSP's litigation, Program attorneys were unlikely to be able to claim direct conflict with a Supreme Court precedent very often, particularly during the Warren Court era. Their opportunities increased as their own litigation established precedents, but the Burger Court was less sensitive to these conflicts, reviewing only 27 percent, compared to the 55 percent reviewed by the Warren Court.[52] Nonetheless, 18 percent (21) of the LSP cases granted review were summarily disposed of in light of a previous Supreme Court decision.[53] Some LSP attorneys made rapid use of the Supreme Court's inclination to insure that its decisions are followed by the lower courts, but even if all LSP attorneys were able to show such conflict in their cases, the Program's 72 percent (118) review rate substantially exceeds the Warren and Burger Court's combined review rate of 41 percent in cases that contained genuine conflicts with Supreme Court precedents.

Ulmer found that both Courts were slightly less likely to grant review in cases that presented genuine instances of circuit conflict, rather than conflict with its own precedents. The Warren Court granted 53 percent of such petitions, and the Burger Court granted 21 percent, with a combined grant rate of 35 percent for the two Courts.[54] Forty-two LSP sponsored cases were petitions from the Courts of Appeals; 57 percent (24) of these were granted review, a

---

[48] Ulmer, "Certiorari Decisions: Conflict."

[49] Perry also notes the importance of conflicts to the justices in their case selection decisions. In addition, he provides some evidence that dissension below provides the justices with information about the case that they may consider relevant in their case selection decisions. He reports that all the justices ask their clerks to include the vote, the composition of the panel, and who wrote opinions in the court below in the cert. memos they write. Perry, "Deciding to Decide," pp. 344–47, 361.

[50] Stern and Gressman's guidebook stresses the importance of conflicts in the case selection process. Stern and Gressman, *Supreme Court Practice*, pp. 154–66.

[51] Ulmer, "Certiorari Decisions: Conflict," p. 906. Ulmer's data encompass the 1947–76 Terms. He presents his data in three categories: the Vinson, Warren, and Burger Courts. I have adopted only his Warren and Burger Court data because it corresponds most closely to the period of the LSP's operation.

[52] Ulmer, "Certiorari Decisions: Conflict," pp. 903–10. See also U.S., Commission, *Recommendations for Change*.

[53] Eighteen cases were remanded, two were reversed, and one was affirmed.

[54] Ulmer, "Certiorari Decisions: Conflict," p. 907.

noticeably higher percentage than we would expect even if all of these petitions contained genuine circuit conflicts. The justices actually cited conflict
between circuits as the reason for granting certiorari in only one LSP case,
*Kokoska v. Belford* (1974). What is more surprising than the 57 percent (24)
review rate in LSP cases that came from the Courts of Appeals is the justices'
decision to review 52 percent (27) of the LSP cases that came from state courts,
even though, traditionally, the review rate is much lower in the latter category.
For instance, Justice Brennan reports that in the 1958 Term, only 7 percent of
the challenges to state court decisions that were brought to the Court were
granted review.[55] While these state cases may have sometimes involved conflicts with Supreme Court precedents, they clearly did not contain circuit conflicts. In the Court's selection of LSP cases for review, conflict does not appear
to have played the seminal role Ulmer has assigned it in the case selection
process generally.[56]

Using the most generous assumptions about the presence of cues in LSP
cases, the Supreme Court still accepted more LSP cases for review than we
would have predicted based on the various versions of cue theory. The inability of cue theory to predict or explain the Court's receptivity to LSP cases does
not, in itself, negate the validity of our cue theories; rather, it suggests that the
Court's review of LSP cases was not simply "business as usual."

## Judicial Values and Case Selection

Some students of the Court have turned to judicial values and ideologies in
attempting to discern the Court's unwritten review criteria, suggesting that the
same values that shape the justices' votes on the merits also influence their
case selection decisions. These scholars hypothesize that the justices are more
likely to vote to review the cases they want to reverse, making the review vote
a preliminary vote on the merits.[57] Using the records of the justices' case selection votes during the 1947–1957 Terms contained in the Burton papers,
Ulmer and Provine have found that all of the justices were more likely to vote
to reverse those lower court decisions that they had voted to review, although

[55] Stern and Gressman, *Supreme Court Practice*, pp. 151–52.

[56] Ulmer finds: "Conflict is clearly the most important predictor of Vinson and Warren Court
decisions on certiorari. An examination of the discriminate function coefficients shows that conflict with Supreme Court precedent is 2 to 3 times as important as federal government as petitioning party. In the Burger Court, it is less than half as important. For the Burger Court, intercircuit
conflict is only one-fourth as significant in explaining variance in decision as federal government
as petitioning party. In the other two Courts, on the other hand, it is again 2 to 3 times as important." Ulmer, "Certiorari Decisions: Conflict," p. 909.

[57] See especially Baum, "Judicial Demand-Screening"; Baum, "Policy Goals"; Brenner, "Certiorari Game"; Perry, "Indices and Signals," p. 25; Provine, *Case Selection*, pp. 106–10; Songer, "Concern for Policy Output"; Ulmer, "The Decision to Grant Certiorari"; Ulmer, "Strict
and Not-So-Strict Constructionists."

there were substantial variations in the correlations.[58] In examining criminal justice cases, Ulmer argued that the justices' attitudes toward government authority explained both the case selection and merits votes.[59] Provine attributed the imperfection and variation in the correlations between the two votes to the justices' different "beliefs about the proper work and workload of the Supreme Court."[60] More generally, the relationship between case selection votes and votes on the merits is suggested by the fact that the Court reverses two-thirds of the cases it reviews.[61]

The extent to which votes to review are preliminary votes on the merits is impossible to test directly without access to records of the individual justices' case selection votes; such data is not yet available for the era in which the LSP was litigating. However, the earlier studies suggest that if judicial views on the merits of the petitioners' claims played their usual role in LSP cases, then the reversal rate in the reviewed cases should be about two-thirds, or 67 percent. In fact, the overall reversal rate in all LSP sponsored cases that the Court reviewed was 60 percent (71), a bit less than two-thirds.[62] When the cases in which the LSP was the petitioner and those in which it was the respondent are considered separately, an interesting pattern emerges. When the LSP was the petitioner, almost exactly two-thirds of the reviewed cases were reversed (68 percent [46] of the sixty-eight cases). Unexpectedly, when Program attorneys represented the respondent, only half of the reviewed cases were reversed (50 percent [25] of the fifty cases), indicating that other factors were at work in the Court's decision to place these cases on its decision agenda. Of course, the rule of four allows merit voting in case selection and an affirmance by the Court on the merits, but only six of the 118 cases that were reviewed had a four-man minority on the merits.[63] It seems likely that Provine's judicial "beliefs about the proper work and workload of the Supreme Court," rather than a desire to reverse on the merits, account for the pattern of decisions in the cases in which the LSP represented the respondent.

---

[58] Ulmer, "The Decision to Grant Certiorari"; Ulmer, "Strict and Not-So-Strict Constructionists"; Provine, *Case Selection*, pp. 107–10.

[59] Ulmer, "Strict and Not-So-Strict Constructionists," p. 27.

[60] Provine, *Case Selection*, p. 129.

[61] In the 1959–62 Terms, in certiorari cases disposed of on the merits, 68 percent of the lower court decisions were reversed. Stern and Gressman, *Supreme Court Practice*, p. 179. See also Brenner, "Certiorari Game"; Songer, "Concern for Policy Output."

[62] As is generally the practice in compiling reversal rates, remanded cases were counted as reversals. Twenty-one cases in which the LSP was the petitioner were remanded. Eleven cases in which the LSP was the respondent were remanded.

[63] For example, Provine reports that, "The percentage of reversals was consistently higher throughout the Burton period when five justices initially voted to reverse. . . . The rule of four thus tends to camouflage the actual similarity between votes to review and votes to reverse." Provine, *Case Selection*, pp. 108–9.

## LSP Cases and the "Proper Work" of the Court

The old adage that where you sit determines where you stand applies to Supreme Court justices as well. Their place at the top of the federal judicial system influences their view of what the "proper work" of the Court should be and, as Provine has shown, those views shape their case selection decisions.[64] When the justices announce in Rule 19 that they will review "important" federal questions, they are engaging in more than tautology; they refer to questions that, for practical or political reasons, should be authoritatively resolved by the highest national tribunal. The justices do not see the Court's role as primarily one of providing individual litigants with "justice"; that is the role of the intermediate appellate courts. Rather, the Supreme Court's role, as the final national arbiter, is to use its limited resources to settle questions of law and constitutional interpretation that have a general import to the citizenry and the polity.[65]

As the once popular terms "judicial activism" and "judicial restraint" suggest, the justices do indeed differ in their conceptions of what is the "proper" work of the High Court,[66] but there are also certain commonalities in their conceptions of what constitutes a case important enough to command the attention of the overburdened Court.[67] At least in recent history, these shared concerns have included the potential impact of the litigation and the protection of those civil liberties and civil rights enshrined in the Constitution but not always honored in the democratic process, or in other words, the substantive sympathies expressed in the Carolene footnote's justification for the exercise of judicial review. Cue theory's data have statistically validated the importance of the latter and, perhaps, its Solicitor General cue has served as a partial surrogate for the former.[68] However, there is more to these shared role conceptions than is captured by quantitative analysis.

The LSP's success is partly attributable to its serendipitous sponsorship of cases that fit the Court's conception of its proper role. The notion that the LSP's cases tapped shared conceptions of the proper work of the Court is buttressed by the essentially equal review rates of 72 percent (72) and 73 percent (46) it enjoyed during and after 1972, when the four conservative Nixon appointees were sitting, and before 1972, respectively (see table 4-4).[69] The fact that 7 percent of all written opinions handed down during the 1966 through 1974 Terms were responses to LSP sponsored cases provides further support for this

---

[64] Provine, *Case Selection*, pp. 86–130, 173–77.

[65] See Stern and Gressman, *Supreme Court Practice*, pp. 149–51, 167–69; Perry, "Deciding to Decide," pp. 291–308.

[66] Provine, *Case Selection*, pp. 104–30; Perry, "Deciding to Decide," pp. 260–64, 302–8.

[67] Provine, *Case Selection*, pp. 74–103.

[68] See Perry, "Deciding to Decide," pp. 294, 301–2.

[69] A year-by-year reporting of the Program's review rates is presented in Appendix B.

TABLE 4-4
Review Rates in LSP Sponsored Cases by Court, 1966–1974 Terms

| Court | LSP | | All Cases (n) |
|---|---|---|---|
| | Appellant/ Petitioner (n) | Appellee/ Respondent (n) | |
| Warren 1967–1971 | 65%(28) | 90%(18) | 73% (46) |
| Burger/Nixon 1972–1975 | 63 (40) | 89 (32) | 72 (72) |
| All Cases | 64%(68) | 89%(50) | 72%(118) |

conclusion. It is this fit with the Court's conception of its proper role that most likely accounts for the Court's willingness to place the LSP's cases on its decision agenda irrespective of petitioning party, Solicitor General support, conflict, or desire to reverse on the merits.

The justices use several criteria in assessing the potential impact of the cases that come before them.[70] First, the Court is more likely to accept cases that affect many people beyond the specific parties to the case. During the 1960s and early 1970s, about two-thirds of the poor received some form of direct financial payment from the government,[71] ensuring that decisions relating to the administration of transfer programs would indeed affect many people. Nineteen states had a substitute parent rule comparable to the one struck down in *King v. Smith*, and more than a third of the states had maximum grant rules similar to the one challenged in *Dandridge v. Williams*. Over forty states employed the type of residency requirements for receipt of welfare that the Court declared unconstitutional in *Shapiro v. Thompson*.[72] These residency requirements denied aid to an estimated one hundred thousand persons annually prior to the *Shapiro* decision. In the single year after *Shapiro* there was a 17 percent increase in the number of AFDC recipients.[73] The Court granted review in 93

[70] Provine, *Case Selection*, pp. 40–75; Perry, "Deciding to Decide," pp. 291–302. Stern and Gressman, in their guidebook to Supreme Court practice, also discuss this factor. *Supreme Court Practice*, pp. 167–77. However, probably due to the nebulousness of "potential impact," there has been little statistical evaluation of this factor. Using a number of criteria, Estreicher and Sexton have concluded that nearly one-fourth of the 164 cases the Court granted review in the 1982 Term "did not merit Supreme Court review." Estreicher and Sexton, "NYU Supreme Court Project."

[71] The bottom 20 percent of America's population received only 5 percent of the nation's goods and services in the early 1960s. Johnson, *Justice and Reform*, pp. 341–42, 345. Piven and Cloward report that in February 1969, 1,545,000 families were receiving AFDC. Piven and Cloward, *Regulating the Poor*, Appendix, Source Table 1.

[72] Shriver, "Law Reform"; Sparer, "Welfare Testing Memo."

[73] Although a variety of factors no doubt accounts for this increase, it has been primarily attributed to the elimination of residency requirements for the receipt of AFDC. Johnson, *Justice and Reform*, pp. 347–48. See also Champagne et al., "The Impact of Courts."

percent (56) of the LSP cases involving transfer programs (see table 4-1); these cases made up almost half of all the LSP cases reviewed by the Court. Decisions in other types of LSP cases were also likely to affect many people beyond the actual litigants in the case. For instance, in 1960 there were 3,684,000 urban slum housing units in the U.S.,[74] and the Court granted review in 47 percent (9) of the shelter cases the LSP sponsored. Furthermore, some LSP cases (e.g., *Goss v. Lopez*) dealt with issues such as education, which would affect the middle class as well as the poor.

Second, the Court considers potential impact in terms of the amount of related litigation pending or anticipated.[75] The LSP's nationwide scope and its combining of the client server and reformer roles ensured that similar litigation would show up in many different court dockets. Although it is difficult to assess the justices' precise awareness level, LSP briefs often included accounts of related litigation in other courts. For example, the *Shapiro* brief listed over twenty recent lower court cases challenging residency requirements for AFDC, although only one such case had ever been decided by an appellate court before the LSP began litigating.[76] *Shapiro* itself was the lead case among three cases the Court decided together. In eight other instances LSP cases were combined with others for review, which indicates that significant related litigation was pending before the Supreme Court.[77] Another example of the prevalence of LSP issues in other court dockets is provided by eight cases brought to the Supreme Court in 1971 presenting issues similar to the one decided two months earlier in *Boddie v. Connecticut*.[78] Given the currency of poverty issues on the Supreme Court's jurisdictional agenda, the Court's review of some LSP cases allowed them to deal with other cases summarily. The Court summarily disposed of fourteen LSP cases alone, based on other full opinion LSP cases. The presence of related litigation stood as testament to the importance

[74] Johnson, *Justice and Reform*, p. 353.

[75] This factor works in two ways. One, it tips the justices off as to the importance of an issue and, two, it allows them to reduce their workload by settling an issue. On the other hand, if other similar litigation is anticipated, it may free the justices to deny review to a particular case without forfeiting the opportunity to address an issue. There is some evidence that the justices see cases as "fungible." Perry reports, "The usual procedure is to grant one case and deny many cases which look very similar to the one selected. We should not conclude from this that the presence of that issue did not convey important information that was somehow used." Perry, "Indices and Signals," p. 9; Perry, "Deciding to Decide," pp. 252–53.

[76] Heydenreich v. Lyons, 1940.

[77] The lead cases in these nine combined cases were: *Fuentes v. Shevin* (1972); *Graham v. Richardson* (1971); *Lascaris v. Shirley* (1975); *Mazer v. Weinberger* (1975); *McKeiver v. Pennsylvania* (1971); *Philbrook v. Glodgett* (1975); *Richardson v. Wright* (1972); *Towsend v. Swank* (1971); and *Shapiro v. Thompson* (1969).

[78] Over the dissent of Justices Black and Douglas, the Court denied review in five of these cases. In one it noted probable jurisdiction and two were vacated and remanded for reconsideration in light of *Boddie*. See Justice Black's and Justice Douglas's dissent from denial of review in Meltzer v. LeCraw & Co. (1971).

of the issues raised in LSP cases and the reviewing of some of them allowed the Court to reduce its own workload and direct the lower courts' decision making in other cases.

Finally, the justices assess the impact of a case in terms of the seriousness of the penalty involved. Although in LSP cases the dollar amount that individual litigants stood to lose or gain was usually small, it often involved their very means of subsistence.[79] Some of the justices acknowledged this in their written opinions. Upon welfare aid, the majority opinion in *Shapiro v. Thompson* declared, ''may depend the ability of the families to obtain the very means to subsist—food, shelter, and other necessities of life.'' Even the majority opinion in *Dandridge v. Williams*, a major loss for the LSP, reiterated this theme. Justice Stewart wrote, ''the administration of public welfare assistance . . . involves the most basic economic needs of impoverished human beings.'' Opinions in other LSP cases are peppered with similar comments.[80] Welfare decisions made a great deal of difference in aggregate dollar amounts going to the poor. The Department of Health, Education, and Welfare estimated that three LSP cases won on the merits—*King v. Smith, Goldberg v. Kelly*, and *Shapiro v. Thompson*—resulted in a $400 to $500 million per year increase in public assistance payments.[81] Between 1967 and 1971, total public assistance payments jumped from $7.8 billion to $17.7 billion. Certainly, LSP's transfer program cases were not solely responsible for this increase, but they contributed to it.[82] Other LSP cases, while not directly involving money grants, related to things commonly considered necessities or near-necessities in the United States, although the Court was not convinced to declare an absolute constitutional right to these ''necessities.'' Some dealt with housing while others involved access to the courts, education, public utilities, transportation, rights of illegitimate children and their parents, and medical care. Although the LSP's Supreme Court cases grew out of individual client representation, they often raised issues whose resolution would have a serious effect on a sizeable proportion of the population.

[79] In 1965, 20 percent of the poor received transfer payments that accounted for 60 percent of their income. ''By 1970, 67.3 percent of families below the poverty line received transfer income in some form and this accounted for 50.5 percent of total income received by these poor families.'' Female-headed households received 67.4 percent of their income from transfer payments. Johnson, *Justice and Reform*, p. 345.

[80] For example, see Justice Black's dissent in *Shapiro v. Doe* (1970); Justice Douglas' dissent in *Dillard v. Industrial Commission of Virginia* (1974); Justice Marshall's concurrence in Johnson v. N.Y. State Education Dept. (1972) and his dissent in *Dandridge v. Williams* (1970); and Justice Black's dissent in Meltzer v. LeCraw & Co. (1971).

[81] Johnson, *Justice and Reform*, pp. 369–70.

[82] U.S., Department of Commerce, *Statistical Abstract*, Table 486, p. 299. The increase is credited to ''the broadening of eligibility rights, the assertion of existing rights, and higher benefit schedules.'' Johnson, *Justice and Reform*, p. 349. LSP cases had a role in the first two factors. See also Piven and Cloward, *Regulating the Poor*, pp. 309, 314.

Not only did the issues raised in LSP cases seem likely to have a substantial enough impact to justify the expenditure of the Court's limited agenda space, but they also provided the Court with the opportunity to fulfill the substantive role it had set for itself in Justice Stone's famous 1938 Carolene footnote.[83] With the decline of economic due process in the late 1930s, the Court turned to heightened scrutiny of governmental intrusion on personal and group rights.[84] By the late 1960s, the Court's role in protecting the civil liberties and civil rights of individuals and minorities from government intrusion was well established. Throughout the 1970s, the Burger Court continued to devote almost three-quarters of its decision agenda to civil liberties and civil rights issues.[85] As the data presented in table 4-2 showed, at least 74 percent (121) of the Program's cases involved constitutional provisions commonly used in support of civil liberties and civil rights claims and the Court granted review in 73 percent (90) of these cases. Furthermore, a full 95 percent (154) of the Program's cases were challenges to state or federal laws and the Court reviewed 75 percent (115) of these cases, whereas it only reviewed 22 percent (2) of the nine challenges to private practices.

Even though, as table 4-1 revealed, very few of the Program's cases dealt directly with the kind of political rights Justice Stone referred to when he wrote of "legislation which restricts those political processes which can ordinarily be expected to bring about the repeal of undesirable legislation," and the Program's cases often interwove economic issues with civil liberties claims,[86] the LSP's cases fit well within the Carolene tradition of providing a forum for groups lacking a voice in the political arenas.[87] The difficulties the

[83] U.S. v. Carolene Products Co. (1938). See also Ely, "The Wages of Crying Wolf." The Court's own recognition of the role of interest groups in this process is articulated in NAACP v. Button (1963). See also Brotherhood of Railroad Trainmen v. Virginia (1964); United Mine Workers v. Illinois Bar Assn. (1967); and United Transportation Union v. State Bar of Michigan (1971).

[84] See Pacelle, "The Supreme Court Agenda"; Pacelle, "The Supreme Court and the Growth of Civil Liberties"; Provine, *Case Selection*, pp. 95–99.

[85] Baum, *The Supreme Court*, pp. 164–66; Baum, "Explaining the Burger Court."

[86] In *Goldberg v. Kelly* (1970) the Court seemed to suggest that it would accept Reich's argument that welfare assistance was "new property" that required special protection by the Court. See Reich, "New Property"; Reich, "Individual Rights and Social Welfare." *Shapiro v. Thompson* (1969) combined a "property" interest in welfare payments with the right to travel. The LSP's argument in *King v. Smith* (1968) combined the same "property" interest with a right to privacy although the Court did not adopt this line of reasoning. In *Lynch v. Household Finance Corp.* (1972) Justice Stewart repudiated the distinction: "The dichotomy between personal liberties and property rights is a false one. Property does not have rights. People have rights. The right to enjoy property without unlawful deprivation, no less than the right to speak or the right to travel, is, in truth, a 'personal' right, whether the 'property' in question be a welfare check, a home, or a savings account. In fact, a fundamental interdependence exists between the personal right to liberty and the personal right in property." See also Redlich, "The Art of Welfare Advocacy."

[87] See Ely, "Representation Reinforcing"; Bickel, *The Supreme Court*, p. 114.

poor face in the legislative and executive branches are well known. As Schattschneider reminds us, "The flaw in the pluralist heaven is that the heavenly chorus sings with a strong upper-class accent."[88] While the problems of poverty had captured the attention of national lawmakers, many of the states were not as sympathetic to the plight of the poor. One hundred and twenty-nine of the LSP's cases were challenges to state or local rules and 72 percent (93) of them were granted review. By turning toward the adjudicatory policy-making process, the poor could rely on the power of reasoned, rational arguments rather than on electoral pressures, which they could seldom successfully bring to bear.[89] Hence, the overwhelming majority of LSP cases presented the Court with opportunities for decision in those substantive areas that it had defined as "important" and within the "proper work" of the Court.

Of course, shared judicial role conceptions do not explain why the Court granted review in some LSP cases and not in others. Nor do they really account for the Program's extraordinary review rate compared to other interest groups who also commonly sponsor cases that fit within the Court's definition of its proper role. Given that the LSP's Supreme Court cases grew haphazardly out of its client service, it is surprising that so many of its cases did indeed fall within the Court's view of its proper role. The serendipitous congruence between the issues raised in LSP cases and the shared judicial role conceptions renders the Program's review rate somewhat less remarkable and suggests some reasons why the Court did not deny review in LSP cases. To understand why the Court was unusually receptive to the particular subject matter of LSP cases, we must turn to those factors that add more specific content to the justices' perceptions of what constitutes an important issue, and when.

## The Role of Political Climate in Shaping Judicial Conceptions of the "Proper Work" of the Court

Most of the traditional explanations of the case selection process give only indirect attention to the political climate in which the justices conduct their work.[90] These traditional theories of case selection do not seem to provide very satiating explanations for LSP's unusual review rate, but taking explicit account of the political climate during the LSP's tenure may render the LSP's success somewhat less perplexing. The Supreme Court is an institution where law and politics mix. Most of the justices were active in politics before joining

[88] Schattschneider, *The Semisovereign People*, pp. 34–35.

[89] See Fuller, "Forms and Limits."

[90] For a broader view of agenda change rather than case selection in the Court, see Pacelle, "The Supreme Court and the Growth of Civil Liberties"; Pacelle, "The Supreme Court Agenda." See also Perry, "Deciding to Decide."

the bench,[91] and undoubtedly, once robed, they remain cognizant of political events outside the Court. It is likely that the rediscovery of poverty and its emergence on the nation's political agenda (which, among other things, changed the parameters of access to the Supreme Court's jurisdictional docket through the creation of the LSP) also affected the justices. Poverty claims came to be incorporated into the justices' conception of the "proper" work of the Court. This argument is begun here and developed more fully in the next chapter as we examine the LSP's success on the merits.

The Court, while protected from direct political pressure, is not immune to prevailing political climates. As Justice Holmes reminds us: "The life of the law has not been logic: it has been experience. The felt necessities of the time, the prevalent moral and political theories, intuitions of public policy, avowed or unconscious, even the prejudices which judges share with their fellowmen, have had a good deal more to do than the syllogism in determining the rules by which men should be governed."[92] During the 1960s and early 1970s the national domestic policy agenda focused on equality and poverty issues. It was an era of changing theories of poverty and reform of the welfare system.[93] With the attention Congress and the President gave to poverty, it is not surprising that the justices would find it to be an important issue and place it on their agenda as well.[94] From a legal standpoint, these issues were ripe for adjudication. Because the poor had been without lawyers for so long, the constitutionality of the legal order which impinged on them had rarely been tested, but potentially favorable doctrinal trends had surfaced in cases addressing other issues such as racial discrimination, loyalty-security dismissals, and criminal procedure.[95] The LSP's cases fit well with the Court's inclination to

[91] Of the fourteen justices serving during the LSP's tenure, twelve of them had held an elective office or an appointive administrative position within government at some point in their career before joining the Court. Compiled from Baum, *The Supreme Court*, pp. 54–55.

[92] Holmes, *The Common Law*, p. 347. Justice Cardozo's method of sociology suggests that this *should* be so. Cardozo, *The Nature of the Judicial Process*.

[93] See Patterson, *America's Struggle*, esp. pp. 157–59; Heclo, "The Political Foundations of Antipoverty Policy."

[94] Similarly, Greenberg argues that the national political climate contributed to the success of the NAACP LDF in the school desegregation cases: "A blueprint of where the country should be going with regard to race was published by President Truman's Committee on Civil Rights in 1948. . . . It called for abolishing segregation in all aspects of American life, including education, as did President Truman's Committee on Higher Education. . . . Americans' views on racial questions had changed markedly during the war. The Supreme Court was a willing collaborator. . . . In granting review [of Brown], the Court deliberately selected five cases from a wide geographic area to consider the national implications of the issue. It reached down and took the District of Columbia school segregation case on its own initiative before judgment in the Court of Appeals. It accelerated the schedule of the Delaware school case. . . . There was a current of history and the Court became part of it." Greenberg, "Litigation for Social Change," pp. 333–34.

[95] For example, though scholars had questioned the legality of "midnight searches" and "suit-

address equality issues. The same societal climate that led to the creation of a Legal Services Program affected the justices. Indeed, some of their earlier decisions, such as Brown v. Board of Education, had played a role in creating that climate. And, several of the justices had in fact endorsed the creation of the LSP.[96] The Court showed itself to be part of the dominant national governing alliance, not by following Mr. Dooley's "illiction returns," but by paralleling its agenda.[97]

The Court's sensitivity to the political environment in its case selection decisions is evidenced by the changing definitions of "civil liberties" adopted by cue-theory students. Teger and Kosinski write:

> Since the cues are, in fact, surrogates for the salient issues, they must be constantly updated. Cue theory ends up saying that the justices tend to accept cases that they think are important. Seen in this light, cue theory is not much of a theory. The fact that Tanenhaus was able to predict fairly well what the justices thought was important does not make the theory any more sound. There are no criteria for defining salience in advance of analysis. . . . The fact that the Court deals with the most salient issues of the day is important not only for those who argue about the role the Supreme Court plays in our society, but also because of the light it sheds on the certiorari decision itself.[98]

Apparently the post–New Deal justices are consistently disposed toward civil liberties cases, but what constitutes an important civil liberty changes over time, both in response to changing litigant claims and changing political climates. Before poverty made its way onto the national political agenda and before Legal Services Program attorneys began petitioning the Court, there was no reason to include poverty issues in an operational definition of the civil liberties cue. When poverty cases were not appealed to the Court, judicial views toward such cases were irrelevant to our understanding of case selection. With little history, the Court's receptivity to these issues could not be predicted. The Legal Services Program's litigation allowed the justices to expand their working notion of civil liberties. The national political climate gave them a reason to do so.

There is other evidence which suggests that the LSP brought cases to the Court at a time when the Court was predisposed to address indigency issues. The Court had struck down a number of criminal justice practices that differ-

---

able home" welfare policies shortly prior to the LSP's efforts, the constitutionality of these two provisions had not been tested. See Note, "Federal Judicial Review of State Welfare Practices," p. 86; Reich, "Midnight Welfare Searches"; Note, "Suitable Home Tests."

[96] See Johnson, *Justice and Reform*, pp. 49–64; Brennan, "Address."

[97] See Dahl, "Decision-Making in a Democracy."

[98] Teger and Kosinski, "Cue Theory: A Reconsideration," p. 845. See also Armstrong and Johnson, "Certiorari Decisions."

entiated between rich and poor.[99] Most notably, in 1962 the Court reached out to overrule Betts v. Brady, and establish a right to counsel in criminal cases. Clerks combed the in forma pauperis petitions in search of an appropriate case. When they found Gideon v. Wainwright (1963) the justices appointed Abe Fortas, a prominent lawyer, to argue Gideon's cause.[100] The process was simpler in LSP cases. The Program brought the cases to the justices. In an era of equal protection adjudication, it is not surprising that the Court would turn its attention to the nation's economically disadvantaged.[101]

Furthermore, other than general caseload pressures, incentives to avoid review of LSP cases were largely lacking. As the "electoral incentive" constrains Congress, the need to maintain legitimacy constrains the Court.[102] Perhaps LSP cases were reviewed because they allowed the justices to address issues they felt were important without threatening the Court's legitimacy. The cost, to the Court, of deciding LSP cases was low.[103] Compared to many other cases the Court has decided in the last thirty years, LSP cases were safe. Unlike the racial segregation cases (and perhaps the women's rights cases), they could be decided without precipitating a reweaving of the fabric of American society. Unlike the reapportionment decisions, they did not, on their face, threaten to radically redistribute political power in the nation. Generally, LSP cases did not push the Court away from textual referents and into controversial areas of constitutional interpretation in the way Griswold v. Connecticut (1965) and Roe v. Wade (1973) did.[104] Indeed, in some LSP cases that the

[99] See Griffin v. Illinois (1956); Eskridge v. Washington Prison Board (1958); Draper v. Washington (1963); Lane v. Brown (1963); Rinaldi v. Yeager (1966); Burns v. Ohio (1959); and Smith v. Bennett (1961).

[100] Lewis, *Gideon's Trumpet*. See also Douglas v. California (1963).

[101] See Funston, *Constitutional Counterrevolution?*, pp. 298–99 for a discussion of the Court's interest in equality during this time. Professor Bickel, following Professor Kurland, has suggested that the goal of the Warren Court was an "Egalitarian Society." Bickel, *The Supreme Court and the Idea of Progress*, pp. 13, 103. Professor Spaeth, noted for his quantitative analyses of Supreme Court decision making writes, "Concerns that bear on equality, such as sit-in demonstrations; sex discrimination; the rights of juveniles, indigents, and illegitimates; and poverty law did not figure prominently in the Court's decisions until the 1960s." Spaeth, "Attitudes and Values," p. 397. See also Pacelle, "The Supreme Court and the Growth of Civil Liberties."

[102] Mayhew, *Congress*; Dahl, "Decision-Making in a Democracy"; Cox, *The Role of the Supreme Court*, pp. 3–30, 99–118.

[103] On the Court's "dodging" or postponing decisions on controversial issues, such as challenges to the Vietnam War or to anti-miscegenation and sodomy statutes, by passing up many seemingly "review-worthy" cases, see Perry, "Deciding to Decide," pp. 295–300; Baum, *The Supreme Court*, pp. 100–101.

[104] Although the Court does indeed decide some of these "dangerous" cases, it seems to be sensitive to its limits. Indeed, the pre-Brown racial discrimination cases were purposefully designed to have minimal political repercussions. See Greenberg, "Litigation for Social Change," p. 333. Furthermore, school desegregation only had to proceed with "all deliberate speed," which the South took to mean not at all. Brown v. Board of Education II (1955). The Court has been careful not to judicially create an Equal Rights Amendment. The Court shied away from the

Court did grant review, such as *San Antonio v. Rodriguez* and *Dandridge v. Williams*, the Court overturned potentially disruptive, textually tangential, lower court decisions.

LSP cases largely dealt with bureaucracies invisible to middle America. Most Americans would not feel any direct effects of these decisions except, perhaps, in terms of higher tax rates to cover increased public assistance payments at a time when Congress was already appropriating large sums for poverty programs.[105] The Supreme Court's decisions in LSP cases were not seen as judicial usurpations of power. The Court's legitimacy was not threatened by addressing poverty issues. There was never active public opposition to the Supreme Court's decisions in LSP cases. These cases never served as a catalyst for grass-roots interest mobilization in the way Brown, Roe, and the school prayer decisions have. To the extent there was political opposition to the decisions in LSP cases, it came largely from state and local government officials and was directed toward the Program not the Court. Indeed, much of this political opposition was the result of lower court cases rather than Supreme Court decisions.[106] These local battles may have made the Supreme Court hesitant to issue broad, sweeping rulings favorable to the poor as a class, but these battles did not lead the Court to foreclose the poor's access to its decision-making process by refraining from reviewing their cases.

Perhaps more important, LSP cases were legitimate Supreme Court fare in that they addressed the interaction between the citizen and the state. It is the protection of individual liberties against government infringement that provides one of the theoretical justifications for judicial review in a democratic regime.[107] In many of these cases, the Court was simply applying the rule of law to the administrative state,[108] and enforcing accepted federal policy.

The LSP cases, while quite important to nearly one-fifth of the population, were politically salient but relatively safe cases for the Court to decide. By

---

reapportionment decisions for many years. See Shapiro, Law and Politics, pp. 174–252. Friedman has suggested that there is a political compromise transpiring between the Court and Congress on the abortion issue. Friedman, "Conflict." (The LSP did file an amicus curiae brief in Roe v. Wade, but amicus cases are not included in this discussion of case selection.) Of course, the "switch in time that saved nine" was the Court's most famous legitimacy saving move. See Jackson, *The Struggle for Judicial Supremacy*; Leuchtenburg, "Roosevelt's Court-Packing Plan"; Baker, *Back to Back*.

[105] The Court backed away from decisions that would obviously, substantially, reallocate public resources. See *Dandridge v. Williams* (1970) and *San Antonio v. Rodriguez* (1973), both of which reversed lower court decisions; and the certiorari denials in Meltzer v. LeCraw & Co. (1971).

[106] See George, "Development."

[107] See U.S. v. Carolene Products (1983); Choper, *Judicial Review*; Corwin, "The 'Higher Law' Background"; Ely, *Democracy and Distrust*; Mason, "New Foundations"; Murphy, "The Art of Constitutional Interpretation"; Perry, *The Constitution, the Courts, and Human Rights*.

[108] On the implications of the English courts' failure to do this, see Shapiro, *Courts*, pp. 111–25.

reviewing poor people's cases the Court could reinforce the myth of equality before the law. Indeed, it brought reality a bit closer to the myth. The Court had little to lose and something to gain by accepting LSP cases for review.

## CONCLUSIONS

As Kingdon reminds us: "The patterns of public policy, after all, are determined not only by such final decisions as votes in legislatures, or initiatives and vetoes by presidents [or decisions on the merits by the Supreme Court], but also by the fact that some subjects and proposals emerge in the first place and others are never seriously considered."[109] Litigants and the justices both play a crucial role in determining which "subjects and proposals" will "emerge in the first place." Who has the ability to appeal to the Supreme Court and how the justices respond to those requests for review are important determinants of the patterns of doctrine emanating from the Court. By removing the burdens of the de facto assistance of counsel requirement, the LSP provided the poor with an ability to bring their civil claims to the Supreme Court that they had not enjoyed before. This newfound access and the justices' responsiveness to the heterogeneous collection of cases that it produced, account for the emergence of poverty law as a substantial component of the Court's jurisprudence.

But this begs the question of why the justices agreed to place the poverty issues raised in LSP cases on their decision agenda. That scholars' attempts to unveil the unwritten criteria that guide case selection and provide a systematic model of the process do not seem to account for the LSP's exceptional 64 percent (68) review rate or its opponents' remarkable 89 percent (50) review rate, should not necessarily surprise us. Others who have studied Congress and the executive branch have provided us with some excellent descriptions and explanations of agenda setting that illustrate an intricacy that defies predictive model building.[110] Indeed, we have not agreed on a systematic explanation of why poverty emerged as such an important issue on the national political agenda in the 1960s and 1970s that would allow us to predict when it will receive such beneficent attention again.[111] Instead, the studies show agenda

---

[109] Kingdon, *Agendas*, p. 2.

[110] Kingdon, *Agendas*; Light, *The President's Agenda*; Nelson, *Making an Issue of Child Abuse*; Peterson, *Legislating Together*; Polsby, *Political Innovation in America*; Walker, "Setting the Agenda in the U.S. Senate."

[111] Patterson, *America's Struggle*, provides an excellent history of the cycles of attention to poverty that have characterized national policy making. As a historian, Patterson does not attempt to develop a social science type model to explain these cycles. Heclo, "The Political Foundations of Antipoverty Policy," adopts Kingdon's model to explain the emergence of the Great Society. He adds an excellent analysis of the political weaknesses that have been most damaging to an overt commitment to an antipoverty policy and the role of public attitudes. The explanations Piven

setting to be a rather messy process; our national political agenda is set by complex combinations of separate phenomena that have lives of their own. It is almost impossible to systematically predict when these phenomena will ripen and combine to push an issue onto the agenda.[112]

And so it is with the Supreme Court. We can specify the prerequisites to an issue's appearance on the Court's agenda, such as litigant access and compatibility with the justices' conceptions of the Supreme Court's role, and we can specify those variables that correlate with review grants, such as support of the Solicitor General, conflict, and desire to reverse the court below; but we cannot systematically predict precisely what subjects the Court will choose to focus on, and when, or how many cases it will take in those areas. The importance the justices assign to different issues varies as the political climate and the pool of litigant claims placed before the Court change. This does not make the Court's "decision to decide" capricious; rather, it renders it, in some measure, responsive to the "felt necessities of the times."

Once we acknowledge that the political climate of an era will affect the justices' conceptions of the "proper work" of the Court and their conceptions of what issues are most important for the highest court in the land to resolve, it is not so surprising that the Court would accept so many cases brought by a group so recently created by the national executive and legislative branches. Unlike other interest groups, the LSP did not have to create, or wait to seize, the right political moment; it was the product of such a time. The justices' case selection decisions allowed the LSP to move the issues of the poor onto the Supreme Court's policy-making agenda. The Program's litigation had passed its first hurdle. Next, the final substantive policy decisions were at stake. And, not surprisingly, there too the political climate of the era shaped the Court's response.

---

and Cloward put forth in *Regulating the Poor* have come under considerable attack. See Trattner, *Social Welfare*.

[112] See Kingdon, *Agendas*, pp. 75–94, 173–204.

# CHAPTER FIVE

# Decision Making in LSP Cases

THE COURT'S case selection decisions gave Legal Services Program clients access to the Supreme Court's policy-making agenda. Through the LSP, the poor were enfranchised in the judicial development of national policy. From the perspective of democratic theory, access to the policy-making forum was crucial. From the perspective of the poor clients, prevailing in that forum was crucial. And prevail they did. LSP attorneys secured victories for their clients in 62 percent (74) of the 119 cases the Supreme Court reviewed.[1]

The LSP's victories, mirroring its cases, defy simple classification. They ranged across a variety of sources, targets, subjects, and constitutional issues. They were not the flowering of a nurtured and highly cultivated litigation plan, nor were they the fruit of the labors of an exceptionally skilled, experienced bar. They were not the final product of patient cross-breeding of favorable precedents over time. Nor were they simply what we would expect from the Supreme Court. LSP attorneys were far more successful than typical Supreme Court decision patterns suggest they should have been.

How can the LSP's relative success be explained? Access was the key prerequisite. Through LSP attorneys, the poor finally overcame the burden of the de facto assistance of counsel requirement and were able to present the Court with opportunities for decision in areas that were significant to them. Furthermore, LSP attorneys were able to bolster their poor clients' claims with legal arguments and precedents recently developed in other areas and tap the justices' sympathies for civil liberties and civil rights issues. Perhaps most important, the LSP came to the Court at a time when poverty and equality issues were on the national political and judicial agendas. Poverty law took root in the Supreme Court because the seeds were introduced to fertile soil.[2]

In this chapter, the deviations between decisions in LSP cases and customary decision patterns are explored. The breadth of the LSP's victories and patterns of judicial support for the LSP show that who is *before* the Court can be as

---

[1] The Program's seventy-four wins includes twenty-three cases that were remanded. It lost forty-five cases, nine of which were remanded. Remanded cases were read and substantively analyzed, then coded as an LSP win or loss depending upon whether the remand and accompanying instructions to the lower court advantaged the LSP's client (see Appendix D).

[2] A different configuration of justices or lack of a suitable national policy climate could have rendered the soil barren and the LSP unsuccessful. However, as shown later, both the Warren and Burger Courts were receptive to the LSP's arguments. The fertility of the soil was earlier evidenced by the justice's case selection decisions.

important as who is *on* the Court for understanding judicial policy making. We will examine the confluence of various legal and political factors that seem to explain the Program's success better than the organizational factors usually associated with interest group litigation success. Here the focus is on examining the Court's and the individual justices' response to the Program's litigation in the aggregate. In the next chapter, we will examine the substantive and doctrinal import of the LSP's victories and losses.

## Breaking With Prediction

The LSP was considerably more successful than predictions based on the Court's treatment of its civil docket as a whole would lead us to anticipate. The LSP's 62 percent (74) win rate was not simply business as usual.

The Supreme Court generally rules for the petitioner in two-thirds of the cases it hears.[3] Had this pattern held for LSP cases, the Program would have secured victories in 53 percent of its cases rather than 62 percent (74). As expected, when the LSP was the petitioner, it won 61 percent (42) of its cases. Contrary to expectations, the LSP's petitioning opponents only secured victories in 36 percent (18) of their cases. The LSP won over 60 percent of the time, regardless of whether it was on the offensive or defensive, which is a statistically significant variation from the Court's usual pattern of decision making (see table 5-1).

TABLE 5-1
LSP Success Compared to the Supreme Court's Usual Reversal Pattern

| Petitioner | LSP | |
|:---:|:---:|:---:|
| | Won (n) | Lost (n) |
| LSP | 42 | 27 |
| | (46)[a] | (23) |
| Other | 32 | 18 |
| | (17) | (33) |

$x^2 = 23.05$, df $= 1$, p $> .001$.

[a] Expected frequencies. These expected frequencies were computed based on the Supreme Court's general pattern of reversing two-thirds of the cases it reviews. Brenner, "Certiorari Game," p. 655. The chi square here indicates that the difference between the LSP's actual success rate (62 percent) and the predicted win rate based on the usual pattern of Supreme Court reversals (53 percent) is significant. For the use and meaning of chi square, see Blalock, *Social Statistics*, pp. 279-325.

[3] Brenner, "Certiorari Game," p. 655. See also Stern and Gressman, *Supreme Court Practice*, p. 179.

The LSP's success as a petitioner and as a respondent is even more remarkable given that government was the opponent 87 percent (103) of the time. During the 1966–1974 Terms, the Court ruled for government units in 60 percent of their cases.[4] This pattern predicts a 52 percent LSP win rate[5]; in fact, the LSP won 64 percent (66) of the cases in which it opposed a government unit.

The LSP's victories against the federal government are particularly notable. Between 1966 and 1974, the Court ruled against the federal government in only 28 percent of its civil cases. In LSP cases, the Solicitor General lost 47 percent (6) of the thirteen cases in which the federal government was the opponent. He lost 73 percent (8) of the eleven cases in which he opposed the LSP by filing an amicus brief or serving as cocounsel with another LSP opponent. Although the LSP secured a substantially higher proportion of victories against the federal government than one would expect, it was less successful in opposing the federal government than in opposing other parties.

State governments are notably less favored in the Supreme Court than is the federal government, sustaining defeats in 56 percent of their civil cases.[6] State governments suffered even more in LSP cases, losing 67 percent (60) of the contests. Half of all LSP cases reviewed by the Court resulted in victories over state governments. These cases were particularly salient because state-administered bureaucracies impinged most directly on the poor's lives.

The LSP not only secured an unpredicted number of victories, but also an unpredicted number of written opinions. The Court, between 1966 and 1974, issued written opinions in only 47 percent of the cases it decided. In contrast, 67 percent (80) of the LSP's cases received plenary consideration. The proportion of written opinions favorable to the LSP (63 percent [50] of 80) corresponds to the proportion of cases the Program won (62 percent [74] of 119). In terms of the entire work of the Court during this time, 7 percent of all written opinions were responses to LSP cases; 4 percent were pro-LSP opinions. Hence, the LSP was not just winning; it was shaping the development of the law and policy articulated by the Court.

The surprising number of LSP victories does not correspond to hypotheses involving expertise of counsel. The LSP, itself, did not have the organizational attributes generally associated with interest group litigation success such as

[4] Unless otherwise noted, all figures in this chapter on the Court's business, decision patterns, and judicial voting patterns were compiled from "The Supreme Court, 1966–1974 Terms: The Statistics." LSP cases were considered as a subset of all Supreme Court cases. Had a dichotomous variable been used (e.g., LSP cases versus non-LSP cases), the differences in percentages would have been slightly higher. During the 1966 through 1974 Terms, the Supreme Court decided a total of 2559 cases, giving plenary consideration to 1193.

[5] The prediction is four LSP wins against the federal government and fifty wins against state governments in 103 cases.

[6] Compiled from "The Supreme Court, 1966–74 Terms: The Statistics." See also Baker and Asperger, "Foreword: Toward A Center for State and Local Legal Advocacy"; Ulmer, "Government Litigants."

longevity, group coordination and cohesion, and a sharp issue focus,[7] nor did the Program employ a particularly experienced or expert legal staff. The LSP secured victories in 63 percent (43) of the cases argued alone by an individual attorney from one of the 265 local projects (see table 5-2). By and large, much like the Galanter's one-shotter attorneys, this was the only case the attorney had ever argued before the Supreme Court.[8] While, undoubtedly, most project attorneys received some advice from the LSP back-up centers, many of their opponents had more experience arguing before the Supreme Court.[9] Occasionally the back-up centers participated directly as counsel, and the LSP's success rate was slightly higher in these cases. However, the relationship is not statistically significant and the back-up center cases only constituted 23 percent (17) of the LSP's victories.[10] The LSP was less successful in cases cosponsored with

Table 5-2
LSP Success Rates by Presence of Expert Counsel

| Cosponsor | Success Rate (n) |
|---|---|
| OEO-LSP Back-up Center | 68%(17) |
| Other Cosponsors | 54　(14) |
| NAACP LDF | 56　(5) |
| ACLU | 33　(1) |
| Other interest groups; private, appointed by Court or faculty attorney | 50　(6) |
| Federal Government | 100　(2) |
| None | 63　(43) |
| All Cases | 62%(74) |

Cosponsorship/none with case outcome: Yule's Q = −0.05 (N = 119). Excluding non-LSP cosponsored cases, back-up center cosponsorship/none with case outcome: Yule's Q = 0.11 (N = 93). Non-LSP cosponsorship/back-up center cosponsorship and none with case outcome: Yule's Q = −0.25 (N = 119). Yule's Q is a statistical measurement of association for dichotomized dependent variables that takes into consideration the fact that the marginals for the dependent variable are fixed by the method of research. It is used here because the data represent a universe rather than a sample. Q = 0.0 when the variables are completely independent, and Q = 1.0 (positive or negative) when they are perfectly associated. See Blalock, *Social Statistics*, pp. 306–7.

[7] See Sorauf, *Wall*, p. 73; O'Connor, *Women's Organizations'*, pp. 16–28; Hahn, "NAACP Legal Defense and Education Fund," pp. 387, 390; Epstein, *Conservatives*, pp. 12–14, 150–55.

[8] Galanter, "Why the 'Haves.' "

[9] Furthermore, there was a high turnover rate among LSP attorneys. See Katz, "Lawyers for the Poor." On the characteristics of Legal Services attorneys generally, see Handler et al., *Lawyers*, pp. 135–53. On the back-up centers, see Johnson, *Justice and Reform*, pp. 180–82, 274.

[10] The association between back-up center cosponsorship and case outcome is not statistically

other expert litigators such as the NAACP-LDF and ACLU, winning only 54 percent (14) of these cases.[11] The participation of more experienced or skilled counsel in some cases does not account for the LSP's success rate.

The current literature provides few guidelines for predicting victories based on the filing of supportive amicus curiae briefs.[12] The LSP's success pattern suggests that these briefs may not have explanatory value. Amicus curiae briefs were filed in support of the LSP in 45 percent (54) of the Program's cases. As table 5-3 shows, the LSP was slightly less successful in these cases than in those Program attorneys argued without the aid of friends.[13] The Program did win five of the eight cases in which the Solicitor General filed a supportive amicus brief.[14] Among the twenty-four cases in which the LSP participated only as a friend-of-the-court, "its" side prevailed 71 percent (17) of the time.[15]

TABLE 5-3
LSP Success Rates by Filing of Amicus Curiae Briefs

| Amicus Brief(s) Filed in Support of LSP | Success Rate (n) |
| --- | --- |
| Yes | 59%(32) |
| No | 65   (42) |
| All Cases | 62%(74) |

Yule's Q = −0.11.

significant. Yule's Q = 0.11. Cosponsorship by a back-up center yielded a 68.0 percent (17) success rate. Most of these cases involved transfer programs. The LSP won 70.0 percent (39) of its transfer payment cases. It is impossible to determine which factor had a greater causal impact on the outcomes in these cases.

[11] More difficult or radical cases may have provoked cosponsorship thereby depressing win rates.

[12] Puro reports that between 1920 and 1973, the U.S. as amicus was successful in 74 percent of the political cases in which it filed, surpassed only by the NAACP's 84 percent success rate. Puro, "The United States as *Amicus Curiae*," pp. 223–24. See also O'Connor and Epstein, "Beyond Legislative Lobbying," esp. p. 143.

[13] This is not to argue that amicus briefs do not influence the Court, but rather that their influence may be more subtle than simply calculating wins and losses reveals. The win rate may be slightly lower in cases with amicus briefs because the characteristics of the cases that attract amicus briefs may also make them difficult cases. O'Connor and Epstein found that between 1969 and 1981 amicus briefs were cited by majority, concurring, or dissenting opinions in 18 percent of the cases where at least one amicus brief was filed. O'Connor and Epstein, "Court Rules and Workload."

[14] The support of the Solicitor General does not seem to have been as critical to the LSP's success as it was to the NAACP's and Jehovah's Witnesses'. Vose, *Caucasians Only*, pp. 172–73; Manwaring, "The Flag Salute Case."

[15] This may only suggest that the back-up centers were adept at choosing cases in which to file

In sum, the LSP won substantially more often than could be predicted by the overall decision patterns of the Court. Particular qualities of counsel and the filing of amicus curiae briefs do not suggest that such predictions should be revised upwards, nor do they provide an explanation of the Program's exceeding of the predictions. The LSP's pursuance of the poor's claims to the nation's highest judicial tribunal met with an unusual degree of success.

## VICTORIES ACROSS THE BOARD

The diversity of the LSP's victories is as great as the diversity of cases it appealed to the Court. The Court supported the LSP across the agenda that the poor provided the Program. There are no clear-cut differences in the descriptive characteristics of LSP wins and losses. The LSP's success rate was not the result of multiple favorable decisions in similar cases.

The route to the Supreme Court traveled by an LSP case did not affect the ultimate decision of the Court. The LSP's success rate was consistent regardless of what kind of lower court had previously decided the case, winning 65 percent (15) of the cases from the Courts of Appeals, 61 percent (42) from three-judge federal district courts, and 63 percent (17) from state courts.[16] Cases that came to the Court under its certiorari jurisdiction were only slightly less favored (59 percent of 44) than cases that came to the Court on appeal (64 percent of 74).[17]

The source and kind of rule challenged had little effect on the LSP's ability to persuade the Court. Federal rules were slightly less vulnerable than state and local rules, with the LSP winning 59 percent (13) of its challenges to the former and 64 percent (61) of its attacks on the latter.[18] The LSP lost both of its two challenges to private practices. There is not a statistically significant association between any of these case attributes and case outcome.

There is some variance in the LSP's success rates across subjects. The LSP was the most successful in cases involving transfer programs, personal well-being, legal procedures, and Indian Rights (see table 5-4), and the least so in cases involving political rights. In other subjects, the Program won about half its cases. When the subject variable is dichotomized as transfer program and other, there is a weak positive association between transfer program cases and LSP success.[19]

There is a moderate relationship between absence of a constitutional issue

---

amicus curiae briefs. Counting these cases as "LSP wins" along with sponsored cases only increases the LSP's win rate 1.4 percent, from 62.2 percent to 63.6 percent.

[16] State/federal court with case outcome: Yule's Q = 0.02.

[17] Excluding the petition for an injunction: Yule's Q = $-0.09$ (N = 118).

[18] Excluding the two challenges to private practices, federal/state rules with case outcome: Yule's Q = $-0.11$ (N = 117).

[19] Yule's Q = 0.29. Definitive conclusions are not, and should not, be drawn from small differences in success rates across subjects presented in table 5–4. The small N sizes of some categories make the percentages somewhat misleading.

TABLE 5-4
LSP Success Rates by Subject

| Subject | Success Rate (n) |
|---|---|
| Transfer Programs | 70%(39) |
| Criminal Justice | 46 (6) |
| Shelter | 44 (4) |
| Personal Well-Being | 60 (6) |
| Financial Relationships | 55 (6) |
| Legal Procedures | 64 (7) |
| Political Rights | 25 (1) |
| Indian Rights | 100 (5) |
| All Cases | 62%(74) |

*Note*: Transfer programs/other with case outcome: Yule's Q = 0.29.

and LSP success, with the Program winning 81 percent (17) of such cases. However, cases without constitutional issues only account for 23 percent (17) of the LSP's victories (see table 5-5). Among those cases that did raise a constitutional issue, the LSP's success rate was fairly consistent, resulting in a combined success rate of 58 percent (57) in all constitutional cases.[20] Over two-thirds of the Program's victories involved due process or equal protection claims.

In sum, the LSP was successful across the board. No definable set of cases met with a great deal more success than others. Though the Program was noticeably more successful when no constitutional issues were presented, such cases account for less than a quarter of the Program's victories. The diversity of these cases demonstrates that LSP attorneys were not simply scoring redundant victories.

## THE JUDICIAL VARIABLE

The business litigants bring to the Court is the first determinate of Supreme Court doctrine and policy, but the justices remain crucial in determining the substantive direction of the Court's response to its opportunities for decision. During the nine terms the LSP participated in the Supreme Court's docket, the personnel of the Court was in flux. The LSP began its work with the Warren Court firmly in place; by the time the Program ended, Nixon had appointed

[20] Again, small N sizes in some categories require caution in drawing definitive conclusions based on variations.

TABLE 5-5
LSP Success Rates by Constitutional Issue

| Constitutional Issue | Success Rate (n) |
|---|---|
| Equal Protection, 5th and 14th Amendments | 57% (29) |
| Due Process, 5th and 14th Amendments | 65 (22) |
| First Amendment | — (0/1) |
| Criminal Procedure Amendments | 40 (2) |
| Right to Access to the Courts | 60 (3) |
| Other | 50 (1) |
| None | 81 (17) |
| All Cases | 62% (74) |

*Note*: Constitutional issue/none with case outcome: Yule's Q = −0.51.

TABLE 5-6
LSP Success Rates by Court

| Court | Success Rate (n) |
|---|---|
| Warren, 1967–1971 | 62% (29) |
| Burger/Nixon, 1972–1975 | 63 (45) |
| All Cases | 62% (74) |

Yule's Q = −0.02.

four justices and the Burger Court era was in full swing. The LSP's success before five natural Courts underscores the importance of litigants in shaping the development of judicial policy.

Intuitively, we would expect a liberal Court, such as the Warren Court, to be more favorably inclined toward the poor's claims than a more conservative Court, such as the Burger/Nixon Court. But, as table 5-6 shows, the Program's success rate on the merits, like its review rate, is essentially the same both before and after the four Nixon appointees assumed the bench.[21] The LSP's success was clearly not a Warren Court phenomena. Chief Justice Warren only participated in nine LSP cases before he left the bench in 1969, of which the Program won seven, whereas between 1969 and 1975, Chief Justice

[21] 1972 was the first year in which there were four Nixon appointees on the bench. The Court's composition then became three liberals: Brennan, Douglas, and Marshall; four conservatives: Burger, Blackmun, Powell, and Rehnquist; and two moderates: White and Stewart. A year-by-year reporting of the Program's success rates is presented in Appendix B.

Burger participated in 108, 60 percent (65) of which the LSP won.[22] Eighty-eight percent (65) of the LSP's victories were achieved after Burger had assumed the chief justiceship and 61 percent (45) were accomplished after Burger had been joined by the three other Nixon appointees.

Of course, the chief justice is only the first among equals. Like any other justice, he must convince four of his brethren to join him to prevail on the merits.[23] The core of the LSP's support came not from the chief justices (see table 5-7), but rather, as we would expect, from those justices most often

TABLE 5-7
Ranking of the Justices by LSP Support Score and Spaeth's Equality Scale

| Rank Order of Justices' Support for LSP in All LSP Cases[a] (n) | | Spaeth's Equality Scale[b] (Scale Scores) |
|---|---|---|
| Douglas | 81.3%(91) | Douglas (.76) |
| Marshall | 76.5 (88) | Fortas (.64) |
| Brennan | 72.6 (85) | Warren (.61) |
| Fortas | 66.7 (4) | Brennan (.58) |
| Warren | 66.7 (6) | Marshall (.57) |
| White | 59.3 (70) | White (−0.7) |
| Stewart | 57.6 (68) | Stewart (−0.8) |
| Blackmun | 57.3 (55) | Powell (−.26) |
| Powell | 53.7 (36) | Blackmum (−.27) |
| Harlan | 52.4 (22) | Harlan (−.36) |
| Rehnquist | 45.5 (30) | Burger (−.42) |
| Burger | 45.4 (49) | Black (−.55) |
| Black | 45.2 (19) | Rehnquist (−.58) |

[a] Support scores were computed as the number of times the justice voted for the LSP's position divided by the number of LSP cases the justice participated in. In addition, Justice Clark participated in one LSP case in 1967; he voted with the majority in support of the LSP's position.

[b] Spaeth, *Supreme Court Policy Making*, p. 135.

[22] The Court decided two cases in favor of the LSP without the participation of either chief justice.

[23] The special duties of chief justices do provide them with a few extra tools to use in persuading their colleagues, but incumbents have varied in their inclination and ability to use these tools. Burger is generally not viewed as a particularly persuasive chief justice. Murphy, *Elements of Judicial Strategy*, pp. 82–89; O'Brien, *Storm Center*, pp. 186–89, 241–43.

characterized as liberal—particularly Douglas, Marshall, and Brennan. The ordering of judicial support for the LSP roughly corresponds to Spaeth's equality rankings.[24] Until 1969, liberals could command a five-man majority on the Court.[25] By 1972, the four Nixon appointees were voting as a conservative bloc.[26] Nonetheless, the LSP still won over 60 percent (45) of its cases. There are two possible voting patterns that would account for the LSP's continued success as more conservatives took the bench. First, the three liberal justices still on the Court, Douglas, Brennan, and Marshall, may have been able to cajole two or three conservative or moderate justices to join them in some LSP cases. Alternately, a majority of the justices may have had a propensity to support the LSP's position irrespective of their usual ideological orientation. Although neither explanation minimizes the importance of who litigates, the second emphasizes it.

Table 5-7 provides some support for the first explanation. The traditionally liberal justices were indeed the most supportive of the LSP: Douglas, Marshall, Brennan, Fortas, and Warren. Conservative justices and most of the Nixon appointees were less so: Black, Harlan, Burger, Powell, and Rehnquist. The three moderates, White, Stewart, and Blackmun, had support scores just under the LSP's win rate. The dissent matrix presented in table 5-8 shows evidence of small liberal and conservative blocs operating in LSP cases. Douglas, Marshall, and Brennan constitute the former, and Burger, Powell, and Rehnquist constitute the latter.[27] Blackmun and White joined the liberals frequently enough to provide the LSP with considerable success. That Blackmun and White voted with the majority 94 and 96 percent of the time, respectively, suggests they were swing votes in LSP cases (see table 5-9).

Nonetheless, the swing-vote explanation can be challenged. If valid, we would expect many of the cases to be one-vote decisions. Only 6 percent (4) of the LSP's victories and 9 percent (4) of its losses were decided by a single vote (see table 5-10). Furthermore, 58 percent (42) of the LSP's wins were unanimous. In contrast, only 40 percent (18) of its losses were unanimous, which corresponds to the Court's usual unanimity rate.[28] There is a moderate association between LSP success and unanimity and between LSP defeat and

[24] Spaeth, *Supreme Court Policy-Making*, p. 135.

[25] Douglas, Marshall, Brennan, Fortas, and Warren. Although Justice Black has often been classified as a liberal, at this point in his career the label did not clearly fit. Spaeth found that he had the second lowest support score on equality claims. Of course, one cannot equate all poverty claims with equality claims. Particularly in the instance of Black, his score was depressed by his position in the sit-in cases. Nonetheless, of the available ranking scales, "equality" seems to come closest to poverty issues. Spaeth, *Supreme Court Policy-Making*, pp. 128–37. See also Grossman, "A Model for Judicial Policy Analysis."

[26] See Howard, "Is the Burger Court a Nixon Court?"

[27] Stewart also joined the conservative bloc from time to time; however, his dissent agreement with the liberals is almost as frequent as with the conservatives.

[28] During this era 42 percent of all the Court's decisions were unanimous.

TABLE 5-8
Supreme Court Dissent Matrix in LSP Cases

| | Burger | Black | Douglas | Marshall | Brennan | Blackmun | White | Stewart | Rehnquist | Powell | Harlan |
|---|---|---|---|---|---|---|---|---|---|---|---|
| Burger | X | 26 | 1 | 0 | 0 | 4 | 2 | 6 | 9 | 5 | 0 |
| Black | | X | 13 | 5 | 5 | 0 | 0 | 12 | — | — | 5 |
| Douglas | | | X | 15 | 14 | 1 | 1 | 5 | 3 | 2 | 0 |
| Marshall | | | | X | 15 | 2 | 1 | 3 | 0 | 0 | 0 |
| Brennan | | | | | X | 2 | 1 | 2 | 0 | 0 | 0 |
| Blackmun | | | | | | X | 2 | 0 | 2 | 2 | 0 |
| White | | | | | | | X | 1 | 0 | 0 | 0 |
| Stewart | | | | | | | | X | 5 | 3 | 0 |
| Rehnquist | | | | | | | | | X | 8 | — |
| Powell | | | | | | | | | | X | — |
| Harlan | | | | | | | | | | | X |

The methodology outlined in Howard, "Is the Burger Court a Nixon Court?" was used in constructing this table.

one-vote decisions. The high incidence of unanimous victories and the dearth of one-vote decisions, especially among the Program's successes, indicates that the LSP's good fortune cannot be explained simply by traditional liberal/conservative voting patterns and swing votes. Rather, it suggests that a consensus explanation may be more appropriate.

The evidence shows that all the justices, except Black, seemed to have an unusual propensity to vote for the LSP. Comparing agreement rates between pairs of justices in Legal Services cases and in the docket as a whole during the same time period controls for some of the nonideological factors that influence judicial voting patterns such as small group dynamics and freshmen effects. Indeed, the newness of the issues presented in LSP cases would lead us to expect lower agreement rates in the Program's cases, as all the justices were in the process of developing positions on these issues, a situation that would create considerable flux in the coalitions. The newness of the specific issues raised in LSP cases also decreased the constraint of law and precedent on judicial value-based voting.[29] In LSP cases, liberal and conservative justices have

[29] See Murphy, *Elements of Judicial Strategy*, pp. 37–90; Howard, "On the Fluidity."

TABLE 5-9
Ranking of the Justices by Agreement with the Majority in LSP Cases

| Justice | Percentage of Votes With Majority (n) | |
|---------|------|------|
| Fortas | 100% | (6) |
| Clark | 100 | (1) |
| White | 96 | (113) |
| Blackmun | 94 | (90) |
| Harlan | 93 | (39) |
| Powell | 93 | (62) |
| Stewart | 89 | (105) |
| Warren | 89 | (8) |
| Marshall | 85 | (98) |
| Rehnquist | 85 | (56) |
| Brennan | 84 | (98) |
| Burger | 83 | (90) |
| Douglas | 71 | (80) |
| Black | 60 | (25) |

higher agreement rates than in the Court's docket as a whole. Table 5-11 lists the pairs of justices in rank order based on the difference between their agreement rates in LSP cases and in the entire work of the Court. Only 15 percent (10) of the pairs agreed less often in LSP cases. Among this 15 percent there are no liberal/conservative pairs. The lowest scoring liberal/conservative pair, Douglas and Harlan, agreed 5 percent more often in LSP cases than in the entire docket.[30]

The top of the ranking is dominated by liberal/conservative pairs, indicating that they agreed much more often in LSP cases than usual. Indeed, if one excludes the pairs that include Fortas or Warren, who only participated in six and nine LSP cases respectively, the top two pairs are Rehnquist with Douglas

[30] See Appendix E for each set of agreement rates. Four of the ten negative pairs include Black who showed an amazing propensity to disagree with everybody during this time. Black's dissenting opinions in LSP victories indicate that while he was sympathetic to the LSP's claims, his conception of the proper judicial role prevented him from joining the majority. If one excludes pairs involving either Black or Warren (who only participated in nine LSP cases before leaving the Court), there are only three negative pairs.

TABLE 5-10
Vote Divisions in LSP Cases

| Votes in Minority | LSP Wins (N = 73) | | | | | | Votes in Majority — LSP Losses (N = 45) | | | | | | All LSP Cases (N = 118) | | | | | |
|---|---|---|---|---|---|---|---|---|---|---|---|---|---|---|---|---|---|---|
| | 9 | 8 | 7 | 6 | 5 | 4 | 9 | 8 | 7 | 6 | 5 | 4 | 9 | 8 | 7 | 6 | 5 | 4 |
| 0 | 38 | 2 | 2 | | | | 17 | 0 | 1 | | | | 55 | 2 | 3 | | | |
| 1 | | 5 | 0 | 1 | | | | 4 | 1 | 1 | | | | 9 | 1 | 2 | | |
| 2 | | | 4 | 4 | 2 | | | | 2 | 3 | | | | | 6 | 7 | 2 | |
| 3 | | | | 6 | 5 | 2[a] | | | | 10 | 2 | | | | | 16 | 7 | 2[a] |
| 4 | | | | | 2[a] | | | | | | 4[a] | | | | | | 6[a] | |
| Unanimous Decisions | 42 (58%) | | | | | | 18 (40%) | | | | | | 60 (51%) | | | | | |
| One Vote Decisions | 4 (6%) | | | | | | 4 (9%) | | | | | | 8 (7%) | | | | | |

*Note*: Figures presented here exclude one application for an injunction. Win/loss with unanimous/split: Yule's $Q = 0.34$. Win/loss with one Vote/other: Yule's $Q = -0.37$.

[a] One vote decisions.

and Brennan agreeing over 20 percent more often in LSP cases than in the docket as a whole. They are followed by Blackmun with Douglas and Brennan agreeing about 20 percent more often in LSP cases and Powell with Douglas and Brennan agreeing about 19 percent more often. Rehnquist, Blackmun, and Powell voted with Douglas over 54 percent of the time in LSP cases, but on the entire docket, none of them voted with Douglas more than 40 percent of the time. Rehnquist, Blackmun, and Powell voted with Brennan over 65 percent of the time in LSP cases, but on the entire docket, none of them voted with Brennan more than 55 percent of the time. There was more consensus on LSP cases than on the Court's docket as a whole, even though we would not expect LSP cases to tap a particular value dimension upon which the traditionally liberal and traditionally conservative justices would be likely to agree.[31]

[31] All three of Spaeth's scale score rankings place Douglas and Brennan at opposite ends from Rehnquist, Blackmun, and Powell. Spaeth, *Supreme Court Policy-Making*, p. 135. Cappell's structural analysis of the opinion-joining behavior of the justices also confirms this characterization of particular justices as liberal or conservative. The agreement rates in LSP cases indicate that the geometric configuration of the justices was compressed in these cases. Cappell, "A Structural Analysis." These characterizations of the justices' value positions subsume both ideological policy preferences and judicial role conceptions. See Baum, *The Supreme Court*, pp. 143–45; Spaeth, *Supreme Court Policy-Making*, pp. 109–39.

TABLE 5-11
Difference Between Agreement Rates of Justices in LSP Cases and the Court's Entire
Docket, 1966–1974 Terms

| | | | |
|---|---|---|---|
| Stewart-Warren | + 28.9 | Marshall-White | + 10.2 |
| Fortas-Stewart | + 28.0 | Fortas-Harlan | + 9.6 |
| Harlan-Warren | + 25.0 | Powell-Stewart | + 9.5 |
| Douglas-Rehnquist | + 24.8 | Brennan-Burger | + 9.0 |
| Brennan-Rehnquist | + 21.6 | Marshall-Powell | + 8.6 |
| Fortas-White | + 21.2 | Brennan-White | + 8.4 |
| Blackmun-Douglas | + 20.8 | Douglas-Stewart | + 8.3 |
| Blackmun-Brennan | + 19.5 | Rehnquist-White | + 8.1 |
| Brennan-Fortas | + 18.8 | Black-Stewart | + 7.9 |
| Brennan-Powell | + 18.6 | Brennan-Douglas | + 6.8 |
| Douglas-Powell | + 18.5 | Harlan-Marshall | + 6.7 |
| Blackmun-Marshall | + 18.2 | Brennan-Stewart | + 6.3 |
| Blackmun-Harlan | + 17.9 | Burger-Douglas | + 5.4 |
| Black-Burger | + 15.7 | Douglas-Harlan | + 5.1 |
| Blackmun-Stewart | + 14.9 | Warren-White | + 5.0 |
| Stewart-White | + 14.9 | Blackmun-Rehnquist | + 4.4 |
| Harlan-White | + 14.6 | Harlan-Stewart | + 4.4 |
| Brennan-Harlan | + 14.4 | Brennan-Marshall | + 4.2 |
| Fortas-Marshall | + 14.4 | Douglas-Fortas | + 4.1 |
| Marshall-Rehnquist | + 14.2 | Black-Warren | + 4.0 |
| Blackmun-White | + 13.3 | Burger-Marshall | + 3.5 |
| Powell-Rehnquist | + 12.7 | Marshall-Stewart | + 2.8 |
| Rehnquist-Stewart | + 12.5 | Black-Marshall | + 2.8 |
| Burger-Stewart | + 11.2 | Fortas-Warren | + 2.8 |
| Powell-White | + 11.0 | Black-Fortas | + 2.5 |
| Douglas-White | + 10.7 | Burger-White | + 2.4 |
| Blackmun-Powell | + 10.4 | Black-Harlan | + 1.1 |
| Douglas-Marshall | + 10.2 | Burger-Powell | + 0.3 |

TABLE 5-11 (*cont.*)

| | | | |
|---|---|---|---|
| Blackmun-Burger | −0.3 | Brennan-Warren | −5.0 |
| Burger-Rehnquist | −0.5 | Black-Brennan | −6.1 |
| Marshall-Warren | −1.8 | Douglas-Warren | −7.3 |
| Burger-Harlan | −2.0 | Black-White | −13.9 |
| Black-Blackmun | −3.2 | Black-Douglas | −15.4 |

( + ) Indicates a higher agreement rate in LSP cases given plenary consideration.

( − ) Indicates a lower agreement rate in LSP cases given plenary consideration.

*Note*: Agreement rates (percentage of cases that both justices voted in which they voted together) on the Court's entire docket were compiled from "The Supreme Court, 1966–74 Term: The Statistics." Pairs with N sizes of less than 5 in LSP cases are omitted. See Appendix E for actual agreement rates in LSP cases and in the entire docket.

Indeed, in examining a group of poverty law cases decided by the Court during the 1971 Term, Spaeth also found much more consensus among the justices than he had predicted based on his analysis of judicial value systems.[32]

The conservatives' propensity to vote with liberals in LSP cases suggests that the LSP's success was not simply the function of a liberal Court. Without the votes of conservative justices, the LSP could not have won 62 percent (74) of its cases. The Program owes its success as much to the conservatives as to the liberals.

EXPLAINING THE SUCCESS

The consensus among the justices that led to the LSP's success can be described as resulting from a fruitful confluence of three separate, but interactive, factors influencing judicial decision making. The Court's decisions in LSP cases were the product of the joining of (a) newly enfranchised litigants presenting new opportunities for decision; (b) available legal bases for favorable decisions developed independently in other areas; and (c) judicial attention to and sympathy for the subjects and issues presented. The political climate of the era influenced each of these factors and provided a "window of opportunity" for their fruitful coupling.[33]

As we have seen, the LSP was responsible for introducing a new class of

[32] Spaeth, *Supreme Court Policy-Making*, pp. 150–52.

[33] Some of the language used here and, more important, the notion of explaining processes as a confluence of factors or streams was adapted from Kingdon, *Agendas*. In developing his model of agenda setting, Kingdon draws on Cohen et al., "A Garbage Can Model of Organizational Choice." For an application of this model to antipoverty policy in the political branches, see Heclo, "The Political Foundations of Antipoverty Policy."

litigant claims to the Supreme Court beginning in 1967. Prior to the establishment of the LSP, the poor had seldom been before the Court independent of an interest group litigation strategy. In sixty-eight of the 119 reviewed cases, LSP attorneys sponsored the appeal. In the fifty reviewed cases in which LSP attorneys represented the respondent, the Program's willingness to take their clients' claims to trial and mount appellate litigation was the essential prerequisite to an appeal to the Supreme Court. Particularly during the Warren Court era, the LSP, as respondent, focused on the endorsement of its lower court victories rather than on the possibility of reversals.[34] Indeed, the Court's affirmance of half, rather than the usual third, of the LSP's opponents' lower court defeats provides some ex post facto justification for this optimism.[35] The LSP's petitions to the Court and the Program's responses to its opponents' petitions increased the poor's access to Supreme Court decision making and changed the pool of opportunities for judicial choice.[36]

Both the availability of favorable legal bases and judicial interest in equality and poverty-related concerns are demonstrated by the prevalence of due process and equal protection claims on the Court's agenda during this era. Pacelle reports that the Court's attention to due process claims grew from 21 percent of its decision agenda in the 1958 through 1962 Terms to 31 percent during the 1968 through 1972 Terms. Attention to equality claims grew from five percent of the Court's decision agenda in the 1958 through 1962 Terms to 12 percent during the 1968 through 1972 Terms.[37] The earlier loyalty-security dismissal, criminal procedure, reapportionment, voting rights, and civil rights

[34] Interview with an LSP attorney.

[35] Furthermore, seven of the twenty-five cases counted as reversals were actually remands with instructions to the lower court favorable to the LSP's client. Supreme Court affirmance of the Program's lower court victories was important because many states had rules similar to those under review. For example, approximately forty states had residency requirements similar to those overturned in *Shapiro v. Thompson* (1969). Shriver, "Law Reform and the Poor." Nineteen states had "substitute father rules" similar to the one disallowed in *King v. Smith* (1968). Johnson, *Justice and Reform*, p. 346. Of course, in some cases the Supreme Court did reverse the lower court decisions that condemned widespread practices challenged by the LSP. For example, more than a third of the states set maximum limits on family welfare grants similar to those upheld in *Dandridge v. Williams* (1970). Sparer, "Social Welfare Law Testing," p. 21. Virtually all states financed public schools through district property taxes as allowed in *San Antonio v. Rodriguez* (1973). Johnson, *Justice and Reform*, pp. 215–16. But see Serrano v. Priest (1971), and Robinson v. Cahill (1973). See also Lehne, *The Quest for Justice*.

[36] On the importance of the "occasions for decision," litigants and their counsel present to the Court in shaping the development of judicial policy, also see Casper, *Lawyers Before the Warren Court*, esp. pp. 191–94.

[37] Due process claims accounted for 14 percent of the Court's decision agenda during the 1948–52 Terms and equality claims accounted for 5 percent during those Terms. Pacelle, "The Supreme Court and the Growth of Civil Liberties," p. 32. See also Pacelle, "The Supreme Court Agenda"; Cox, "The Supreme Court 1965 Term"; Cox, *The Role of the Supreme Court*, pp. 56–75; Funston, *Constitutional Counterrevolution?*, pp. 298–99; Bickel, *The Supreme Court and the Idea of Progress*, pp. 13, 103.

cases are illustrative of the Court's emerging focus on due process and equal protection issues during this era.[38] These cases provided doctrinal developments that could be borrowed in LSP cases. In the early 1960s, articles developing potential legal bases for decisions favorable to the poor began to appear in well-respected publications such as *Harvard Law Review* and *Yale Law Journal*.[39] Perhaps most important, the central applications of the due process clause to criminal proceedings and the equal protection clause to racial discrimination had already been achieved, easing expansion of the scope of those guarantees in LSP cases.

Even before LSP began appealing cases, the Court had shown some interest in poverty-related claims. For example, in 1963 the Court had acknowledged and reduced the handicaps that indigent criminal defendants face in Gideon v. Wainwright.[40] In Harper v. Virginia Board of Elections (1966), the Court struck down poll taxes, finding that "lines drawn on the basis of wealth or property, like those of race, are traditionally disfavored."[41] The LSP's provision of counsel to indigents with civil claims greatly expanded the justices' opportunities to address other poverty-related issues. As we have seen, the justices were willing to expand their working definition of "important" civil liberties and civil rights issues to provide these new opportunities with a place on the Court's decision agenda.

Each of these three elements—new litigants and claims, available legal bases, and judicial sympathy—were influenced by a favorable political climate in which poverty and equality issues were salient.[42] Such issues had

[38] See Schmidhauser, *Constitutional Law in American Politics*, esp. pp. 429–96. This case book, organized by historical epochs rather than constitutional issues, provides an interesting overview of change in the Court's work in relation to change in the political system.

[39] Articles in *Harvard Law Review* and *Yale Law Journal* include Van Alstyne, "The Demise of the Right-Privilege Distinction"; Michelman, "On Protecting the Poor"; Reich, "Midnight Welfare Searches"; Reich, "The New Property"; Reich, "Individual Rights and Social Welfare"; Note, "Neighborhood Law Offices"; Note, "Suitable Home Tests." For example, two of Reich's articles were cited by Justice Brennan in his majority opinion in *Goldberg v. Kelly* (1970). Krislov has suggested that the LSP's failure to convince the Court to declare a right to the necessities of life in *Dandridge v. Williams* (1970) is partly attributable to the insufficient time for such extra-Court development of supportive legal arguments. Krislov, "The OEO Lawyers Fail," p. 245.

Articles published in other prominent journals during the early 1960s include Carlin and Howard, "Legal Representation"; Note, "Federal Judicial Review of State Welfare Practices"; Note, "The Right to Counsel in Civil Litigation"; Silver, "How to Handle a Welfare Case"; Sparer, "The Role of the Welfare Client's Lawyer."

[40] See also Griffin v. Illinois (1956), Douglas v. California (1963), and *Argersinger v. Hamlin* (1972).

[41] In Bullock v. Carter (1972) and Lubin v. Panish (1974) the justices invalidated filing fee requirements for candidates.

[42] See Patterson, *America's Struggle*. Of course, the political system did not generally pursue pure equality. With the exception of Nixon's Family Assistance Plan, the effort was largely limited to a reduction of inequalities in opportunities rather than results. The Court's decisions in LSP

reached the agendas of all three branches. The same forces that allowed the creation of the LSP provided the climate for its securance of Supreme Court decisions favorable to its clients. As the LSP began litigating, the War on Poverty was being waged. As Patterson's study of "changing perspectives, especially of reformers, toward poverty and welfare,"[43] notes: "The war on poverty, finally, dramatized the contemporary rediscovery of poverty. . . . The result was to lift poverty from benign neglect to a place on the public agenda. . . . The focus on poverty was one of many elements that made public officials a little more responsive to the newly articulated demands of the poor."[44] It is not unreasonable to suggest that the justices were among these public officials affected by poverty's new place on the national agenda.

Poverty remained a salient political issue throughout the LSP's tenure and, unlike in the 1980's, it then received beneficent attention from all three branches.[45] Although Nixon attempted to dismantle the Office of Economic Opportunity in 1973, between 1969 and 1972 he kept poverty issues on the national political agenda by embarking upon "the most ambitious effort for welfare reform in the forty years since the creation of the welfare state in 1935." Nixon's proposed Family Assistance Plan, which guaranteed all families with children a minimum income, reflected the then current consensus among experts that the War on Poverty's "doors" of opportunity were neither sufficient nor bureaucratically efficient. By 1969, conservatives and liberals began looking to income "floors," as a "quick, cheap solution to the 'crisis' of welfare." In sharp distinction from earlier approaches, "they sought not only equality of opportunity, but equality of result," by establishing a basic entitlement to a minimum level of support. Although public opinion polls showed that the majority of Americans continued to hold negative views of the poor, poverty and welfare issues remained on the national political agenda and in the headlines until the early to mid-seventies.[46] By then, the LSP's national leadership had begun de-emphasizing appellate litigation. In 1973, new

cases are consistent with this American emphasis on equality of opportunity rather than of results—for the individual rather than for groups, and in political rights rather than in economic status. See Verba and Orren, *Equality in America*, esp. pp. 1–20. See also Pole, *The Pursuit of Equality*, esp. pp. 253–92; 325–58.

[43] Patterson, *America's Struggle*, p. vii.

[44] Ibid., pp. 153–54.

[45] As Patterson reports, "The goal of social policy in the Johnson (and even Nixon) years had started with the question, 'How can we help the poor?' Reagan, in contrast, tended to ask, 'How can we cut costs, and how can we get people to work?' " Poverty received renewed agenda status in the 1980s with the emergence of a "near-hysterical, alarm over the specter of what many contemporaries termed an 'underclass' . . . [which] threatened to undermine all that was good and promising in national life." This was mixed with a "continuing skepticism—not to say cynicism—about the 'failures' of liberal welfare policy in the 1960s." Patterson, *America's Struggle*, pp. 212, 215, 216. See also Danziger and Weinberg, *Fighting Poverty*.

[46] Patterson, *America's Struggle*, pp. 185–98, 172, 202; Heclo, "The Political Foundations of Antipoverty Policy," esp. pp. 326–32.

LSP guidelines were issued informing local project directors that "law reform will no longer be a primary or separate goal of the Program or the chief criterion in evaluating or refunding projects."[47]

In 1974, legislation was signed that replaced the LSP with a new Legal Services Corporation designed to be insulated from the types of parochial political attacks that had been launched against the LSP as the national government groped for a bipartisan poverty policy. Spurred on by state and local officials who were affronted by some of the LSP's local law reform successes, as early as 1967, conservative members of Congress attempted to limit the LSP's activities. Republican George Murphy (R-CA) introduced an amendment in 1967 that would have, in practice, severely curtailed the LSP's appellate work. It provided that "no project under such program may grant assistance to bring any action against any public agency of the United States, any State, or any political subdivision thereof."[48] The Murphy Amendment was defeated 52-36 in the Senate, but Congress did pass an amendment restricting criminal representation, which limited the LSP's juvenile justice work.[49] In the 1969 legislative session, Senator Murphy introduced an amendment providing state governors with a veto over funding of local LSP projects that was checked by another amendment allowing the President to override such vetos. The House rejected both amendments and the conference committee excluded them. Such attacks continued throughout the life of the LSP and provided the impetus for the creation of the independent Legal Services Corporation. But these attacks focused on the LSP's local successes, not its Supreme Court litigation or the Court itself.[50]

[47] *Poverty Law Reporter*, 2:9787.

[48] U.S. Congress, Senate, 90th Cong., 2d sess., 1967, *Congressional Record* 113:27871. The prevailing wisdom is that Senator Murphy was responding to the California Rural Legal Assistance Program's successful suits against the state of California. The CRLA's work stimulated many of the national political problems of the LSP. The most famous controversy was Governor Reagan's veto of its federal appropriations in 1970, later overridden by President Nixon. See Champagne, "Legal Services," pp. 135–37; Schardt, "Legal Services"; Arnold, "Wither Legal Services"; Lenzer, "Legal Services Fights for the Poor"; George, "Development." Although CRLA was considered one of the most innovative and activist of the LSP grantees, it was actually one of the few projects operating fully within the national LSP guidelines. See Pious, "Policy," pp. 378–86. Eleven of the 164 LSP Supreme Court appeals came through the California state courts. This is twice as many as any other state, and testifies to the reformist activity of the California projects. Had more of the projects pursued the national Program's law reform priority with such vigor, there undoubtedly would have been more political controversy surrounding the LSP in Congress, the Executive branch, and the localities. For instance, in a much later study of Legal Services Corporation funded projects, Kessler has found that a project's involvement in law reform activities is heavily conditioned on the local political environment's tolerance or support of such work. Kessler, *Legal Services for the Poor*.

[49] *Economic Opportunity Act, Amendments of 1967*, H.R. Rep. No. 012, 90th Cong., 1st sess. (1967).

[50] George, "Development"; Pious, "Congress," esp. pp. 430–31; Johnson, *Justice and Reform*, pp. 193–94; Cramton, "Promise and Reality."

The introduction of hostile amendments forced Congress to review the LSP's work, and its rejection of the amendments resulted in a limited congressional endorsement of the Program's appellate advocacy. Some members of Congress used the occasion to explicitly encourage and praise such litigation. For example, in 1967, the Senate Committee on Labor and Public Welfare concluded that "more attention should be given [by the LSP] to test cases and law reform."[51] In 1970, Senator Mondale asserted that the LSP "has probably caused more hope and trust in the system and more basic legal reform per dollar then has any other program. . . . It is that opportunity to be a part of social reform—of legal reform within the system on an honest basis—which I think is the most exciting aspect of this program." He added, "We are aware of the fact that this remarkable organization [LSP] has brought an awful lot of important lawsuits [some of which have] led to a fundamental change in the Nation's welfare laws."[52] A 1973 GAO report to Congress recommended that the OEO Director take steps to increase local projects' commitment to law reform.[53] Congress speaks with many voices and some were clearly supportive of the LSP's representation of the poor in appellate tribunals.[54]

It was this attentive, and largely supportive, political climate that provided a "window of opportunity" for the fruitful coupling of LSP cases, disparate legal bases, and judicial attention and sympathy, resulting in the LSP's extraordinary success, both in gaining review and securing rulings for its clients. Throughout the era of the LSP's litigation, the justices lived in a world that was rediscovering and addressing poverty. Although members of the legislative and executive branches often held conflicting views on appropriate solutions to the problem of poverty, there was bipartisan agreement that it was a problem deserving of the national government's attention. The lack of a political consensus on remedies may account for the justices' unwillingness to embrace some of the LSP's more ambitious doctrinal arguments in cases such as *Dandridge v. Williams* and *San Antonio v. Rodriguez*, but it did not prevent the justices from turning the Court's attention to the problems of poverty as presented to it by LSP clients and issuing many rulings favorable to those litigants. Partly as a result of the Court's decisions in LSP cases, but also as a result of the civil rights movement and a general rise in expectations in a seemingly more affluent America, welfare increasingly came to be characterized as a

[51] U.S. Congress, Senate, Committee on Labor and Public Welfare, *Legal Services Program of the Office of Economic Opportunity, Hearings Before the Subcommittee on Employment, Manpower, and Poverty*, 91st Cong., 2d sess., 7 and 9 Oct. 1970, p. 135.

[52] U.S. Congress, Senate, Committee on Labor and Public Welfare, S. Rept. 563, 90th Cong., 1st sess., 1967, p. 40.

[53] U.S. Comptroller General, "Report to Congress: The Legal Services Program—Accomplishments Of and Problems Faced By Its Grantees, B-130515," p. 18.

[54] The Legal Services Program enjoyed substantial, though not unanimous, congressional support throughout its tenure. See Pious, "Congress"; Pious, "Policy"; George, "Development"; Champagne, "Legal Services"; Failinger and May, "Litigating Against Poverty."

"right," rather than a "privilege" in general parlance.[55] The justices, though partially responsible for this transformation, could find support for pro-LSP decisions in the attitudes this linguistic change signaled.

## LEARNING FROM THE LSP'S SUCCESS

While this picture has some of the characteristics of a post hoc explanation, it describes a process, allows comparisons with other litigation-oriented groups, and suggests some unique and common factors in the LSP's success.

The LSP did present the Court with opportunities for decision under a particularly fortuitous set of circumstances compared to other litigation-oriented interest groups such as the NAACP LDF and ACLU. Most notably, LSP attorneys were able to invoke prepackaged precedents and present their arguments during an era hospitable to such claims. In contrast, the NAACP LDF campaign, which set the prototype for interest group litigation, had to create its own favorable precedents to counterbalance earlier negative decisions in an environment that was only slowly becoming receptive to a change in race relations.[56] When the ACLU defends the politically unpopular, the influence of political climate works against it.[57] Indeed, to the extent that interest groups use the courts to overturn recent unfavorable political outcomes or because they perceive the political branches to be unreceptive to their goals, few interest groups will find themselves litigating with such a wide-open "window of opportunity" as the LSP enjoyed.[58] Unlike most litigation-oriented groups, the LSP was not designed to pursue policy goals rejected elsewhere. Of course, many interest groups have successfully used litigation to achieve policy pronouncements unattainable in the legislative and executive arenas; but none have matched the LSP's record of prevailing in 62 percent of 119 decisions ranging over a variety of subjects in as few as nine years.[59] In some measure,

[55] See Patterson, *America's Struggle*, pp. 153–54, 179–80; Sosin, "Legal Rights and Welfare Change"; Mead, "Comment."

[56] See Greenberg, "Litigation for Social Change"; Kluger, *Simple Justice.*

[57] For example, see Downs, *Nazis in Skokie*; Donahue, *The Politics of the American Civil Liberties Union.*

[58] Twenty years ago, Cortner suggested that these are the primary motivations for interest group litigation. Cortner, "Strategies and Tactics." It seems that his observation still holds true for liberal interest groups. Sorauf, *Wall*; O'Connor, *Women's Organizations*; Barker, "Third Parties"; Berry, *Lobbying for the People*; Greenberg, "Litigation for Social Change"; and Manwaring, *Render Unto Caesar*. However, Epstein finds that conservative groups have become involved in litigation because they "view themselves as disadvantaged *only* in the judicial forum" which they see as allied with liberal interests. Epstein, *Conservatives.* See also O'Connor and Epstein, "Rebalancing the Scales of Justice."

[59] See Appendix C for success rates of other litigation-oriented interest groups. See Barker, "Third Parties"; Cortner, "Strategies and Tactics"; Handler, *Social Movements*; Kluger, *Simple Justice*; O'Connor, *Women's Organizations*; Manwaring, *Render Unto Caesar*; Sorauf, *Wall*; Vose, *Caucasians Only.* To a degree, the orchestration of litigation strategies by interest groups

the LSP was successful in convincing the Supreme Court to rule for its clients because a national political coalition let it be.

Still, the LSP's success may not be as idiosyncratic as the traditional view of interest group litigation suggests. It is clear that the LSP lacked the organizational attributes that studies of other litigation efforts have emphasized, such as longevity, financial viability, devoted expert staff, and single issue concentration, when explaining group success.[60] Some of these characteristics may actually be the usual prerequisites to group participation in Supreme Court litigation rather than causes of success. Furthermore, many accounts of successful group litigation campaigns also provide some evidence that the three factors whose confluence accounts for the LSP's success were present in those instances as well.

Often interest group litigation, like LSP litigation, presents the Court with its first and only significant opportunity to address the issues being pressed. Frequently, the claims presented by groups would have never reached the Court without their sponsorship.[61] This is particularly true when groups represent individuals burdened by the de facto assistance of counsel requirement.

Various interest groups have found available legal bases for their claims in the form of previously ignored constitutional provisions, new statutory language, or seemingly unrelated lines of precedent.[62] Often though, groups have had to create their own favorable precedents, which is why longevity is usually considered to be such an important factor in a group's success.[63]

Group litigation has tested and, when successful, taken advantage of, the judicial attention and sympathy factor and the justices shared conceptions of the judicial role. On a general level, the rise of liberal interest group litigation has coincided with the Court's increasing focus on civil liberties and civil rights claims since addressing economic issues became politically dangerous in the 1930s. And, as the Nixon appointees turned the Court in a more conservative direction in the 1970s, conservative interest groups' participation tripled.[64] O'Connor and Epstein provide a more specific example, noting that the ACLU's Women's Rights Project and Reproductive Freedom Project "were established at a time when ACLU leaders recognized that the Court was willing

---

may allow them to succeed without full measure of the three factors and a favorable political climate. But see Wasby, "Civil Rights Litigation"; Greenberg, "Litigation for Social Change."

[60] Barker, "Third Parties"; Cortner, "Strategies and Tactics"; Epstein, *Conservatives*, pp. 12–14, 150–55; Handler et al., *Lawyers*; Kluger, *Simple Justice*; Manwaring, *Render Unto Caesar*; O'Connor, *Women's Organizations*; Sorauf, *Wall*; Vose, *Caucasians Only*.

[61] Greenberg, "Litigation for Social Change," pp. 331–32; O'Connor, *Women's Organizations*; O'Connor and Epstein, "Beyond Legislative Lobbying"; and Sorauf, *Wall*, esp. pp. 30–31.

[62] Greenberg, "Litigation for Social Change," pp. 326–32; Kluger, *Simple Justice*; Sorauf, *Wall*, pp. 18–19.

[63] See, for example, Kluger, *Simple Justice*.

[64] O'Connor and Epstein, "The Rise of Conservative Interest Group Litigation," pp. 481–82.

to expand interpretations of the Constitution. Thus, the ACLU acted quickly to take full advantage of a favorable judicial climate.''[65] Of course, beyond shared role conceptions, the objects of judicial concern may be personal and ideosyncratic to the justices, but they are also susceptible to the influence of political climate.

Some groups have succeeded in Court without a broadly favorable political milieu because judicial insulation from majoritarian procedures allows the justices to respond to elite opinion even when it conflicts with mass opinion. Rarely are groups successful in using litigation to replace or override legislation without considerable elite opinion on their side. For example, in explaining Brown, Greenberg points to several examples of elite opinion favoring desegregation such as Solicitor General briefs supporting the plaintiffs in racial discrimination cases beginning in the mid-forties, reports of Truman's Committees on Higher Education in 1947 and on Civil Rights in 1948, and a change in American views toward race resulting from the World War II experience. Greenberg concludes that "there was a current of history and the Court became part of it. . . . Tourgee would have won Plessy in 1954. The lawyers who brought Brown would have lost in 1986.''[66] The LSP's ability to capitalize on a wide-open "window of opportunity" created by a broadly supportive political climate explains its unusually high success rate without detracting from the importance of a coupling of these factors in other litigation campaigns.

Thinking of Supreme Court decisions and doctrinal development as precipitated by a confluence of litigant claims, available legal basis, and judicial sympathy joined by a hospitable political climate, has several advantages. Unlike accounts that focus on the organizational attributes of group litigants, this confluence picture suggests additional factors that influence litigant success, and, more important, it incorporates group litigation efforts into a comprehensive description of the judicial decision-making process by revealing the importance of the opportunities for decision presented to the Court. In contrast to accounts that focus solely on judicial values and behavior, this description of a confluence of factors reminds us that the justices are powerless to act without a case. The volume of certiorari petitions notwithstanding, the pool of cases litigants provide can constrain or encourage judicial choice. Who has access to the Court's jurisdictional agenda is an important variable in explaining the course of doctrinal development. This description also reminds us that "the law," to the extent that it must be sufficiently developed to provide a basis for litigant claims and a justification for judicial preferences, matters in

[65] O'Connor and Epstein, "Beyond Legislative Lobbying," p. 138.

[66] Greenberg, "Litigation for Social Change," pp. 333–34. On the interaction between political climate, elite opinion, and the Court's decisions on abortion, see Friedman, "Conflict"; Steiner, "Abortion Policy and the Potential for Mischief." On the political context of church-state litigation, see Sorauf, Wall, esp. pp. 11–29, 230.

adjudicatory policy making. And finally, conceptualizing Supreme Court decision making as determined by a confluence of these factors shows us that while judicial values and ideologies are an important determinate of Court output, they are not an independent determinate. It suggests that while the underlying dimensions of judicial values may be stable,[67] the political environment plays an important role in determining the issues to which those values adhere.

In terms of precipitating doctrinal developments, the LSP's experience suggests that the introduction of new litigants and their claims can nudge, but not shove, the Court into new applications of constitutional and statutory provisions. The LSP's history suggests a corollary to the notion that litigation successes are only meaningful when combined with attempts to influence the other branches at the implementation stage.[68] Multi-forum strategies may be important in obtaining favorable court decisions in the first place.[69] Judges are surely not simply political animals, but neither are they impervious to political and societal conditions. Some measure of political acceptability may be as important as organizational attributes for litigation success.

The Legal Services Program enjoyed considerable success, at least in part, because it was in the right place at the right time. The importance of the confluence of a particular configuration of claims, legal bases, and judicial sympathies set in an attentive political climate, underscores how easy it is for groups and litigants to be in the wrong place at the wrong time. Litigation is not always simpler than legislation. Judicial values alone do not produce doctrinal change.

CONCLUSIONS

The LSP persuaded the Court to rule for its clients in 62 percent (74) of their cases. The Program was much more successful, across a heterogeneous group of cases, than we would have anticipated based on usual patterns of Supreme Court decision making and hypotheses that correlate success with experience and expertise of counsel. While, as we would anticipate, the liberal justices were more supportive of the LSP's claims than the conservative justices, there was an unusual degree of consensus in these cases. At least in the LSP's cases, both the liberals and conservatives seemed to defer to Justice Cardozo's prescription: "My duty as a judge may be to objectify in law, not my own aspi-

---

[67] See Baum, *Supreme Court*, pp. 140–42.

[68] See, for example, Johnson and Canon, *Judicial Policies*; Olson, *Clients and Lawyers*; Scheingold, *Politics of Rights*.

[69] Indeed, interest mobilization precipitated by an unpopular Supreme Court decision may also make future Supreme Court victories less likely. See Friedman, "Conflict."

122 of Chapter Five

rations and convictions and philosophies, but the aspirations and convictions of the men and women of my time."[70]

The picture of the judicial decision-making process developed from an examination of the Court's response to LSP cases suggests that judicial doctrine is the product of those litigant claims, legal bases, and judicial sympathies that the temper of the times create and join together. The Court's decisions, like those of the other branches, are the result of a complex interplay of forces. Created by the President and Congress, and shaped by activists and the bar, the LSP provided the Court with a new set of opportunities for decision at a time when the other conditions for favorable judicial decisions in the poor's cases were present.

To assign political climate such an important role in shaping the course of judicial policy development is not to claim that the poor were not disadvantaged in the political process, nor does it mean that the Court will only aid the powerful. The Carolene footnote's promise to protect the civil liberties and civil rights of those who cannot rely on the political process does not oblige the Court to only befriend the totally friendless and ignored. The poor clearly did still lack power in the political branches; national bureaucrats and social scientists, not the poor, lobbied for the War on Poverty.[71] While the problems of poverty had captured the imagination of the national government, many of the states remained uninterested or hostile and, most often (80 percent of the time [95]), it was state laws that the Court was reviewing. In the LSP's litigation the Court subtly showed itself to be part of Dahl's national political alliance by paralleling its agenda and substantive sympathies; but, by critically reviewing state legislation, its role went beyond that of mere legitimacy conferer.[72] The LSP's Supreme Court litigation provided the Program's poor clients with a significant new avenue of participation in an important crucible of policy-making power. Whether they won or lost on the merits, the poor's cases changed the course of judicial policy development.

[70] Cardozo, *The Nature of the Judicial Process*, p. 173.

[71] Patterson, *America's Struggle*, p. 138; Moynihan, *Maximum Feasible Misunderstanding*; Heclo, "The Political Foundations of Antipoverty Policy."

[72] Dahl, "Decision-Making in a Democracy." On the importance of the Supreme Court's policy-making power through the review of state legislation, see Casper, "The Supreme Court and National Policy Making."

# CHAPTER SIX

# The LSP's Role in the Development of Law

THE POOR'S PARTICIPATION in Supreme Court policy making significantly affected the development of law during the late 1960s and early 1970s. During the 1966 through 1974 Terms, 7 percent of all written opinions handed down by the High Court were responses to Legal Services Program sponsored cases. These eighty cases most frequently involved due process or equal protection claims, two particularly salient issues in the Court's jurisprudence during this era. Almost a score questioned the congruence between state policies and federal directives and another dozen involved the interpretation of federal statutes, the Fourth and Sixth Amendments, or the rights of Native Americans (see table 6-1). These issues arose in a wide variety of contexts, including the administration of transfer programs, criminal and civil court procedures, education, and consumer contracts. The influence of the decisions rendered in LSP cases is disparate yet pervasive, reflecting the diversity of the claims LSP attorneys brought to the Court.*

In studying the policy-making process, influence is frequently equated with success; the winner is traditionally labeled as the influential actor. But this definition of influence ignores the agenda-setting stage, the complexity of the processes by which decisions are made, and the nuances in results that can differentiate one success from another. These problems of definition arise in defining litigant influence and success before the Court as well.[1] Thus far, in examining the justices' response to LSP cases, a decision has been characterized as an LSP success if the LSP was the petitioner and the Court reversed the lower court decision, if the LSP was the respondent and the Court upheld the lower court decision, or if the Court remanded the case with instructions favorable to the LSP's client. This measure indicates whether or not the LSP client received the specific legal result she requested, but it does not tell us whether the Court based its decision on the desired reasoning, creating a favorable precedent for future cases. The latter is particularly important in assessing the influence and success of interest groups that are pursuing policy change through doctrinal change. It is this latter definition of success that is often used in assessing poverty law in the Supreme Court, leading to conclusions that the

---

* Here, as throughout, Supreme Court cases sponsored by the LSP are set in italics, while all other cases are set in roman.

[1] See Casper's critique of Dahl's assessment of influence based on who wins. Casper, "The Supreme Court and National Policy Making," pp. 60–63.

TABLE 6-1
Issue Distribution and Success in LSP Plenary Cases

| Issue | Decided on Jurisdictional Grounds | | Decided Substantive Claim | | Total | |
|---|---|---|---|---|---|---|
| | N | Success Rate (n) | N | Success Rate (n) | N | Success Rate (n) |
| Due Process | 12 | 50% (6) | 16 | 56% (9) | 28[a] | 54%(15) |
| Equal Protection | 4 | 75 (3) | 18 | 57 (10) | 22[b] | 59 (13) |
| Conflict between Federal and State Law, Supremacy Clause | 3 | 100 (3) | 15 | 80 (12) | 18 | 83 (15) |
| Federal Statutory Interpretation | — | — | 2 | 0 (10) | 2 | 0 (0) |
| Fourth Amendment | — | — | 2 | 0 (0) | 2 | 0 (0) |
| Sixth Amendment | — | — | 3 | 67 (2) | 3 | 67 (2) |
| Indian Rights | 1 | 100 (1) | 4 | 100 (4) | 5 | 100 (5) |
| All Cases | 20 | 65%(13) | 60 | 62%(37) | 80 | 63%(50) |

[a] Includes two LSP victories in which the Court also addressed equal protection clause issues, but does not include cases where the Court only used the Fourteenth Amendment due process clause for incorporation purposes.

[b] Includes two LSP victories and one LSP defeat in which the Court also addressed due process clause issues, and three LSP defeats in which the Court also addressed a claimed conflict between federal and state laws (one of which was decided on jurisdictional grounds).

poor litigants in these cases were not very influential or, consequently, important actors in Supreme Court policy making.

In this chapter, we will review the common wisdom about the Court's poverty decisions, noting some doctrinal successes that are frequently overlooked or undervalued. In addition, I argue that in assessing LSP litigation it is valid to also use the Court's issuance of the specific legal result that the litigant requested as a measure of success. As we have seen, the LSP was representing clients, not pursuing a litigation strategy designed to produce particular doctrinal reforms. Furthermore, in assessing the influence of litigants (i.e., the effect of the parameters of access to the Court), success on the merits, under either definition, may not be the crucial determinate. Rather, given the Court's passive stance, the significance of the Court's response to the opportunities for decision presented by litigants provides a fuller indication of their influence and importance in setting the agenda and determining the course of judicial policy development. The success of litigants and their attorneys in persuading the Court to adopt particular legal arguments in its substantive opinions provides a second measure of influence, not the only measure.

In evaluating the influence of the LSP, we cannot just ask whether the Court created new constitutional doctrines and precedents that would revolutionize the relationship between the poor and the state and then conclude that since it did not, the poor's participation in Supreme Court decision making had little influence or importance. We can ask how successful the LSP was in achieving legal reform that would benefit its clientele, but we must also consider how important it was in shaping the Court's agenda. We must ask what role the LSP cases played in the broader doctrinal developments of the era and to what extent our current jurisprudence is indebted to the opportunities for decision the poor presented to the Court. This chapter explores these questions by examining the role of LSP cases in the Court's development of its due process and equal protection jurisprudence.

## SUCCESS OR FAILURE?

The common wisdom is that the justices were ultimately unresponsive to the Legal Services Program's litigation and poverty issues.[2] Most of the traditional accounts focus on welfare litigation. The chroniclers begin with the early, big victories. The most frequently discussed cases are *King v. Smith* (1968), striking down "man-in-the-house" rules; *Shapiro v. Thompson* (1969), holding that state residency requirements for the receipt of AFDC unconstitutionally burden the right to travel, and *Goldberg v. Kelly* (1970), holding that due process guarantees adhere to statutory entitlements such as welfare. The Court's clear focus on poverty in holding filing fees in divorce actions unconstitutional usually merits the inclusion of *Boddie v. Connecticut* (1971) in a litany of the poor's early successes. Occasionally, *Fuentes v. Shevin* (1972), holding state replevin laws authorizing prehearing seizure of goods violative of the due process clause, is included as well.

Commentators then turn to the big defeats. The Court's failure to establish a right to the necessities of life or to find an equal protection violation in maximum family welfare grants in *Dandridge v. Williams* (1970),[3] and the Court's unwillingness to find an equal protection violation in district property-tax based financing of public schools in *San Antonio v. Rodriguez* (1973), are read as sounding the death knell for poverty litigation. Additional evidence of defeat is gleaned from the Court's unwillingness to extend the combined rationales of *Goldberg* and *Boddie* in challenges to filing fees for appellate review

[2] See Bennett, "The Burger Court"; Krislov, "OEO Lawyers"; Law, "Economic Justice"; Rosenblatt, "Legal Entitlements"; Johnson, *Justice and Reform*, pp. 192–224.

[3] But see the 1974 LSP victory *Graham v. Richardson* (1971) holding the denial of welfare benefits to resident aliens unconstitutional under the equal protection clause.

of welfare administrative hearings[4] or in bankruptcy proceedings[5] and its backing off from the *Fuentes* decision in *Mitchell v. W. T. Grant* (1974).[6] The Supreme Court's failure to extend the spirit of its earlier decisions in cases such as *Wyman v. James* (1971),[7] and *Edelman v. Jordan* (1974)[8] are cited as final logs on the funeral pyre.

This assessment of the Program's litigation comes from viewing the LSP as an interest group pursuing widespread reform of the welfare system and attempting to create a constitutional right to the necessities of life. Judged from this perspective, the LSP's litigation did fail.

As we would anticipate, given the role we have assigned to the national political climate in explaining judicial decision making, the Court sought to accommodate the claims of the poor in a more limited manner. By and large, the Court, like the Office of Economic Opportunity, focused on procedural issues and on equalizing opportunities, not necessarily results.[9] Much as in women's rights litigation where the Court issued many favorable decisions but refused to judicially create an Equal Rights Amendment, the Court was reluctant to preempt the political process by creating broad-sweeping new rights that the electorally-accountable branches were already considering adopting. Nixon's call for a Family Assistance Plan in 1969 put the question of a guaranteed minimum income before Congress; the Court was not going to "jump the gun" and create a constitutional right to one. Furthermore, by the late 1960s the cocky optimism of the early sixties had worn off and there was an emerging consensus that poverty was a much more obstinate problem than the architects of the Great Society had hoped.[10] In 1970, the Court, too, found that public welfare assistance programs presented "intractable economic, social, and even philosophical problems," and that the "difficult responsibility of allocating limited public welfare funds among the myriad of potential recipients" was best left to the political branches.[11] Not so surprisingly, the Court refused to restructure wealth distribution by judicial fiat.

[4] *Ortwein v. Schwab* (1973).

[5] *U.S. v. Kras* (1973).

[6] In *Mitchell v. W. T. Grant Company* (1974) the two new members of the Court, Rehnquist and Powell, joined the three dissenters in *Fuentes* to hold that writs of sequestration issued without preseizure notice and hearing did not violate due process. Four members of the *Mitchell* majority distinguished *Fuentes* on the facts, while Justices Powell (in concurrence) and Brennan (in dissent) expressed the view that the Court had overruled *Fuentes*. *Shepard's Citations* does not list *Fuentes* as overruled; however, it was distinguished in eight subsequent Supreme Court cases. See also North Georgia Finishing, Inc. v. Di-Chem, Inc. (1975).

[7] Fourth Amendment does not prohibit warrantless searches by welfare case workers.

[8] The Eleventh Amendment prohibits the federal government from requiring states to award retroactive benefits.

[9] Patterson, *America's Struggle*, pp. 185–98.

[10] Ibid.

[11] Justice Stewart for the majority in *Dandridge v. Williams*, at p. 487.

But, as we have seen, the LSP's Supreme Court litigation was not orchestrated to achieve that goal. The Program's enfranchisement of the poor in the processes of Supreme Court decision making was an extension of its client service. Its performance should be evaluated from this perspective as well. When we view the LSP as a mechanism by which a new class of litigants was able to place its civil claims before the Supreme Court and influence the decisions emanating from that institution, the doctrinal defeats that the traditional accounts focus on do not completely erase the picture of success one gains from the simple frequency of Supreme Court judgments for LSP clients. Although some cases with major policy implications were lost on the merits, 62 percent (74) of the clients LSP attorneys represented before the Court achieved the specific legal result, if not the doctrine, they sought. These victories also benefited many people beyond the individual litigants in the cases. For example, when the Supreme Court disallowed substitute parent rules in *King v. Smith* (1968) and residency requirements in *Shapiro v. Thompson* (1969), the Department of Health, Education, and Welfare predicted a $300 million to $400 million increase in public assistance payments to the poor, even though the Court did not declare welfare to be a fundamental right for the purposes of equal protection analysis in either case.[12] The LSP's losses, while not inconsequential, generally merely allowed the political branches to proceed as they wished, rather than preventing innovations designed to benefit the poor as the Court had done in an earlier era in such cases as Lochner v. New York (1905) and Adkins v. Children's Hospital (1923).

In addition, the poor achieved both the specific legal result and the doctrine they sought in a number of cases that are generally overlooked in accounts of the Court's response to poverty. As we have seen, the poor presented a diverse collection of claims to the Court, many of which were not directly related to the welfare system or poverty per se. Indeed, about half of the LSP cases given plenary consideration involved issues that could affect the middle class as well as the poor.[13] The catalogue of LSP success includes a number of doctrinally important cases that are not generally associated with the Program. For example, in *Stanley v. Illinois* (1973) the Court extended the application of the due process clause in civil proceedings to require the states to provide unwed fathers with a hearing before depriving them of custody of their illegitimate children. The Court also expanded the scope of the due process clause's prior notice and hearing requirements to include school suspensions in *Goss v. Lopez* (1975). Turning to the equal protection clause, the Court added aliens to the list of "suspect" categories that provoke "heighten scrutiny" in *Sugar-*

[12] In the single year following the *Shapiro* decision, there was a 17 percent increase in AFDC recipients. The Court's decision has been given substantial credit for this increase. Johnson, *Justice and Reform*, pp. 203–4, 347–48. See also Champagne et al., "The Impact of Courts."

[13] There is no significant difference between the Program's success rate in these two groups of cases, winning over 60 percent in each.

*man v. Dougall* (1973). The Court created an "irrebuttable presumptions" doctrine in *Vlandis v. Kline* (1973), disallowing a statutory presumption of nonresidence for the purpose of determining tuition at state schools. In *Jiminez v. Weinberger* (1974), the Court, using a "rational basis" test, found an equal protection violation in the Social Security Act's classifications of illegitimate children for the purposes of determining a parent's disability insurance benefits.

Of course, there were doctrinally important losses that are generally not attributed to the LSP either, such as the Court's refusal to find state action in a privately-owned, though heavily regulated, utility company's termination of electrical service without prior notice or hearing in *Jackson v. Metropolitan Edison Co.* (1974). The Court also drew boundaries on the scope of the equal protection clause in rejecting LSP challenges to California's requirement that low-income housing projects be approved in local referendums in *James v. Valtierra* (1971), and to California's exclusion of pregnancy from disability insurance coverage in *Geduldig v. Aiello* (1974).

To acknowledge that the Court's interpretation of the constitution and federal statutes in LSP cases did not serve to drastically reform the welfare system or dramatically redistribute wealth and privilege, does not mean that the LSP's successes were doctrinally unimportant. Given the judicial system's reliance on precedents to guide or justify its decisions, a rough quantitative approximation of the relative significance of the various LSP decisions in the development of law is provided by the frequency of citation of those cases in subsequent court decisions. Table 6-2 provides these frequencies and confirms the doctrinal importance of those explicitly poverty-related cases that often form the core of an analysis of the Supreme Court's response to the poor. *Shapiro v. Thompson* (1969) and *Dandridge v. Williams* (1970) lead the ranking, each being cited over one hundred times in subsequent Supreme Court decisions and approximately two thousand times in other courts' decisions. As the top pair indicates, both the LSP's victories and its losses served as important precedents. However, the Program's successes disproportionately dominate the top of the citation frequency ranking. Indeed, among the eleven cases cited by the Supreme Court at least fifty times and by lower courts at least six hundred times, 73 percent (8) were LSP victories. Of the twenty-nine LSP cases cited at least twenty times by the Supreme Court, 76 percent (22) were LSP victories. These figures do not belie the significance of the LSP's losses in *Dandridge* and *Rodriguez*, but they also show that many of the LSP's successes were very important contributions to the development of the Court's jurisprudence as well.[14]

[14] Sixty-eight percent (1299) of the total 1899 citations of LSP cases by the Supreme Court were citations of LSP victories. Sixty-six percent (1248) of the 1899 citations were "approving" of the LSP's position in the cited case. Citations counted as favorable to the LSP were: LSP wins that were explained, followed, harmonized, parallel, "blank" (citation not characterized by *Shepard's*), or

TABLE 6-2

Citation of LSP Plenary Cases: Ranking by Number of Citations by the Supreme Court, 1967–1983

| Case | Supreme Court Citations | Lower Federal Court Citations | State Court Citations | Citations in Con Law Texts | Citations in Law Reviews | LSP Win/Loss |
|---|---|---|---|---|---|---|
| Shapiro v. Thomson | 139 | 982 | 1006 | 7 | 16 | W |
| Dandridge v. Williams | 127 | 943 | 1057 | 5 | 10 | L |
| Goldberg v. Kelly | 90 | 1581 | 1436 | 7 | 11 | W |
| Edelman v. Jordan | 83 | 860 | 84 | 6 | 15 | L |
| San Antonio v. Rodriguez | 83 | 536 | 772 | 7 | 25 | L |
| Stanley v. Illinois | 70 | 312 | 1129 | 6 | 21 | W |
| Boddie v. Conn. | 67 | 386 | 845 | 6 | 25 | W |
| Rosando v. Wyman | 64 | 558 | 171 | 0 | 3 | W |
| Fuentes v. Shevin | 61 | 748 | 988 | 5 | 63 | W |
| Graham v. Richardson | 59 | 303 | 345 | 6 | 0 | W |
| King v. Smith | 58 | 544 | 421 | 0 | 14 | W |
| Argersinger v. Hamlin | 48 | 234 | 914 | 4 | 43 | W |
| Hagans v. Lavine | 43 | 561 | 66 | 0 | 7 | W |
| Weinberger v. Salfi | 42 | 614 | 151 | 3 | 6 | L |
| Goss v. Lopez | 41 | 486 | 399 | 5 | 39 | W |
| McClanahan v. Ariz. State Tax Com. | 40 | 142 | 122 | 1 | 4 | W |
| Sugarman v. Dougall | 37 | 113 | 66 | 6 | 2 | W |
| Vlandis v. Kline | 36 | 187 | 246 | 7 | 11 | W |
| Jefferson v. Hackney | 34 | 216 | 150 | 6 | 4 | L |
| Mitchell v. W. T. Grant Co. | 31 | 228 | 393 | 3 | 38 | L |
| Towsend v. Swank | 28 | 105 | 104 | 0 | 1 | W |
| O'Connor v. Donaldson | 27 | 178 | 302 | 3 | 25 | W |
| Jiminez v. Weinberger | 27 | 97 | 103 | 5 | 2 | W |
| Lindsey v. Normet | 24 | 145 | 220 | 4 | 9 | W |
| Lynch v. Household Finance Corp. | 23 | 336 | 65 | | | |

TABLE 6-2 (*cont.*)

| Case | Supreme Court Citations | Lower Federal Court Citations | State Court Citations | Citations in Con Law Texts | Citations in Law Reviews | LSP Win/ Loss |
|------|------|------|------|------|------|------|
| Dept. of Agriculture v. Moreno | 22 | 165 | 132 | 5 | 6 | W |
| Lau v. Nichols | 21 | 142 | 19 | 5 | 2 | W |
| Mourning v. Family Publications Service, Inc. | 21 | 326 | 148 | 3 | 2 | W |
| Jackson v. Metropoliton Edison Co. | 20 | 406 | 174 | 7 | 11 | L |
| Damico v. California | 18 | 213 | 15 | 2 | 0 | W |
| Gonzales v. Automatic Employees Credit Union | 18 | 123 | 7 | 0 | 5 | L |
| James v. Strange | 18 | 49 | 109 | 4 | 2 | W |
| Thorpe v. Housing Authority of Durham | 18 | 328 | 135 | 0 | 2 | W |
| Williams v. Illinois | 18 | 110 | 336 | 7 | 13 | W |
| Breed v. Jones | 15 | 63 | 443 | 1 | 12 | W |
| McKeiver v. Penn | 15 | 121 | 579 | 2 | 19 | L |
| Fusari v. Steinberg | 14 | 83 | 67 | 0 | 1 | W |
| Geduldig v. Aiello | 14 | 145 | 126 | 6 | 12 | L |
| James v. Valtierra | 14 | 65 | 47 | 7 | 18 | L |
| U.S. v. Kras | 14 | 126 | 154 | 6 | 14 | L |
| Calif. Dept. of Human Resources v. Java | 13 | 64 | 111 | 1 | 1 | W |
| Carleson v. Remillard | 13 | 79 | 74 | 0 | 4 | W |
| Morton v. Ruiz | 13 | 195 | 26 | 0 | 2 | W |
| N.Y. State Dept. Social Services v. Dublino | 13 | 166 | 94 | 1 | 3 | L |
| Indiana Employment Division v. Burney | 12 | 28 | 5 | 0 | 0 | W |
| Philbrook v. Glodgett | 12 | 284 | 20 | 0 | 2 | W |
| Richardson v. Ramirez | 11 | 47 | 31 | 6 | 5 | L |
| Shadwick v. Tampa | 11 | 20 | 98 | 0 | 4 | L |

TABLE 6-2 *(cont.)*

| Case | Supreme Court Citations | Lower Federal Court Citations | State Court Citations | Citations in Con Law Texts | Citations in Law Reviews | LSP Win/ Loss |
|---|---|---|---|---|---|---|
| Burns v. Alcala | 10 | 64 | 70 | 0 | 3 | L |
| Richardson v. Perales | 10 | 776 | 119 | 2 | 2 | L |
| Keeble v. U.S. | 9 | 81 | 85 | 0 | 2 | W |
| Perez v. Campbell | 9 | 199 | 109 | 3 | 5 | W |
| Phillips v. Martin Marietta Corp. | 9 | 90 | 41 | 2 | 5 | L |
| Richardson v. Wright | 9 | 37 | 3 | 3 | 1 | W |
| Wyman v. James | 9 | 81 | 120 | 3 | 24 | L |
| Kennerly v. District Court | 8 | 26 | 68 | 0 | 3 | W |
| Overmyer Co. v. Frick Co. | 8 | 77 | 138 | 2 | 1 | L |
| Williams v. Oklahoma City | 8 | 27 | 73 | 0 | 1 | W |
| Carter v. Stanton | 7 | 112 | 13 | 1 | 0 | W |
| Shea v. Vialpando | 7 | 83 | 80 | 0 | 1 | W |
| Wheeler v. Montgomery | 7 | 48 | 35 | 1 | 3 | W |
| Dept. of Game of Wash. v. Puyallup Tribe | 6 | 25 | 26 | 1 | 0 | W |
| Swarb v. Lennox | 6 | 64 | 79 | 0 | 1 | L |
| Shapiro v. Doe | 5 | 26 | 14 | 0 | 1 | W |
| Lewis v. Martin | 5 | 147 | 127 | 0 | 1 | W |
| Preiser v. Newkirk | 4 | 106 | 8 | 0 | 1 | L |
| Christian v. N.Y. State Dept. of Labor | 4 | 17 | 9 | 0 | 1 | W |
| Sanks v. Georgia | 3 | 9 | 6 | 1 | 1 | L |
| Ortwein v. Schwab | 3 | 55 | 151 | 6 | 4 | L |
| Kokoszka v. Belford | 3 | 98 | 33 | 0 | 4 | L |
| Schmidt v. Lessard | 2 | 72 | 78 | 0 | 0 | L |
| Philpott v. Essex County Welfare Board | 2 | 28 | 104 | 0 | 1 | W |
| Wyman v. Rothstein | 1 | 44 | 6 | 0 | 0 | L |

TABLE 6-2 (*cont.*)

| Case | Supreme Court Citations | Lower Federal Court Citations | State Court Citations | Citations in Con Law Texts | Citations in Law Reviews | LSP Win/ Loss |
|---|---|---|---|---|---|---|
| *Pease v. Hansen* | 1 | 2 | 4 | 0 | 0 | W |
| *Patterson v. Warner* | 1 | 4 | 0 | 0 | 1 | W |
| *Matthews v. Little* | 1 | 2 | 0 | 0 | 0 | W |
| *Jennings v. Mahoney* | 1 | 8 | 41 | 0 | 0 | L |
| *Dillard v. Industrial Commission of Va.* | 1 | 5 | 0 | 0 | 1 | L |

| Totals | |
|---|---|
| Supreme Court Citations[a] | 1,899 |
| Lower Federal Court Citations[a] | 17,171 |
| State Court Citations[a] | 16,115 |
| Citations in Seven Constitutional Law Texts[b] | 194 |
| Citations in Law Reviews[c] | 613 |

[a] Compiled from *Shepard's Citations* 1966–1983.

[b] Compiled from Barrett and Cohen, *Constitutional Law*; Barron and Dienes, *Constitutional Law*; Brest, *Processes of Constitutional Decision-Making*; Chase and Ducat, *Constitutional Interpretations*; Gunther, *Cases*, 10th ed.; Lockhart, Kamisar, and Choper, *Constitutional Rights and Liberties*, 5th ed.; and Tribe, *American Constitutional Law*.

[c] Compiled from *The Index to Legal Periodicals*, 1966–1984.

Depending on what goals we ascribe to the LSP's litigation and what measure of success we employ, the proverbial glass can be labeled half empty or half full, but we cannot deny that the LSP put something important in the glass that was not there before. When examining the whole panoply of cases sponsored by the LSP and evaluating it in terms of its ability to get its poor clients the legal decisions they requested, the Program fares much better than when it is evaluated in terms of the achievement of the particular policy goals often ascribed to it but not systematically pursued. The LSP's most doctrinally im-

---

cited in a dissenting opinion; and LSP losses that were distinguished, criticized, limited, overruled, or questioned. Omitting all citations in dissenting opinions, 65 percent (823) of the 1274 citations were "approving" of the LSP position. Of the 275 citations in majority opinions characterized by *Shepard's*, 52 percent (144) were "approving" of the LSP position.

Data on the frequency of citation as recorded by *Shepard's* has not been published for other groups of cases. Consequently, the data on LSP cases is not put into a comparative context. However, perhaps one example will be suggestive: Brown v. Board of Education (1954) was cited 142 times by the Supreme Court, 1158 times by lower federal courts, and 639 times by state courts in reported decisions between 1954 and 1982.

portant cases, whether ultimately won or lost, provided the justices with new and different opportunities to refine their understandings of the due process and equal protection clauses. Poor litigants, represented by LSP attorneys, shaped the judicial landscape and affected the constitutional development of this era.

## INFLUENCE: THE COURT'S DUE PROCESS AND EQUAL PROTECTION JURISPRUDENCE

Two-thirds of the Legal Services Program's cases given plenary consideration provided the justices with occasions for the development of due process and equal protection doctrines. While the Court has not used the precedents established in LSP cases to revolutionize poverty law and policy, it has invoked them to support decisions in other areas. Most traditional accounts of the Court's due process and equal protection jurisprudence are peppered with references to LSP sponsored cases.[15] Without embarking upon an exhaustive doctrinal exegesis of the Court's Fourteenth Amendment jurisprudence during the last three decades, the next several pages demonstrate the influence of both the LSP's victories and defeats in the Court's development of due process and equal protection doctrine.[16]

### Due Process

In the 1970s, the Court began expanding the reach of the due process clause beyond the criminal justice process, requiring that certain procedural standards be adhered to in other relationships between the citizen and government. The Legal Services Program's cases played an important role in this development. The LSP's first major due process case, *Goldberg v. Kelly* (1970) has been credited with "launching the modern procedural due process revolution."[17] *Goldberg*, which extended procedural due process protections to welfare recipients prior to termination of their benefits, is seen as a rejection of

---

[15] Of course, these accounts generally do not acknowledge the LSP's sponsorship. See especially Gunther, *Cases*, 11th ed., pp. 566–68, 578–85, 665–66, 670–87, 787–99, 830–54; Chase and Ducat, *Constitutional Interpretation*, pp. 631–39, 738–41, 895–96; Tribe, *American Constitutional Law*, pp. 500–564; Nowak et al., *Constitutional Law*, pp. 451–520, 630–47, 652–59, 678–83, 766–82, 789–801; Lockhart, Kamisar, Choper, and Shiffrin, *Constitutional Rights*, pp. 259–96, 938–45, 1027–75, 1233–36.

[16] This section is intended to be accessible to readers with a cursory familiarity with Supreme Court doctrine. More sophisticated readers may find the discussion lacking in depth, though they will find it useful in alerting them to the source of the vehicles for some of the Court's innovations in these areas. Some of the doctrinal points are given more thorough treatment in the accompanying notes.

[17] Gunther, *Constitutional Law*, 11th ed., p. 567.

the right-privilege distinction that had previously characterized civil due process adjudication.[18]

*Goldberg* was followed by a spate of cases in the early 1970s extending pretermination hearing rights to debtors,[19] employees,[20] students,[21] automobile drivers,[22] parolees,[23] and prisoners.[24] By the late 1970s, the Court seemed reluctant to extend these rights further. The right-privilege distinction was replaced with a judicial requirement of entitlement under statutes or the Bill of Rights, thereby limiting the range of interests entitled to due process procedural protections.[25]

---

[18] Justice Holmes is credited with first articulating this distinction while serving on the Massachusetts Supreme Judicial Court. See McAuliffe v. Mayor of New Bedford (1892). See also Sherbert v. Verner (1963) and Sniadach v. Family Finance Co. (1969). See Van Alstyne, "The Demise of the Right-Privilege Distinction"; Van Alstyne, "Cracks in 'The New Property' "; Reich, "New Property"; Reich, "Individual Rights and Social Welfare."

[19] *Fuentes v. Shevin* (1972), but see *Mitchell v. W. T. Grant Company* (1974).

[20] Perry v. Sinderman (1972), but see Board of Regents v. Roth (1972); Arnett v. Kennedy (1974); Bishop v. Wood (1976); and Codd v. Velger (1977).

[21] *Goss v. Lopez* (1975) and *Vlandis v. Kline* (1973); but see Ingraham v. Wright (1978) and Board of Curators of the University of Missouri v. Horowitz (1978).

[22] Bell v. Burson (1971) and *Jennings v. Mahoney* (1971); but see Dixon v. Love (1977) and Mackey v. Montrym (1979).

[23] Morrissey v. Brewer (1972).

[24] Vitek v. Jones (1980), but see Meachum v. Fano (1976); Greenholtz v. Nebraska Penal Inmates (1979); Connecticut Board of Pardons v. Dumschat (1981); Hewitt v. Helms (1983); and Olim v. Wakinekona (1983).

[25] See especially Bishop v. Wood (1976) where Justice Brennan, in dissent, concluded that the Court's reliance on state laws for determinations of the existence of a due process protected property interest "is a resurrection of the discredited rights/privileges distinction, for a State may now avoid all due process safeguards attendant upon the loss of even the necessities of life, c.f. *Goldberg v. Kelly*, by merely labeling them as not constituting 'property.' " As recently as 1979, however, in Califano v. Westcott, the Court rejected a federal government argument that AFDC benefits are a "privilege" rather than a "right" and therefore not subject to the guarantee of equal protection.

In other due process cases, the Court has generally not found a state created property interest in public employment. See Board of Regents v. Roth (1972) and Bishop v. Wood (1976); but see Perry v. Sindermann (1972) and Arnett v. Kennedy (1974). In Arnett, the Court found an entitlement, but no denial of due process. The Court has also looked for, but not found, a state-created liberty interest in reputation (see Paul v. Davis [1976]) or prison assignments (see Meachum v. Fano [1976], Greenholtz v. Nebraska Penal Inmates [1979], Connecticut Board of Pardons v. Dumshat [1981], Hewitt v. Helms [1983], and Olim v. Wakinekona [1983]; but see Vitek v. Jones [1980]). See also Parham v. J. R. (1979) holding that formal adversary hearings are not required prior to parental commitment of children to state mental institutions and O'Bannon v. Town Court Nursing Center (1980) holding that the state is not required to hold hearings prior to the revocation of a nursing home's certification to receive Medicare and Medicaid payments since there is no entitlement or right to residence in a particular nursing home. But see Logan v. Zimmerman Brush Co. (1982) where the Court unanimously held that the state had created a property that could not be denied without due process procedures, in its establishment of remedies for discrimination against the physically handicapped.

The Court also retreated on *Goldberg*'s requirement that due process be accorded prior to the deprivation. In holding that due process did not require a hearing before the termination of Social Security disability insurance benefits in Mathews v. Eldridge (1976), Justice Powell's majority opinion introduced a more restrictive balancing test for determining what process was due when.[26] After 1976, using the Mathews balancing approach and limiting *Goldberg* to its facts, the Court frequently rejected due process hearing claims.[27] Even when the Court did require pretermination hearings, it generally did not require the quasi-judicial procedures outlined in *Goldberg*, preferring to adapt the due process requirements to the particular institution and situation as it had in a later LSP case, *Goss v. Lopez* (1975).[28]

In applying the due process clause to civil trials, the Court's *Boddie v. Connecticut* (1971) decision, striking down filing fees for indigents in divorce actions, did not lead to a broadening of access to civil courts comparable to that witnessed in the criminal process during the last four decades.[29] Almost immediately, it became apparent that the justices would not apply the *Boddie* precedent to other civil cases,[30] leaving them open to the charge of having

[26] Justice Powell wrote in Mathews, ''Identification of the specific dictates of due process generally requires consideration of three distinct factors: first, the private interest that will be affected by the official action; second, the risk of an erroneous deprivation of such interest through the procedures used, and the probable value, if any, of additional or substitute procedural safeguards; and finally, the government's interest, including the function involved and the fiscal and administrative burdens that the additional or substitute procedural requirement would entail.'' Employing this test, the Mathews majority distinguished *Goldberg*, finding that since ''the disabled worker's need is likely to be less than that of a welfare recipient . . . there is less reason . . . to depart from the ordinary principle, established by our decisions, that something less than an evidentiary hearing is sufficient prior to adverse administrative action.''

[27] See Ingraham v. Wright (1977); Dixon v. Love (1977); Smith v. Organization of Foster Families (1977); Board of Curators of the University of Missouri v. Horowitz (1978); Barry v. Barchi (1979); Mackey v. Montrym (1979); Lassiter v. Department of Social Services (1981); and Landon v. Plasencia (1982). But see Little v. Streater (1981) and Santosky v. Kramer (1982).

[28] For example, in a more favorable ruling than *Jackson v. Metropolitan Edison Co.* (1974), the Court, using the Mathews test, accepted a utility customer's due process claim but found that it only required that he have an opportunity to meet with a responsible employee empowered to resolve billing disputes before termination of service in Memphis Light, Gas, and Water Division v. Craft (1978). More recently, see Vitek v. Jones (1980) requiring that prisoners be accorded a hearing prior to a transfer to a mental hospital similar to that necessary to commit an ordinary citizen.

[29] On criminal defendants' access to the courts, see esp. Burns v. Ohio (1954); Smith v. Bennett (1961); Griffin v. Illinois (1956); Long v. District Court of Iowa (1966); Mayer v. Chicago (1971); and Douglas v. California (1963).

[30] The majority opinion in *Boddie* emphasized that filing fees in divorce actions, as applied to indigents, violated due process solely because resort to the state courts is the *only* avenue open for ''dissolution of untenable marriages.'' Speaking through Justice Harlan, the Court said, ''The legitimacy of the State's monopoly over techniques of final dispute settlement, even where some are denied access to its use, stands unimpaired where recognized, effective alternatives for the

elevated a right to divorce.[31] Nonetheless, the following year, in another LSP case, *Lindsey v. Normet* (1972), the Court did find an equal protection violation in Oregon's requirement that tenants wishing to appeal from an adverse decision post bond for twice the amount of rent expected to accrue pending appellate decision, but the majority did not employ *Boddie*'s due process analysis.[32]

In the welfare area, the Court refused to follow the combined rationales of *Goldberg* and *Boddie* in *Ortwein v. Schwab* (1973). The Court held that filing fees for appeals from pretermination hearings did not violate due process. The refusal to require waivers of filing fees for indigents in bankruptcy proceedings in *U.S. v. Kras* (1973) seemed to be the definitive confinement of *Boddie*.

However, *Boddie* can be read as an early signal of the Court's willingness to consider, and sometimes accept, due process claims in the context of state actions that impinge on family relationships, an area in which the Burger Court has been particularly active, if not consistent.[33] In an LSP case decided two months before *Boddie*, *Wyman v. James* (1971), the Court found that since the purpose of social workers' visits to the homes of AFDC recipients was

adjustment of differences remain. . . . We do not decide that access for all individuals to the courts is a right that is, in all circumstances, guaranteed by the Due Process Clause.''

[31] See especially Justices Black's and Douglas's dissents to denial of certiorari in Meltzer v. LeCraw (1971) and four similar cases. Justice Black heavily criticized the ''exclusive'' means and ''fundamental'' subject matter distinctions drawn in *Boddie*, adding, ''I would either overrule *Boddie* at once or extend the benefits of government paid costs to other civil litigants. . . . There is simply no fairness or justice in a legal system which pays indigents' costs to get divorces and does not aid them in other civil cases which are frequently of far greater importance to society.'' Justice Black could find no appropriate grounds on which to distinguish *Boddie* from the five denied cases: Meltzer v. LeCraw, which involved double rent penalties for tenants who challenge their eviction in court but lose; Beverly v. Scotland Urban Enterprises, Inc., which involved penalty bonds required to appeal from adverse judgments in housing eviction cases; Bourbeau v. Lancaster, which involved fees for docketing appeals in child guardianship claims; *In Re Garland*, which involved filing fees for a petition for discharge in bankruptcy; and *Kaufman v. Carter*, which involved a request for court-appointed counsel by an indigent mother to defend herself in a state civil suit to declare her an unfit mother and take five of her seven children away from her. Black found the last case particularly shocking. Justice Douglas's dissent rested on his view that these five cases contained an ''invidious discrimination based on poverty, a suspect legislative classification'' under the equal protection clause. See also the dissenting opinions in *Ortwein v. Schwab* (1973) and *U.S. v. Kras* (1973).

[32] The Court upheld, in the face of due process and equal protection challenges, the statute's provisions that (1) trial be held between two and six days after service of the complaint, unless security for accruing rent is provided; and (2) litigable issues are limited to those involving the tenant's default.

[33] See Burt, ''The Burger Court and the Family,'' and cases cited therein. Burt writes, ''The Court's repeated attention during the 1970s to abortion and gender discrimination, as well as adoption and foster placement proceedings and disputes between children, parents, and school authorities, has elaborated new constitutional doctrine to adjudicate relations both within the family and between the family unit and outsiders.'' Burt, ''The Burger Court and the Family,'' p. 92, citations omitted. See also Gunther, *Constitutional Law*, 11th ed., pp. 550–59.

to protect the dependent children, such a visit did not constitute a search that would require a warrant under the Fourth Amendment.[34] In an LSP case decided the year following *Boddie*, the Court held in *Stanley v. Illinois* (1972) that an unwed father, like other parents, is entitled to a hearing on fitness before his illegitimate children are taken from him in dependency proceedings.[35] In 1981, returning to *Boddie* and following the spirit of *Stanley* while distinguishing *Ortwein* and *Kras*, the Court unanimously held that due process entitled indigent defendants in paternity support actions to state-subsidized blood grouping tests in Little v. Streater (1981).[36] The Court has been willing to impose some due process restrictions on state supervision of the family unit.

In other LSP cases, the Court adopted and then abandoned a controversial "irrebuttable presumptions analysis" which allowed heightened scrutiny of legislative classifications on procedural due process rather than equal protection grounds.[37] Under this doctrine, legislative classifications found to create "irrebuttable presumptions" were struck down and individualized determinations and hearings were required. Justice Stewart launched the doctrine in *Vlandis v. Kline* (1973), overturning Connecticut's statute that set tuition rates on the basis of "irrebuttable presumptions" of nonresidence, which were not necessarily or universally true in fact. Without elevating education or equal tuition fees to a constitutionally protected right, the Court found that there

[34] Justice Blackmun noted, in a footnote to his majority opinion, that "there are indications that all was not always well with the infant Maurice (skull fracture, a dent in the head, a possible rat bite)," at p. 322n.9. Burt reconciles *Wyman v. James* (1971) with other seemingly contradictory decisions related to parental authority such as Parham v. J. R. (1979) and Wisconsin v. Yoder (1972) by suggesting that "the operative principle that gives consistency to this [conservative] bloc's various decisions is rather that only parental authority exercised in a traditional authoritarian format requires constitutional deference." Burt, "The Burger Court and Family Law," p. 98.

[35] In Caban v. Mohammed (1979), the Court invalidated a New York statute denying the fathers of illegitimate children the same rights as mothers to block the adoption of their illegitimate children, but in Lehr v. Robertson (1983) the Court held that fathers who had not had a significant relationship with their illegitimate children were not entitled to notice and hearing prior to the child's adoption. The denial of a father's right to sue for the wrongful death of his illegitimate child was upheld in the face of an equal protection challenge in Parham v. Hughes (1979).

[36] However, in Lassiter v. Department of Social Services (1981), decided the same day, a split Court held that due process did not require the appointment of counsel to indigent mothers involved in state court parental status determinations. Gunther, *Cases*, 11th ed., p. 832. See also Zablocki v. Redhail (1978) invalidating a Wisconsin statute requiring court approval before parents with child-support obligations could remarry; Smith v. Organization of Foster Families (1977) finding due process satisfied by informal hearing procedures used before a foster child is removed from a foster home; and Santosky v. Kramer (1982) allowing a "fair preponderance of the evidence" standard in proceedings to terminate parental rights because of permanent neglect. For an overview of the Court's positions on illegitimacy classifications and marriage and family rights, see Nowak et al., *Constitutional Law*, pp. 647–60 and 689–94, respectively.

[37] The irrebuttable presumptions doctrine is frequently characterized as an ominous mix of due process and equal protection analysis. See Gunther, *Cases*, 11th ed., pp. 853–54 and sources cited therein; and Nowak et al., *Constitutional Law*, pp. 481–83 and sources cited therein.

were "reasonable alternate means" available to the state to determine residency; consequently, due process required that individuals have the opportunity to present evidence showing that they were bona fide residents and entitled to the in-state rates.[38]

Illustrative of the waivering history of the irrebuttable presumptions doctrine, in *Mourning v. Family Publications Service* (1973), decided in the same spring as *Vlandis*, the Court failed to find an irrebuttable presumption violation of the due process clause in the Federal Reserve Board's Four Installment Rule.[39] During the following 1973 October Term, the Court found due process violations under the irrebuttable presumptions doctrine in *Dept. of Agriculture v. Murry* (1973), involving classifications of households under the Food Stamp Act, and in Cleveland Bd. of Education v. LaFleur (1974), involving employment restrictions on pregnant teachers.[40]

In 1975, in *Weinburger v. Salfi*, upholding the Social Security Act's duration of relationship requirement, the Court essentially abandoned the irrebuttable presumptions doctrine. It expressly overruled the district court's use of the doctrine, though it did not overrule its own *Vlandis* decision.[41] Justice Rehnquist, writing for a six-man majority, including *Vlandis'* author Justice Stewart, found that the due process clause only bars statutory classifications that are "patently arbitrary" and "utterly lacking in rational justification." *Weinberger* suggested that an irrebuttable presumption claim alone would no longer render a classification unconstitutional.[42]

---

[38] The Court found no constitutional bar against states charging nonresidents higher tuition rates than residents. See Starns v. Malkerson (1971). However, Justices Marshall and Brennan, concurring, disapproved of states imposing a one-year residency requirement for in-state tuition benefits. Justice White did not join in the irrebuttable presumption analysis, concurring in the result on equal protection grounds. Justices Burger, Rehnquist, and Douglas dissented.

[39] 12 CFR 226.2(k). The Rule, designed to prevent creditors from concealing finance charges, required credit disclosures in sales of certain consumer goods when either a finance charge was, or could be, imposed, or when the agreement allowed payments to be made in more than four installments. Chief Justice Burger, writing for five members of the Court, found that the Four Installment Rule did not create an irrebuttable presumption of concealment of credit charges, rather it imposed a disclosure requirement with which the seller had refused to comply. Justice Stewart, along with Justices Douglas and Rehnquist, dissented on jurisdictional grounds.

[40] See also Turner v. Department of Employment Security (1975).

[41] The Court held that the fact that the duration of relationship requirement "undoubtedly" excluded some surviving wives and stepchildren who were not in the factual situation that had generated congressional concern did not render the statute unconstitutional. In contrast to *Vlandis*'s insistence that "reasonable alternative means" were open to the state to determine the truth of what it was assuming, the *Weinberger* majority allowed Congress to rationally conclude that ease and certainty of operation justified any inherent imprecision in the prophylactic rule. Rejecting the individual's right to a hearing to determine her actual motives, the Court turned to minimal scrutiny under the equal protection clause requiring only that the classification be free from invidious discrimination and bear a sufficiently close nexus with underlying policy objectives to appear to be rationally based.

[42] In analyzing the Court's use of the irrebuttable presumptions doctrine, Gunther found that

In these LSP cases, poor clients provided the Court with opportunities to reshape its due process jurisprudence. The Court's decisions provided the poor with a few mechanisms for checking the exercise of discretion by government officials, but the Court certainly did not use the due process clause to fundamentally change the substantive policy of government vis-à-vis the poor.

## Equal Protection

Since the Warren Court's resuscitation of the equal protection clause in Brown v. Bd. of Education (1954), the Court's equal protection jurisprudence has been characterized by a multi-tiered analysis.[43] The Court invokes strict scrutiny, requiring a compelling state interest, when government classifications impinge on a "suspect class" or a "fundamental right." When neither of these components are present, the Court merely requires a showing of some reasonable, rational basis for the state's classification. However, the Court appears to have also silently developed an intermediate level of scrutiny for some suspect classes such as gender,[44] illegitimacy,[45] and alienage,[46] as well as for some fundamental rights, such as voting[47] and travel.[48] The charge that the Court is using intermediate scrutiny in these areas is based on the ease with which it has found a "compelling" state interest in some cases, its use of a "substantially related" or "important state interest" test in some cases, and its failure to articulate any standard in other cases. For many, Justice Marshall's dissenting opinions in two LSP cases, *Dandridge v. Williams* (1970) and *San Antonio v. Rodriguez* (1973), remain the seminal judicial expositions and critiques of the Court's multi-tiered approach to equal protection jurisprudence. Legal Services Program cases provided the Court with vehicles for

---

the Court's dicta in Usery v. Turner Elkhorn Mining Co. (1976), Elkins v. Moreno (1978), and Toll v. Moreno (1979) suggests that the doctrine may resurface when there are "independent reasons for heightened scrutiny, as when fundamental interests are affected, . . . but there is no longer any basis for claiming that heightened scrutiny across the board can be triggered by asserting an irrebuttable presumptions claim." Gunther, *Cases*, 11th ed., p. 854.

[43] See especially Gunther, "Foreword"; Mendelson, "From Warren to Burger."

[44] See especially Reed v. Reed (1971); Frontiero v. Richardson (1973); Craig v. Boren (1976); Califano v. Goldfarb (1977); Califano v. Westcott (1979); and Mississippi University for Women v. Hogan (1982). See also *Geduldig v. Aiello* (1974) and *Phillips v. Martin Marietta Corp.* (1971).

[45] See especially Levy v. Louisiana (1968); Labine v. Vincent (1971); New Jersey Welfare Rights Organization v. Cahill (1973); Lalli v. Lalli (1978); Mills v. Habluetzel (1982); and Pickett v. Brown (1983). See also *Jimenez v. Weinberger* (1974).

[46] See especially *Graham v. Richardson* (1971); *Sugarman v. Dougall* (1973); In Re Griffiths (1973); Ambach v. Norwick (1979); and Bernal v. Fainter (1984).

[47] See especially Ball v. James (1981); Clements v. Fashing (1982); Bullock v. Carter (1972); and Lubin v. Panish (1974).

[48] See especially *Shapiro v. Thompson* (1969) and Zobel v. Williams (1982). *Shapiro*, and its progeny are discussed infra.

some of its expansion and limitation of the suspect class and fundamental rights categories, and for its development of intermediate level scrutiny.

In an LSP case, *Graham v. Richardson* (1971), the Court struck down state regulations that made aliens who had not resided in the United States for a specified number of years ineligible for welfare. The Court held that aliens were a suspect class triggering strict scrutiny of legislative classifications. Two years later, the Court struck down restrictions on alien's practice of law in In Re Griffiths (1973) and New York's bar on aliens holding civil service jobs in *Sugarman v. Dougall* (1973), another LSP case. In 1976, the Court extended *Sugarman* to the federal government, holding that, in the absence of a foreign policy justification, resident aliens could not be barred from competitive federal civil service, in Hampton v. Mow Sun Wong. The inclusion of aliens in the suspect class category was reaffirmed in 1977 in Nyquist v. Mauclet,[49] and again in 1982 in Plyler v. Doe, striking down a Texas statute authorizing public schools to deny enrollment to children who were not "legally admitted" to the United States.[50]

While alienage remains a suspect class, the Court has not disallowed all legislative classifications based on it, permitting the states to discriminate if they can demonstrate that requiring citizenship promotes "self-governance." While the *Sugarman* majority found that this justification was not compelling for state competitive civil service jobs, the Court has accepted the "self-governance" justification in the context of the appointment of state police officers, and peace officers more generally, as well as public school teachers.[51]

The Court's majority has consistently refused to declare "wealth"—or more to the point, "indigency"—a suspect class, an invitation primarily put forth in LSP cases, especially in *Shapiro v. Thompson* (1969), *U.S. v. Kras* (1973), and *San Antonio v. Rodriguez* (1973). The Court rejected arguments that discrimination against the poor is motivated by racial bias and therefore suspect in *James v. Valtierra* (1971), upholding California's requirement of public referendum approval for construction of low-income housing, and in *Jefferson v. Hackney* (1972), upholding Texas' greater reduction of AFDC benefits from the standard of need, even though minorities constituted a greater proportion of recipients of AFDC than other welfare programs. However, the Court has been willing to strike down classifications based on wealth when they impinge upon the exercise of fundamental rights.[52]

[49] Nyquist struck down a state law that conditioned aliens' eligibility for aid for higher education on their intent to apply for citizenship.

[50] In Mathews v. Diaz (1976) the Court seemed to suggest that federal government classifications based on alienage would not be subject to strict scrutiny.

[51] Foley v. Connelie (1978), Cabell v. Chavez-Salido (1982), and Ambach v. Norwick (1979).

[52] See Justice Marshall's dissent in *Dandridge v. Williams* (1970), *Lindsey v. Normet* (1972), and *San Antonio v. Rodriguez* (1973). See also Arlington Heights v. Metro. Housing Development Corp. (1977) and Schweiker v. Wilson (1981). The Court has upheld classifications based on

In defining fundamental rights for the purposes of equal protection analysis, the Court has not strayed far from the specific language of the Bill of Rights, adding only the right to vote,[53] the right of access to the judicial process for criminal defendants, and the right to travel.[54] Legal Services Program cases provided the Court with its vehicles for inclusion of the right to travel in its list of fundamental rights triggering strict scrutiny under the equal protection clause.

*Shapiro v. Thompson* (1969) involved one-year residency requirements for the receipt of AFDC benefits that almost forty states employed.[55] To find an equal protection violation in *Shapiro* required more than a simple application of precedents or specific constitutional language. The Court could have rested its decision on a finding that these particular residency requirements made a distinction based on a suspect class—wealth—as the dicta in Justice Brennan's majority opinion suggests.[56] Or, the Court could have found a fundamental

wealth even when combined with the right protected by Roe v. Wade (1973). See especially Harris v. McRae (1980) and Williams v. Zbaraz (1980). But see *Williams v. Illinois* (1970) where the Court held that imprisoning indigents convicted of a crime for longer than the maximum statutory term because of their inability to pay fines and court costs violates the equal protection clause without finding a suspect class or fundamental right, but using intermediate scrutiny.

LSP attorneys also argued that pregnant women should be declared a suspect class in one case, *Geduldig v. Aiello* (1974). The Court rejected the argument, holding that California's exclusion of pregnancy from coverage by the state's disability insurance program did not invidiously discriminate against one sex and that classifications in social welfare programs need only be rationally based. The Court adopted a similar analysis in General Electric Co. v. Gilbert (1976) upholding a similar private exclusion challenged under Title VII of the 1964 Civil Rights Act, which was later overturned by Congress in its 1978 amendments to Title VII. See also *Phillips v. Martin Marietta Corp.* (1971), Nashville Gas Co. v. Satty (1977), and Newport News Shipbuilding & Dry Dock Co. v. EEOC (1983).

The Court has refused to declare illegitimacy a suspect class, but it generally applies intermediate level scrutiny to such classifications. See especially Levy v. Louisiana (1968) and Pickett v. Brown (1983). In one LSP case, *Jiminez v. Weinberger* (1974), the Court, using the language of minimal scrutiny, struck down federal Social Security Act regulations that differentiated between classes of illegitimate children.

[53] But see *Richardson v. Ramirez* (1974) where the Court upheld California's denial of the right to vote to convicted felons who have completed their sentence and parole. Justice Rehnquist's opinion for the Court found that the equal protection claim was superceded by Section Two of the Fourteenth Amendment that allows states to deny the right to vote "for participation in rebellion, or other crime."

[54] See Gunther, *Cases*, 11th ed., pp. 787–89.

[55] See *Shapiro v. Thompson*, at p. 639n.22; Shriver, "Law Reform"; Champagne et al., "The Impact of Courts."

[56] Justice Brennan wrote that a state "could not, for example, reduce expenditures for education by barring indigent children from its schools. Similarly, in the cases before us, appellants must do more than show that denying welfare benefits to new residents saves money. The saving of welfare costs cannot justify an otherwise invidious classification." One might have cited Edwards v. California (1941), especially Justice Jackson's concurrence, for support. However, in striking down California's statute penalizing those who knowingly brought indigents into the state, the majority rested its decision on the commerce clause.

right to the necessities of life, here in the form of welfare payments.[57] In fact, the Court adopted neither of these arguments, preferring to elevate the right to travel to a fundamental right triggering strict scrutiny.[58] In *Shapiro* the Court found no compelling state interest served by distinctions based on length of residence. In a per curiam opinion handed down a year and a half later, *Pease v. Hansen* (1971), the Court reaffirmed its *Shapiro* decision and extended it to welfare programs that do not receive federal funds.

*Shapiro*'s addition of the right to travel to the fundamental rights strain of equal protection analysis has served as the basis for the Court's disallowance of residency requirements in a variety of contexts.[59] The Court struck down one-year residency requirements for subsidized nonemergency hospitalization and medical care for indigents in Memorial Hospital v. Maricopa County (1974). Fifteen-month residency requirements for voting were struck down in Dunn v. Blumstein (1972), although fifty-day requirements were upheld in Marston v. Lewis (1973) and Burns v. Fortson (1973).[60] The Court also invalidated schemes that distributed benefits to its citizens based on the length of their residence in the state in Zobel v. Williams (1982), or conditioned benefits on residence in the state before a certain date in Hooper v. Bernalillo County Assessor (1985).

Still, the Court has not invalidated all residency requirements and it has seemed to employ only intermediate level scrutiny in some right to travel cases. In Sosna v. Iowa (1975), over Justices Marshall's and Brennan's objections that the Court was abandoning *Shapiro*, the majority held that residency requirements for divorce actions were reasonably justified by considerations due more deference from the Court than the budgetary or administrative concerns that had motivated the states in *Shapiro*. The Court again appeared to employ less than strict scrutiny in Jones v. Helms (1981), upholding a state statute that increased the penalty for willful abandonment of a child if the parent left the state. Since Starns v. Malkerson (1971), the Court has upheld residency-based tuition schemes at state universities.[61] Nonetheless, the right

---

[57] In a footnote, Justice Brennan's majority opinion asserted that "this constitutional challenge cannot be answered by the argument that public assistance benefits are a 'privilege' and not a 'right.' "

[58] Justice Brennan wrote, "We have no occasion to ascribe the source of this right to travel interstate to a particular constitutional provision," and proceeded to characterize it as a long-recognized elementary right, citing U.S. v. Guest (1966) in particular. See the interchange between Justice Stewart (concurring) and Justice Harlan (dissenting) on the persuasiveness of U.S. v. Guest as applied in *Shapiro*.

[59] *Shapiro v. Thompson* (1969) dealt only with interstate travel. In considering restrictions on international travel, the Court balances the right with the federal government's power over foreign affairs. See especially Haig v. Agee (1981) and Regan v. Wald (1984).

[60] See also Rosario v. Rockefeller (1973) and Kusper v. Pontikes (1973).

[61] But see *Vlandis v. Kline* (1973) which cited Starns with approval, but struck down Connecticut's statutory definition of nonresidents as creating an irrebuttable presumption. In 1983, in

to travel developed in *Shapiro* remains a viable basis for findings of equal protection violations.

The Court was also asked to add education to its list of fundamental rights triggering strict scrutiny in several LSP cases. Its most noted refusal to declare a right to education came in *San Antonio v. Rodriguez* (1973), when it upheld Texas's district-based school financing scheme that created inequalities between the funding of schools in property-rich and property-poor districts. While the Court suggested that there might be a right to some minimal level of education based on the fundamental freedoms of speech and voting, it found that, since under the Texas scheme all children retained access to at least a minimum education and the state had a legitimate interest in facilitating local control of schools, there was a reasonable enough relationship between district-financing and state interests to meet minimal scrutiny standards under the equal protection clause.[62]

The Court was nervous that no "logical limitations on the appellees' nexus theory" linking education to the exercise of other constitutional rights could be developed. The majority opinion said:

> How, for instance, is education to be distinguished from the significant personal interests in the basics of decent food and shelter? Empirical examination might well buttress an assumption that the ill-fed, ill-clothed, and ill-housed are among the most ineffective participants in the political process, and that they derive the least enjoyment from the benefits of the First Amendment.[63]

The Court was not willing to be led down the path to a judicial restructuring of the system of wealth distribution that both sustains and circumscribes our democracy. Justice Powell's majority opinion carved a more limited role for the Court.[64]

---

Martinez v. Bynum (1983), the Court upheld a state statute that authorized schools to deny tuition-free education to children whose parents or guardians were not residents of the school district. The right to interstate travel was not directly at issue in this case since the child's parents lived in Mexico.

[62] The majority also noted that it could find no definable class that was being discriminated against since "the poor" is an amorphous group and there was no perfect correlation between family wealth and district property wealth. Nor were blacks found to be concentrated in poverty-poor districts. Furthermore, it pointed to the controversy over whether there is a demonstrable correlation between expenditures and the quality of education. But see the lower courts' decisions in Serrano v. Priest (1971) and Robinson v. Cahill (1973).

[63] *San Antonio v. Rodriguez*, at p. 37.

[64] Powell reminds us of the self-imposed limits on judicial power. He wrote, "The Court has long afforded zealous protection against unjustifiable governmental interference with the individual's rights to speak and to vote. Yet we have never presumed to possess either the ability or the authority to guarantee to the citizenry the most *effective* speech or the most *informed* electoral choice. That these may be desirable goals . . . is not to be doubted. . . . But they are not values to be implemented by judicial intrusion into otherwise legitimate state activities." *San Antonio v. Rodriguez*, at p. 36.

Two years later, the Court did hold that students in public schools were entitled to some form of due process before being suspended in *Goss v. Lopez* (1975). However, the Court was careful to emphasize that there is not a constitutional right to education; rather, in *Goss* state statutes had created an entitlement to a public education that constituted property and liberty interests protected by the due process clause. Unlike the students in poor districts in *San Antonio v. Rodriguez* (1973), the student in *Goss* was totally deprived of public education during her suspension.[65]

In 1982, without finding a constitutional right to education, the Court used intermediate level scrutiny to overturn a Texas statute that allowed local school districts to bar illegal aliens from the public schools and denied state funding for the education of such children in Plyler v. Doe (1982).[66] The Court referred to the importance of education and the statute's denial of all educational benefits to illegal aliens in justifying intermediate level scrutiny, but it reiterated its holding that there is not a constitutional right to education triggering strict scrutiny. In contrast to the five-four decision in Plyler, the following year eight members of the Court employed minimal scrutiny in Martinez v. Bynum (1983), holding that states may deny free public education to children who reside in a school district only for the purpose of attending schools in that district while their parents or guardians live elsewhere.[67] Again, the Court held that education is not a fundamental right.

The Supreme Court's most noted refusal to elevate welfare and other government assistance programs to a fundamental right in its equal protection jurisprudence came in the LSP case, *Dandridge v. Williams* (1970), upholding Maryland's maximum family-grant rule for the distribution of AFDC payments.[68] As in *Rodriguez*, the Court found that, in practice, the regulation did not deprive any children of all aid. The Court, noting the refusal of HEW and Congress to disallow maximum grant rules, held that the states retained the power to "balance the stresses that uniform insufficiency of payments would

[65] But see Ingraham v. Wright (1977) upholding the use of corporal punishment, even over the objections of parents. However, the infliction of corporal punishment does not deprive students of their state-created entitlement to education.

[66] The Court also declined to classify illegal aliens as a suspect class. The Court did note that the statute had the effect of punishing children for the unlawful acts of their parents.

[67] Not only did the Court appear to depart from *Shapiro*'s ban on residency requirements, it seemed to abandon the spirit of Plyler, since the parents of the child involved in Martinez were nonresident aliens living in Mexico.

[68] Under Maryland's administrative regulations, AFDC payments were distributed based on a computation of the standard of need for each eligible family based on the number of children in the family, with the standard of need increasing in proportionately smaller increments based on each additional person in the household. The regulations set a family maximum of approximately $250 per month, depending on the cost of living in each particular locality. Members of large families, including appellees, had standards of need, as computed under the Maryland scheme, that exceeded the maximum grant they actually received.

impose on all families against the greater ability of large families—because of the inherent economies of scale—to accommodate their needs to diminished per capita payments.''[69] Justice Stewart's majority opinion concluded:

In the area of economics and social welfare, a State does not violate the Equal Protection Clause merely because the classifications made by its laws are imperfect. If the classification has some ''reasonable basis,'' it does not offend the Constitution. . . . The Equal Protection Clause does not require that a State must choose between attacking every aspect of a problem or not attacking it at all. . . . We do not decide today that the Maryland regulation is wise, that it best fulfills the relevant social and economic objectives that Maryland might ideally espouse, or that a more just and humane system could not be devised. Conflicting claims of morality and intelligence are raised by opponents and proponents of almost every measure, certainly including the one before us. But the intractable economic, social and even philosophical problems presented by public welfare assistance programs are not the business of this Court.[70]

The Court clearly held that it would employ minimal scrutiny in reviewing classifications used by welfare and government assistance programs, requiring only a rational basis for distinctions made between classes of potential recipients. The Court has reiterated this position and upheld a variety of classifications employed in administering public assistance programs.[71]

Despite the continuing vitality of *Dandridge*, the Court, in reviewing public welfare programs, has occasionally applied ''rationality review with bite,'' using minimal scrutiny yet still finding an equal protection violation.[72] In *Dept. of Agriculture v. Murry* (1973) and *Dept. of Agriculture v. Moreno* (1973), the Court found that classifications that excluded households with members over 18 years old that had been claimed as tax dependents by another

[69] *Dandridge v. Williams*, at pp. 479–80.

[70] Ibid., at p. 487.

[71] See *Jefferson v. Hackney* (1972) upholding differential benefit levels for recipients of Old Age Assistance, Aid to the Blind, Aid for the Permanently and Totally Disabled, and AFDC; *Geduldig v. Aiello* (1974) upholding state's denial of disability insurance to pregnant women; *Weinberger v. Salfi* (1975) upholding the Social Security duration-of-relationship requirement for receipt of death benefits (see also Matthews v. De Castro [1976]); Cleland v. National College of Business (1978) upholding distinctions between educational institutions used in awarding education payments under the G.I. Bill; Califano v. Aznavorian (1978) upholding denial of Social Security benefits to recipients who left the United States for thirty days; United States Railroad Retirement Bd. v. Fritz (1980) upholding elimination of dual retirement benefits for some classes of railroad workers; Schweiker v. Wilson (1981) upholding reduction of Medicaid benefits to those institutionalized in one category of mental care institutions; Schweiker v. Hogan (1982) upholding a distinction between ''medically needy'' and ''categorically needy'' in determining reimbursement of states providing Medicaid benefits; and Maher v. Roe (1977), Beal v. Doe (1977), Harris v. McRae (1980), and Williams v. Zbaraz (1980) upholding federal and state governments' exclusion of abortions from medical assistance program coverage.

[72] Gunther, *Cases*, 11th ed., p. 604.

household the preceding year or with unrelated members, from eligibility for food stamps were "clearly irrelevant to the stated purpose of the act . . . [and] wholly without any rational basis."[73] The majority suggested that the challenged classifications were thinly veiled attempts to discriminate against hippies. In *Jiminez v. Weinberger* (1974), without finding a right to government benefits or defining the effected class as suspect (hence employing minimal scrutiny), the Court found an equal protection violation in the Social Security Act's exclusion of nonlegitimated children born after the onset of the parent's disability in computing parent's disability insurance benefits. The challenged classification was found to be both over- and under-inclusive in the context of any legitimate government objective. As recently as 1985, the Court applied "rationality review with bite" in City of Cleburne v. Cleburne Living Center where it found an equal protection violation in a city zoning ordinance that prohibited the operation of a group home for the mentally retarded. The Court concluded that the classification was based on "an irrational prejudice against the mentally retarded," which it rejected as an illegitimate governmental purpose.[74] The Court does appear to be giving some scrutiny to government's choice of ends, even under its seemingly deferential minimal scrutiny test.

The LSP's equal protection arguments met with mixed success. Poor clients provided the Court with some of its opportunities to extend its equal protection jurisprudence beyond race-related claims. Clearly, the Court articulated a thorough rejection of some of the LSP's arguments that held the potential to extensively restructure some of the government's distributive and redistributive policies. The justices preferred the safer ground of prohibiting some distinctions between subgroups with the poverty community, rejecting the more fundamental challenges to de jure and de facto classifications that worked to distinguish between indigents and the more affluent. Still, in both types of cases, the claims of poor litigants brought forth new explications of the equal protection clause's requirements.

As this brief summary demonstrates, Legal Services Program cases have been of notable consequence in the Court's development of its due process and equal protection doctrines. While some of these doctrinal trends certainly did not redound to the direct benefit of the poor, their litigation played a significant role in the development of our current constitutional jurisprudence.

## CONCLUSIONS

Those who have viewed the Legal Services Program as an interest group pursuing reform of the welfare system and a reduction in economic inequalities through the courts have quite rightly concluded that the LSP failed to accom-

---

[73] *Dept. of Agriculture v. Moreno* (1973).
[74] See also Williams v. Vermont (1985).

plish these goals. Although some LSP attorneys embraced these ambitions, the actual operation of the Program reveals that these goals did not direct the LSP's participation in Supreme Court decision making. Assessing the Program's litigation from this goal-oriented perspective has led commentators to give short shrift to the LSP's success in gaining specific legal results and its doctrinal victories in areas that are not directly related to poverty per se.

Through its representation of indigent clients, the LSP presented the justices with new and different occasions for the development of due process and equal protection doctrines. The LSP's cases provided vehicles for the elimination of the right-privilege distinction and early hints of its replacement with an entitlement test along with a growing flexibility in determinations of what process was due when. The justices flirted with establishment of an irrebuttable presumptions doctrine under the due process clause in LSP cases. Access to the civil courts was expanded for some in cases that provided early indications of the Burger Court's continued attention to family law. Legal Services Program cases were vehicles for the addition of alienage to suspect class analysis and the right to travel to fundamental rights analysis under the equal protection clause. The poor were clearly excluded from the list of suspect classes, and education and welfare, or the basic necessities of life, were excluded from the list of fundamental rights that trigger strict scrutiny under the Court's equal protection jurisprudence. Some of the LSP's equal protection cases divided the justices and appeared to encourage shifting levels of scrutiny under the Court's multi-tiered approach.

The Legal Services Program cases have proved to be important pieces in the mosaic that we call constitutional law. They provided the beginning, and sometimes the whole, of new constitutional configurations that limited some governmental actions while allowing others. Surely, we must conclude that the LSP was influential in shaping the course of judicial policy development even though it did not achieve all the doctrinal reforms some of its proponents were looking for. No account of the Supreme Court's due process and equal protection jurisprudence can ignore the justices' response to the poor's claims.

# CHAPTER SEVEN

## Conclusion: Litigants, the Court, and Democracy

> To no one will we sell, to no one will we refuse or delay, right or justice.
>
> *Magna Carta* (1215)

> All responsible governmental agencies in the Nation today recognize the enormity and pervasiveness of the social ills caused by poverty. The causes and cures for poverty are currently the subject of much debate.
>
> *King v. Smith* (1968)

IT WAS NO ACCIDENT that the Supreme Court entered the national debate on poverty in the 1960s and 1970s. The Legal Services Program's litigation provided the Court with its first opportunity to address a significant number of the civil claims of the poor. The Court accepted the poor's invitation, in part, because their cases were buttressed by a history of legal precedents that had left the poor behind, and, in part, because their cases fit with the justices' shared conceptions of the judicial role. The political climate of the era, the prominence of the debate on the national agenda, encouraged the justices to respond, largely favorably, to the opportunities for decision presented by the poor.

As the history of the LSP's litigation demonstrates, *who* is able to overcome the de facto assistance of counsel requirement, through what type of mechanism, affects the course of judicial decision making. Changing parameters of access affects judicial, as well as legislative and executive, policy making. Assumptions that large caseloads give the justices total freedom to pick and choose their issues has led us to focus on judicial values and ideologies, while giving short shrift to the role of litigants.[1] Our examination of the LSP's liti-

[1] Of course expanding access to the Court will exacerbate the caseload problem that faces the Court. Indeed, the caseload problem itself creates a discongruity between empirical reality and the normative mythology of equal access. Nonetheless, restricting the access of the poor may not be the best way to deal with caseload pressures. First, it generates too much conflict with our other ideals. Second, LSP sponsored appeals to the Supreme Court constituted less than 0.008 percent (164) of all cases the Court was asked to review during the October Terms of 1966 through 1974. We should look very closely before we trade justice and democracy for efficiency. Much too often, seemingly administrative reforms of legal services have been a mere cover for substantive disentitlements. For example, see Champagne, "Legal Services"; Camper and Lubenow,

gation suggests that there is a more complex set of factors at work in shaping judicial decisions. The parameters of access to the Court function as parameters on the justices' opportunities for decision and the changing temper of the times, in combination with judicial values, affects which of those opportunities appear most salient to the Court, and when.

## PROVIDING THE POOR WITH ACCESS TO THE SUPREME COURT

Prior to the establishment of the LSP, the Court had seldom addressed the civil claims of the poor. There is a very simple explanation for this. The de facto assistance of counsel requirement had prevented those poor whose legal claims did not fit into an interest groups' litigation strategy from bringing their cases to the Court. The philosophy of the legal aid societies produced a set of lawyers representing the poor who had little interest in litigation and even less in appellate advocacy. The poor's claims were rarely placed on the Court's jurisdictional agenda.

As America rediscovered poverty in the early 1960s, the placid approach of the legal aid attorneys came under scrutiny. The courts came to be seen as a forum for reform of the laws that impinged on the poor. A new brand of legal representation of the poor was advocated. As it developed, the Legal Services Program came to be an institution that called upon its attorneys to combine client service and reform. The "trustee" model of representation provided by interest group litigation strategies was rejected in policy and in practice. Political realities necessitated a continued commitment to serving the needs of individual clients. The Program's inability to come to a consensus on goals, its decentralized structure, and its local attorneys' demand for autonomy, prevented the coordination and implementation of a litigation strategy. The LSP attorneys who, in serving their clients, appeared before the Supreme Court were the "delegates," rather than the "trustees," of the poor. Contrary to popular impressions, the LSP's Supreme Court litigation was not the product of a handful of activist attorneys pursuing policy reform.[2] One of the most unique and important features of the LSP was its blending of the client server and reformer roles. The stream of indigents pouring through local LSP offices provided the Program with its heterogeneous appellate agenda. Poor individuals, in their capacity as clients, directed the LSP's Supreme Court litigation. The LSP enfranchised one set of individuals that had been barred from the courts by the de facto assistance of counsel requirements.

The Supreme Court was remarkably receptive to the opportunities for de-

---

"The 'Truly Needed' Lawyers"; Gillers, "Repeal by Indirection"; Lewis, "Conserving the Society." More generally, see Lipsky, "Bureaucratic Disentitlement."

[2] This is not to deny that attorney values shape, and sometimes distort, the translation of a client problem into a legal controversy. See Handler, *Social Movements*; Olson, *Clients and Lawyers*; Rosenthal, *Lawyer and Client*.

cision the poor placed on its jurisdictional docket during the 1966 through 1974 Terms. Neither our theories of judicial decision making that point to the advantages of organized litigants or the influence of judicial values, nor our attempts to predict success based on case attributes, seem to account for the justices' decisions to review 72 percent (118) of the 164 LSP sponsored cases and provide the LSP's clients with the specific legal results they requested in 62 percent (74) of the reviewed cases. There was a remarkable consensus among the justices, both liberal and conservative, in the poor's cases. The Court's response to LSP sponsored cases was a function of the congruence between the issues raised and the justices' shared conceptions of the proper work of the High Court; the Court's emerging interest in both equality claims and the poor's disadvantages in the criminal justice system, which resulted in the development of legal precedents and arguments that could be employed to resolve the civil conflicts the poor brought to the Court; and, finally, the national political milieu that defined poverty as a salient issue for the polity while groping for a solution to the newfound crisis. The temper of the times created a "window of opportunity" for the joining of new litigant claims, available legal bases, and judicial attention and sympathy, allowing the poor's participation in Supreme Court decision making to produce significant doctrinal change.

Despite the fact that the Court refused to use LSP cases as an opportunity to restructure the distribution of wealth and privilege in the United States, the LSP's cases have proved to be important components in the development of our due process and equal protection jurisprudence. LSP cases provided the occasion for the Court's repudiation of the right-privilege distinction in civil due process adjudication and its extension of due process hearing guarantees to some. LSP cases provided early hints of the Burger Court's continued attention to family law. In Legal Services Program cases, the Court determined that classifications based on alienage or impinging on the right to travel would receive strict scrutiny under the equal protection clause. The Court drew limits as well, deciding that wealth was not a suspect class and neither education nor the basic necessities of life were constitutionally protected fundamental rights. These cases continue to be employed as precedents in lower courts and in the Supreme Court, often in areas tangentially related to poverty law. Certainly, the Court did not end poverty in the United States or even radically alter its extent. Of course, neither did Congress, the Presidency, or the states.[3] But the Court did interject some measure of procedural fairness into government's interaction with the poor and force policymakers to consider whether their

---

[3] For example, see Danziger and Weinberg, *Fighting Poverty*; Moynihan, *Family and Nation*; Moynihan, *Maximum Feasible Misunderstanding*; Murray, *Losing Ground*; Patterson, *America's Struggle*; Piven and Cloward, *Regulating the Poor*; Schwarz, *America's Hidden Success*.

policies met the tests of the constitution.[4] The Supreme Court became an active participant in the development of national poverty policy.

Furthermore, the Court's response to these cases was quite important to the individual litigants and many similarly situated people. For the litigants, these cases often involved, not only the securance of abstract rights, but their very means of surviving or escaping the deepest depths of poverty. LSP attorneys represented well over a million clients in our nation's courtrooms. They won, on average, about 70 percent of their trials and about 60 percent of their appeals.[5] They brought 164 cases to the Supreme Court. As even relatively narrow precedents were set by these Supreme Court cases, LSP attorneys were able to rely on them in their lower court arguments to secure legal victories for their clients. A substantial number of the poor clearly did benefit from the Program's litigation. The LSP's 62 percent (74) success rate on the merits before the Supreme Court cannot simply be deemed inconsequential because doctrine was not revolutionized. There were real litigants with real problems attached to these cases. By reducing the de facto exclusion of the poor from adjudicatory forums, the LSP brought reality closer to the American ideals of self-government and equal justice. The rule of law was extended to the poor and practice and myth became more congruent in the halls of justice. Certainly some of our nation's poor, if only in the short-run, benefited from the system's attempt to live up to its own ideals.

## SOME THOUGHTS ON DISADVANTAGED LITIGANTS, THE ROLE OF THE COURT, AND SELF-GOVERNMENT

The U.S. Supreme Court functions as a major governing institution in our system. As such, it is often characterized as counter-majoritarian and undemocratic because the justices are not accountable to the citizenry at the polls. For some, this makes the Court suspect in a democratic system, while for others, it makes the Court an essential forum for the protection of the rights of the politically disadvantaged. But both perspectives overestimate the ability or inclination of the Court to operate as a completely independent, autonomous check on the political branches. The focus on electoral accountability of the decision maker as the test of the democraticness of an institution ignores the unique procedures the adjudicatory process allows for self-government. The focus on the formal separateness and independence of the Court from the other branches ignores the fact that all three branches operate in a common political environment that they each play a role in creating.

The analysis of the Court's response to the LSP's litigation presented here

[4] On the effect of some of these due process decisions, see Sosin, "Legal Rights and Welfare Change"; Mead, "Comment"; Katz, "Caste, Class, and Counsel," esp. pp. 275–81.

[5] Johnson, *Justice and Reform*, pp. 188–89. U.S. Office of Economic Opportunity, "The Legal Services Program," 1966/67, p. 42; 1967/68, p. 31; 1969/70, p. 31.

shows that parallels can be drawn between the factors that shape agenda setting and decision making in the judiciary and in the other branches. Kingdon
argues that issues rise on the agendas of the political branches when the independent process streams of "problems, policies, and politics" are joined by
the appearance of "compelling problems or happenings in the political
stream" which serve to open "policy windows."[6] For the Court, litigant
claims, which translate "conditions" into justiciable disputes, function in a
role analogous to Kingdon's "problems." "Policy proposals" take the form
of developing legal doctrines and precedents, new statutes, and innovative
arguments publicized in amicus curiae briefs and law reviews. The justices'
shared conceptions of the proper work of the Court determines which of these
"proposals . . . survive to the status of serious consideration."[7] For the Court,
the "politics" stream is made up of the dynamic conceptions of the judicial
role that vary as the personnel of the Court changes and as political events
outside the Court change the justices' focus of attention. Much as legislators
and presidents hold differing views of the proper role of the federal government, the justices hold differing views of the proper role of the High Court.
These views vary by party and ideology, but they also vary by historical ep-
och. Kingdon's "policy windows" are opened for the Court by compelling
litigant demands and by the prominence of items on the national agenda and
in the public mind. While the fact that the Court is a legal institution means
that the specific procedures for affecting the agendas and decisions of the
Court are different from the procedures for affecting decision making by the
political branches, there are certain commonalities in the broader processes
and influences. Both sets of procedures include opportunities for popular participation.

## Litigation and Self-Government

Much as in the legislative and executive branches, the parameters of access to
the courts affect outcomes. The LSP's role in precipitating the Supreme Court's
development of due process and equal protection doctrine illustrated this process. While in adjudication, the citizenry, either directly or through a representative, does not make the final decision, citizens as litigants are very important participants in the decision-making process.[8] Litigation can provide a
method of individual direct participation, or self-government, in one policy-

[6] Kingdon, *Agendas*, pp. 20–21, 205–18. Kingdon's failure to mention the role of the courts
in affecting the lives of these "streams" and the creation of "policy windows" is largely attributable to his choice of case studies. For instance, had Kingdon looked at education or civil rights
policies, rather than health care and transportation policies, surely he would have found the courts
to be important participants in the agenda setting and alternative specification processes.

[7] Kingdon, *Agendas*, p. 21.

[8] See Chayes, "The Role of the Judge in Public Law Litigation."

making forum. Litigants play a major role in setting the courts' agendas and providing them with opportunities for decision. Furthermore, the evidence and arguments litigants put forth are the judges' primary source of information about the particular controversies they are deciding. Litigants frame the alternatives from which the judges must choose.[9] In the courts, policies are developed with the participation of affected parties that may otherwise be excluded because of their weakness in the electoral process.[10]

Perhaps more important, in the administrative state where many of the decisions that most profoundly affect people's lives are made by unelected administrators and bureaucrats, self-government can only be maintained if we have a mechanism for checking the discretion of these officials and requiring them to act within the confines of the laws our elected representatives have created. The courts provide an effective and powerful forum for such enforcement of the rule of law. Without open access to the courts, we run the risk of returning to the rule of men, rather than of law, with bureaucrats replacing kings. As many of the LSP's cases demonstrated, litigants and judges play a crucial role in enforcing the laws our democracy produces.[11]

In thinking about litigation's role in a system of self-government, we may also want to consider whether the legal process may provide some unique methods of participation that fulfill the purposes of popular participation embodied in classical democratic theory. While modern democratic theory focuses on elections, representation, and pluralist interest group politics, classical theory envisions the citizenry directly engaged in discussions of the public good, reaching decisions based not on which side has the most power to promote its own interests, but based on a consensus built through reasoned arguments that relate the private good to the public good.[12] On the surface, judges appear to impose solutions rather than facilitate consensus building, but if we examine the entire litigation process we see that the overwhelming majority of disputes and cases are resolved through consensual compromise, or in legal parlance, they are settled.[13] It is only when attempts at settlement fail that judges are forced to decide. Once a case goes to court, the success of litigants' arguments often depend on their ability to relate their personal interest at stake in the litigation to a larger common purpose as defined in statutes and the constitution. To some extent, in arguing for different interpretations of those laws that serve as the current definition of the public good, they are

[9] See Cooper, *Hard Judicial Choices*, on the role litigants play in shaping remedial decrees.
[10] See Chayes, "The Role of the Judge in Public Law Litigation," esp. pp. 1310–13.
[11] See Cahn and Cahn, "War on Poverty"; Chayes, "The Role of the Judge in Public Law Litigation," esp. p. 1308; Shapiro, *Courts*; Zemans, "Legal Mobilization."
[12] See Pateman, *Participation and Democratic Theory*; McWilliams, "Democracy and the Citizen"; Walker, "A Critique of the Elitist Theory of Democracy"; Dahl, "Further Reflections."
[13] See Miller and Sarat, "Grievances."

arguing about what the public good should be.[14] The judge's decision and opinion, at least the wise and responsive judge's, is part of an attempt to reach consensus by appealing to the reason of the losing party, using the law as first principles. Often the judge's opinion becomes part of an ongoing conversation that then shifts to those charged with compliance and implementation, or to those empowered to change the first principles of the argument—the law. Of course, compared to the collegiality of the decision-making structures the classical theorists envisioned, litigation is often a rather solipsistic form of political participation.[15] Still, it may be worth considering the extent to which individual, rather than group, participation in the legal process can fulfill the functions given to participation in classical democratic theory: develop responsible, individual social and political action; increase feelings among individuals that they belong to the community; and ensure that all are equally makers and subjects of law.[16] In LSP litigation, it did, at least, promote the final function. From a variety of perspectives, some of which we have yet to fully explore, litigation can be properly thought of as a form of political participation.

## Access to the Courts and Political Equality

In their seminal study of political participation in America, Verba and Nie remind us that

> the extent of democracy in a nation is often measured by the availability of political rights. . . . Such rights can and have been justified as ends in themselves—one of the components of the good polity and society is the equality of access to political rights. But political rights are also justified in terms of their consequences. . . . Political rights give the citizenry control over the government and lead to better public policy, policy more closely attuned to the needs and desires of the citizenry. Though

[14] Of course, the citizen generally must participate through an intermediary—a lawyer—and the client's control over the lawyer, and the nature of the interaction between the two will probably vary in the same direction, with the same socio-economic characteristics, that correlate with other modes of political participation. Perhaps lawyers are simply another "democratic elite" that clients "vote" for with their wallets. But, unlike legislative representatives, the client's relationship with the attorney is individual and direct. The client retains some control and makes the ultimate decision to accept or reject a settlement. The client can, at a moment's notice, "recall" the incumbent, i.e., fire the attorney.

[15] The current solipsistic nature of litigation is part of a much broader phenomena of large-scale society that has also made voting, the now prototypical form of political participation, a rather individualistic enterprise as well. In the complete privacy of the voting booth, we pull a lever and elect representatives who all too often have only the vaguest notion of why they, rather than their opponents, won. In response to direct-mail campaigns, we write a check and thereby "join" an interest group that then claims to represent us. We do not have to reveal or explain our political decisions to anyone, including ourselves. In contrast, litigation seems very public.

[16] Pateman, *Participation and Democratic Theory*, pp. 24–27.

most theorists of democracy have conceded many weaknesses in public control over government policy . . . most agree that public policy arising from free participation of citizens and contention among them is, in the long run, to be preferred to more despotic policy.[17]

Given the courts' role in governing and litigants' role in the courts' decision-making processes, surely, as Zemans has argued, litigation must be considered an activity that promotes the citizenry's control over the formulation and implementation of public policy.[18] A measure of the extent of democracy in a nation must include access to the courts among its list of political rights.

Of course, in the courts, as in the other branches, it is exceedingly difficult to achieve full equality of political rights in the face of economic inequalities that increase the ability and inclination of some to exercise their political rights.[19] In the adjudicatory process, economic differences become inequalities in political rights through the de facto assistance of counsel requirement.[20] When access to the judicial forum is limited, not by the constraints of justiciability but by the financial ability of the aggrieved to retain counsel, the courts' role in governing provides a greater threat to broad-based self-government. The poor are denied an equal opportunity to participate in the making and implementing of public policy.

In the political branches, we have done away with the most obvious legally-imposed economic barriers to basic political rights. We have eliminated property requirements, poll taxes, and racial restrictions on access to the ballot that disproportionately affect the poor. Campaign financing has been subject to repeated reforms designed to reduce the power of large contributors. Legally, there are no economically based barriers to freedom of speech, freedom of association, and some minimal level of education. Less directly, the almost universal ownership of television sets and the ready availability of newspapers allows us all to witness the policy debate that goes on among our leaders. We have been less successful in removing those conditions that produce sociological and psychological impediments to participation and, in many subtle ways, marginalize the politically unpopular in our public discourse.

In the courts, the emergence of a plethora of litigation-oriented interest groups has gone a long way toward removing some of the barriers to participation the de facto assistance of counsel requirement places before the sociologically and psychologically alienated, the financially constrained, and the

[17] Verba and Nie, *Participation*, pp. 334–35.

[18] Frances Kahn Zemans has made this argument very persuasively in several places. See especially Zemans, ''Legal Mobilization''; Zemans, ''Framework for Analysis''; Zemans, ''Fee Shifting.''

[19] See Verba and Orren, *Equality in America*; Verba and Nie, *Participation*, esp. pp. 336–41.

[20] Of course, the economic status of the litigant often also correlates with the quality of counsel and the ability to compile a strong factual record and present expert witnesses.

politically unpopular.[21] Interest group litigation has provided the opportunities for decision that were crucial to the Court's ability to fulfill the role it prescribed for itself in the Carolene footnote. Much as groups do in the political branches, these groups provide "trustee" representation to their clientele. Their leadership is often able to see the opportunities for legal gains that their alienated clientele can not. Groups representing the economically and politically disadvantaged are often more successful in the courts than in the legislative branches, since in the adjudicatory process success is not contingent upon promises to advantage the decision makers in the electoral process. Still, as we have seen, some measure of political acceptability is necessary to get the attention and acceptance of the Court. Groups representing the disadvantaged are in a better position to cultivate such support than are individual litigants, and they would be well advised to do so before, as well as after, asking the Court to intervene. Groups are able to achieve the most for their clientele when they press those concerns that fit the justices' shared conceptions of the judicial role and have some resonance with other national political leaders.

Nonetheless, just as we would not accept interest group activity in the political branches as a complete substitute for voting rights, the kind of "trustee" representation interest groups provide does not completely substitute for direct individual participation in judicial decision making. Litigation-oriented interest groups cannot respond to very many individuals' requests for representation.[22] Although the LSP's experience suggests that groups could still achieve healthy aggregate success rates if they provided such individualized representation, it would not serve their organizational maintenance needs very well. Interest groups' reliance on voluntary giving by foundations, charities, and members, means that they will often minimize their expenses by filing amicus curiae briefs rather than providing primary counsel, committing the sizable resources necessary to sponsor a case only to those most likely to ultimately result in big successes with publicity value.[23] Groups striving for such far-reaching policy reform do need to pursue litigation strategies that will incrementally lead the Court to adopt their arguments as law. But these litigation strategies also set parameters on the poor's access to representation in the Court. Interest group litigation has presented the Court with opportunities to respond to the broad policy interests of many groups disadvantaged by the de facto assistance of counsel requirement; it has not provided a mechanism for direct citizen participation in judicial governance.

---

[21] See generally, Council for Public Interest Law, *Balancing the Scales of Justice*. Various statutory provisions and judicial exceptions to the "American rule" have mitigated the effect of the de facto assistance of counsel requirement by allowing attorney fee shifting in certain kinds of cases. Zemans, "Fee Shifting."

[22] For example, see Halpern, "ACLU Chapters."

[23] See Council on Public Interest Law, *Balancing the Scales of Justice*; Gates and McIntosh, "Classical Liberalism."

The extension of direct participation rights, and abilities, in the courts can better be achieved through an institution such as the LSP that combines client service and reform, thereby allowing clients to have a voice in the setting of appellate court agendas.[24] Contrary to the views of some critics, the LSP's appellate litigation was not a separate enterprise analogous to interest group litigation. It was an extension of the Program's client service. Compared to typical interest group budgets, such a broad provision of a full panoply of legal services, including representation in appellate tribunals, takes tremendous financial resources.[25] Consequently, the existence of such programs is likely to continue to be contingent on the support of the political branches that control the public purse.[26] The history of the LSP suggests that when political support for a program that blends client service and reform again emerges, that political milieu will also allow such a program's litigation efforts to succeed. We,

---

[24] Alternative methods of delivering legal assistance to the poor such as *pro bono* services by private lawyers and judicare programs are generally acknowledged to be likely to provide immediate client service with little reform. See Kessler, *Legal Services for the Poor*, pp. 148–49 and sources cited.

[25] In 1975, for example, the ACLU's $4 million budget was the largest among all public interest law centers, with the NAACP LDF following close behind. Only about 40 percent of the ACLU's budget was devoted to legal work. The combined budgets of all public interest law centers was approximately $40 million in 1975, while in 1972, America's private bar received $10.8 billion in gross receipts. Council on Public Interest Law, *Balancing the Scales of Justice*, pp. 90, 94, 108. The LSP's budget peaked in the early 1970s at $70 to $75 million. Even with this budget, the OEO estimated that 3.2 million poor people had unmet legal needs though the LSP served 1.2 million in 1970. The annual budget of its replacement, the Legal Services Corporation, peaked in 1981 at $321 million. In an attempt to dismantle the Corporation, President Reagan consistently requested zero funding. In 1982, Congress responded by cutting the Corporation's budget to $241 million. Champagne, "Legal Services." The Corporation's budget for fiscal year 1989/90 was $309 million.

These figures should be compared to government subsidies of legal services in other areas and other government expenditures on the democratic process. It has been estimated that by 1982, state and local authorities were spending more than $600 million a year to provide counsel to indigents in criminal cases, as required by Gideon v. Wainwright (1963) and its progeny. In 1981, the five hundred largest corporations in the United States each spent an estimated average of $5 million a year on legal services, all of which was tax deductible as a business expense. Baum, *American Courts*, pp. 72–79. In presidential primaries the government provides $250 million in matching funds to all candidates who raise at least $100,000 in small contributions. The government pays all expenses in the general election if the candidates agree not to spend more than $40.4 million. The federal government also contributes $8 million toward the cost of the national party conventions. Of course, the taxpayers also bear the administrative costs involved in holding elections. Baker, Pomper, and McWilliams, *American Government*, pp. 195–96.

[26] It also seems unlikely that the Court would intervene and declare a right to counsel in civil cases without significant political support. When the Court declared a right to counsel in criminal cases in Gideon v. Wainwright (1963), twenty-three states had indicated their support for such a ruling through the filing of amicus curiae briefs, while only two states had filed amicus briefs opposing it. Lewis, *Gideon's Trumpet*, pp. 145–54. See Falinger and May, "Litigating Against Poverty," pp. 7–13.

as a society, will decide (albeit indirectly) who can come before the Court and who will win.

## The Role of the Court in the Democratic Polity

What does all this mean for an assessment of the role of the Supreme Court in our democratic regime? The Court's responsiveness to the political climate in which it operates is a double-edged sword. On the one hand, it means that the Court's participation in the national policy-making process is not as anathema to self-government as we often assume. On the other hand, it means that expanding access to the Court does not provide a panacea for those disadvantaged in the political processes.

Not only does the Supreme Court provide a unique set of procedures for self-government by allowing direct participation in agenda setting and alternative specification, but the Court also remains responsive to the political winds outside the marble palace. The same political climate that led the political branches to create the LSP also led the Court to accept its claims. "The policy views dominant on the Court are never long out of line with the policy views dominant among the [national] lawmaking majorities of the United States," not simply because presidents select justices that share their policy views, as Dahl has suggested,[27] but because the justices are shaped and influenced by many of the same forces that affect our other national political leaders. They all read the same newspapers, watch the same news broadcasts, and live within the same "beltway." The fact that the justices are appointed by our nation's highest politician means not only that they share his policy views, but also that they share his political world enough to be known and considered for such a plum. The political antennae that made them contenders are not rendered inoperative by the judicial robe.

As the anti-federalists feared two hundred years ago, Supreme Court justices are creatures of the national government and their primary loyalties are to that level. They play an important role not simply as legitimators of congressional and presidential policy, as Dahl suggested, but also, as Casper has argued and the LSP's litigation again showed, as implementors and creators of national policies by which the states must abide.[28] The argument as to whether the states or the national government can best provide self-government has continued for the last two centuries and we will not settle it here. Still, national elections (with their higher voter turnout rates) and the political leaders they produce, can be seen as one, admittedly crude, manifestation of majority will. The "Reagan revolution" notwithstanding, many of our most important pol-

---

[27] Dahl, "Decision-Making in a Democracy," p. 285.

[28] Dahl, "Decision-Making in a Democracy"; Casper, "The Supreme Court and National Policy-Making."

icies are set by the federal government with the Supreme Court as a responsive, willing collaborator.

Consequently, it is a bit unrealistic to look to the Supreme Court to be the stone in David's slingshot. The Court's responsiveness to the national political climate means that expanding access to the Court will not provide the disadvantaged with all the substantive results they seek. Disadvantaged litigants and the interest groups that so often represent them will seldom succeed in the Court without first garnering some measure of success in the political arena. Only occasionally, in isolated instances, will the Court create substantial new policies without at least the tacit support of some political elites. Popular postdecision uproars that force elected representatives to criticize the Court should not blind us to the presence of predecision elite support for many of the Court's most controversial decisions during the last thirty years.

This does not mean that the Court does not provide an important alternate forum for the disadvantaged. In our systems of separate institutions sharing power, different balances can be struck in different institutions. The adjudicatory process provides different procedures for influencing agenda setting and policy making, creating, in the courts, a different set of strategic advantages for those disadvantaged in the political process. The disadvantaged, provided they can cultivate some support among political elites, may be better able to succeed in the courts where they can present reasoned, rational arguments and appeal to the authority of the Constitution, than in the other branches where they must secure majorities in committees and on the floors of two houses and then the public endorsement of the executive. By mixing law and politics as it does, the Court promotes self-government by providing an additional avenue of access to law-making power.

While the Court's decisions are not self-executing,[29] in a culture permeated by the "myth of rights," Supreme Court declarations can be powerful tools for the mobilization of broader political support and the persuasion of additional policy makers and implementers.[30] Although in discussing the LSP we have largely focused on the effect of the national political climate on the Court, the causal arrow also points in the other direction. Supreme Court decisions can, and often do, push issues into greater prominence on the national agenda.[31] The Court does not simply stand aloof judging the constitutionality of policies that are already faits accomplis. Rather, when individuals choose to become litigants, they and the Court actively participate in the development of our national policies.

[29] On implementation and compliance problems generally, see Johnson and Canon, *Judicial Policies*.

[30] Scheingold, *The Politics of Rights*. On presidential power as the power to persuade, see Neustadt, *Presidential Power*.

[31] The school prayer, abortion, and flag-burning cases provide particularly vivid recent examples of this process.

# Research Methods

WHEN I began this study, I naively assumed that the LSP must have kept records of the local projects' appellate litigation. I set out to find such a list of LSP Supreme Court appeals and petitions. After searches in the Legal Services Corporation's archives and numerous conversations with both former Program personnel and students of the Program, I found that the LSP had not kept consistent records of its appellate litigation. No one had, as far as I was able to ascertain, ever seen a comprehensive record of the LSP's participation in the Supreme Court docket.[1] Former LSP director Earl Johnson, Jr., presents aggregate figures on Supreme Court appeals in his book on the Program, *Justice and Reform*, and those figures are often cited in other works. However, in response to a letter, he reported that no list of the cases was currently available; the aggregate figures were arrived at through research assistants' surveys of *Poverty Law Reporter*. The figures I ultimately arrived at are somewhat lower than Johnson's because his seem to include all Supreme Court poverty litigation, not just Legal Services Program cases.[2]

I set out to compile my own list of the Program's Supreme Court litigation. This proved to be a rather complicated process. First, I believed that it was imperative to locate all cases appealed to the Court so as to be able to assess the LSP's success in the case selection process and to compare those cases accepted for review with those rejected. Presumably, one would then go to the certiorari petitions and the jurisdictional statements filed with the Court during the relevant time period. However, in forma pauperis petitions are not available and the paid briefs do not list the organizational affiliation of counsel with any degree of consistency. Furthermore, since the LSP did not channel its Supreme Court litigation through any central organization, there is not a list of "key" LSP attorneys that we would expect to appear on all LSP briefs. Rather, the over twenty-five hundred LSP attorneys (with an average tenure of 3.9 years[3]), employed by 265 local projects, were more or less free to appeal any case they chose. Hence, to use the briefs to locate the LSP's cases would have required cross-checking all attorneys of record against a list of all attorneys

---

[1] One former director of a local LSP project (and later a Legal Services Corporation staff member) told me, "There really isn't a decent listing of the [LSP Supreme Court] cases. I started a list, but I never finished it. It was just too much work."

[2] Johnson, *Justice and Reform*, p. 189. Johnson, Letter, 14 March 1983 and Interview, 10 July 1984.

[3] Handler et al., *Lawyers*, p. 66. Handler's figures are based on attorneys that entered the Legal Services Program in 1967. See also Katz, "Lawyers for the Poor."

ever employed by an LSP project, including their dates of service. Such a list was unavailable. With the demise of the Office of Economic Opportunity in 1973 and the switch from the LSP to the Corporation in 1974–75, and with the accompanying personnel change, most of the LSP's files became scattered. Apparently, many found a home in the private libraries of former LSP personnel. The political climate surrounding the Legal Services Corporation in the 1980s made it quite difficult to gain access to the Corporation's archives and library.[4] It was a challenge to merely acquire a list of all 265 LSP funded projects.

I turned my attention to the LSP's publication, *Clearinghouse Review*. Each issue of the *Review* contains a section entitled "Poverty Law Developments" composed of summaries of appellate litigation brought by LSP attorneys across the country. Since there were substantial incentives for these attorneys to report their appellate cases to the *Review*, I am confident that virtually all Supreme Court petitions or appeals were included.[5] I surveyed all issues of *Clearinghouse Review* published between its inception in September 1967 through 1976 to locate all LSP cases that the Supreme Court decided (i.e., denied review or reached a decision on the merits) during the October Terms of 1966 to 1974. I cross-checked this list of cases and the organizational affiliation of counsel against the aforementioned list of all LSP funded projects. Some cases listed in *Clearinghouse Review* were found not to have been sponsored by an LSP funded program. These cases were excluded from my list.

Next, I surveyed *U.S. Supreme Court Reports* for the October Terms of 1966 through 1974 to acquire a list of all "poverty cases" given plenary consideration during this time period.[6] "Poverty" is a nebulous category. I used three criteria in coding the plenary decisions as poverty cases: (1) the substantive issue in the case involved the poor or poverty, (2) the litigant probably would have been eligible for legal services (based on information available in the decision), or (3) there was an indication in the record that an LSP attorney was counsel or filed an amicus curiae brief. Racial discrimination cases were not counted unless they were explicitly poverty related. Criminal cases in which the LSP participated were included, as were criminal cases in which indigency was the crime or the issue was financial limitations on access to the judicial process. All other criminal cases were excluded. This list of "poverty cases" was cross-checked with my list of LSP cases. Those cases located

---

[4] In 1983, the National Archives reported that it did not have the LSP's files.

[5] Indeed, even some cases that were not brought by LSP attorneys were reported, but they are not included in my LSP figures. All these cases were reported at the request for review stage. Consequently, *Clearinghouse Review* did not provide me with proper citations. Those were acquired later in combination with my survey of constitutional law texts and finally, through the "Table of Cases" published in each volume of *U.S. Reports*. At times, this procedure required considerable investigation since named litigants, such as the Secretary of Health, Education, and Welfare or various state officials, changed during the course of litigation.

[6] I also surveyed the 1963, 1964, 1965, and 1975 Terms although I did not include those Terms in my figures.

through *U.S. Reports*, but not on my list of LSP cases, were researched for LSP participation. Through this effort I was not able to add any cases to my list of LSP sponsored cases,[7] although I did unearth a few more cases in which LSP attorneys only filed amicus curiae briefs.[8]

These procedures yielded a list of 164 LSP sponsored appeals to the U.S. Supreme Court. In addition, I located twenty-four cases where the LSP participated only through the filing of amicus curiae briefs on the merits.[9]

I coded each of these 188 cases for a variety of characteristics or variables. In coding the cases denied review or decided summarily, I relied heavily on the *Clearinghouse Review* summaries, returning to the lower courts' published opinions when necessary. Of course, I relied primarily on the Supreme Court's opinions in coding the cases that received plenary consideration.

All cases were coded for the following characteristics: year of decision; identity of petitioning and responding parties; cocounsel in support of the LSP; method of request for review (i.e., appeal or petition for writ of certiorari); subject (as classified by *Clearinghouse Review*); lower court; target (federal, state, or local, and statute, judicial rule, or administrative rule); and constitutional issue raised.

Cases accepted for review were also coded for: LSP success on the merits; filing of amicus curiae briefs on the merits in support of the LSP's position; Solicitor General participation; type of opinion rendered (signed, per curiam, memorandum); majority size and minority size; the participation and vote of each justice; number of concurring opinions filed; number of dissenting opinions filed; basis of decision (statute, constitutional provision, Supreme Court precedent, etc.). Some of this data was used to compare LSP cases to the Court's overall docket. Data on the latter were gleaned from *Harvard Law Review*'s annual statistical report.[10]

In order to acquire quantitative measures of the significance of the plenary cases, I also researched and recorded the following data: the number of citations of the case in subsequent Supreme Court decisions, lower federal court decisions, and state court decisions, as recorded by *Shepard's Citations* (subsequent Supreme Court citations were also categorized by the signal letter provided by *Shepard's*); and the number of citations of the case in seven major constitutional law texts,[11] and in the *Index to*

---

[7] This further substantiated the reliability of *Clearinghouse Review*'s reporting.

[8] The organizational affiliation of amicus filers is listed in *U.S. Reports*.

[9] For a list of all LSP sponsored and amicus cases, see the Table of Cases, intra.

[10] "The Supreme Court, 1966–1974 Terms: The Statistics."

[11] Barrett and Cohen, *Constitutional Law*; Barron and Dienes, *Constitutional Law*; Brest, *Processes of Constitutional Decision-Making*; Chase and Ducat, *Constitutional Interpretation*; Gunther, *Cases*, 10th ed.; Lockhart et al., *Constitutional Rights and Liberties*, 5th ed.; and Tribe, *American Constitutional Law*. These texts were chosen as major texts based on conversations with publishers about sales and with colleagues about use in graduate programs and "top ten" law schools.

*Legal Periodicals.*[12] In assessing the substantive importance of the LSP's cases in doctrinal development generally, major constitutional law texts and treatises were used to gain an overview of what scholars consider to be the most important components of the Court's jurisprudence.[13] I read the Court's opinions in each of the LSP cases given plenary review.

I also investigated the Program's litigation strategy—or more to the point, its lack of a litigation strategy—and the operation of the Program as it pertained to appellate litigation. Research on these issues was conducted in two ways. First, I relied heavily on the extensive materials published during the operation of the Program and the subsequent studies of its lawyers. The LSP's appellate advocacy efforts, or lack thereof, received extensive attention. Many of these studies were funded by the Program.[14] The national office, having set law reform as a priority, was quite interested in the local project's "compliance." These accounts also had the advantage of being contemporaneous with the Program.[15]

Second, I conducted twenty-four interviews with former Program personnel and affiliates to probe specific issues of concern. My interviewees were promised confidentiality, which was particularly necessary given the political climate surrounding legal services in the 1980s. Interviewees were selected on the basis of their involvement with the Program's appellate litigation and/or the Program's back-up centers. Quite often, one interviewee would suggest another. These interviews were often conversational even though I approached them armed with a set of questions. As is often true in elite interviewing, I quickly found that it was both difficult to keep the respondents hemmed-in by my set of questions and that I would lose much by remaining more interested in my questions than their responses. My questions, which most interviewees did ultimately address, were:

1. What exactly was your position with the LSP? What is your current position? (Generally, I had this information before the interview, but occasionally I asked the respondent to discuss this a bit.)
2. Did the LSP have an overall litigation strategy or plan? (For example, something comparable to the NAACP's plan to challenge "separate but equal" in educational institutions.) What was it? What was it trying to achieve in terms of policy change?

[12] Some of this data is presented in chapter 6. For additional reporting of this data, see Lawrence, "The Poor in Court," pp. 239–55.

[13] In particular, I relied on Gunther, *Cases*, 11th ed.; Chase and Ducat, *Constitutional Interpretation*; Tribe, *American Constitutional Law*; Nowak et al., *Constitutional Law*; and Lockhart, Kamisar, Choper, and Shiffrin, *Constitutional Rights and Liberties*, 6th ed.

[14] See especially, Champagne, "Internal Operation," which summarizes the results of two outside evaluations of local projects funded by the LSP in 1970.

[15] These studies are cited throughout the text, especially in the first three chapters.

3. Did the LSP have specific substantive policy goals? What were they? Did LSP attorneys search for suitable clients and cases to pursue these goals?

4. How was the decision made on whether or not to appeal a specific case to the Supreme Court? Who made the decision?

5. Of course, the national LSP leadership was pushing law reform but there is also evidence that local programs were under a great deal of pressure not to do law reform work. What do you think motivated LSP attorneys to appeal cases to the Supreme Court?

6. In terms of appealing cases to the Supreme Court, what role did the back-up centers play?

7. What effect did the shift to the Burger Court have on the LSP's proclivity to appeal cases to the Supreme Court?

8. Which Supreme Court cases would you say were the most significant?—in terms of the development of legal doctrine, or in terms of their impact on the poor?

9. Do you feel that, overall, the LSP's law reform work was a successful effort? Has the Burger Court reversed whatever progress the LSP had achieved?

Despite the conversational nature of these interviews, I did consistently ask each of my respondents if the LSP had a litigation strategy. This question often required some discussion and clarification, because my respondents, lawyers, were inclined to think of "strategy" and "tactics" as the same thing. They did not automatically make the distinction the political science literature does. As a result, I heard some interesting discussions of the particular tactics involved in specific cases. I followed up with questions about strategy in the sense of the prototypical model, the NAACP LDF's litigation strategy that resulted in the reversal of Plessy v. Ferguson in Brown v. Board of Education. I also consistently asked what the goals of the Program's appellate litigation were. Here, too, I often received answers that focused on the short-term objective of particular cases. When I prodded respondents to discuss the "big-picture" goal of the litigation as a whole, they were frequently at a loss. These interviews provided important information that supplemented the view gained from the literature.

In sum, I identified and examined all Supreme Court litigation in which litigants were represented by LSP attorneys. I present descriptive data and I assess the LSP's Supreme Court litigation in the context of our models of successful interest group litigation efforts; in the context of our current understanding of influences on Supreme Court decision making; and in the context of our qualitative assessments of the poor's contribution to the development of constitutional doctrine. All of this is aimed at demonstrating that *who* has access to the Court, and the nature of the institutions that structure that access, has an important influence on what the Supreme Court decides.

# LSP Review and Success Rates by Year, 1966–1974 Terms

| Year Decided (denied review or decision issued) | Review Rate (n) | Success Rate (n) |
|---|---|---|
| 1967[a] | 67%  (2) | 50%  (1) |
| 1968 | 67%  (2) | 50%  (1) |
| 1969[a,b] | 73%  (8) | 88%  (7) |
| 1970[a] | 70% (14) | 64%  (9) |
| 1971[a] | 78% (21) | 52% (11) |
| 1972 | 79% (19) | 74% (14) |
| 1973 | 68% (17) | 71% (12) |
| 1974 | 67% (22) | 46% (10) |
| 1975 | 78% (14) | 64%  (9) |
| All Cases | 73% (119) | 62% (74) |

[a] Indicates a change in the Court's membership.
[b] Figures include one application for an injunction.

# Review and Success Rates of Selected Groups before the Supreme Court

| Group | Years | Cases Filed (n) | Cases Reviewed by Court (n) | Percent Accepted for Review (%) | Cases Won (n) | Percentage of Accepted Cases Won (%) |
|---|---|---|---|---|---|---|
| Americans for Effective Law Enforcement, sponsorship and amicus filings[a] | 1967–1981 | — | 37 | — | 23 | 62% |
| Americans United for Life, Legal Defense Fund, sponsorship and amicus filings[a] | 1975–1981 | — | 7 | — | 4 | 57 |
| Church-State, Organized Petitioners, sponsorship[b] | 1951–1971 | 17 | 8 | 47% | — | — |
| Church-State, Organized Groups, sponsorship and amicus filings[b] | 1951–1971 | — | 10 | — | 6 | 60 |
| Citizens for Decency Through Law, sponsorship and amicus filings[a] | 1963–1981 | — | 27 | — | 10 | 37 |
| The Equal Employment Advisory Council, sponsorship and amicus filings[a] | 1976–1981 | — | 33 | — | 19 | 58 |
| Jehovah's Witnesses, petitioner, sponsorship[c] | 1947–1957 | 38 | 14 | 37 | — | — |
| Jehovah's Witnesses, Hayden C. Covington, sponsorship[d] | 1937–1977 | — | 87 | — | 75 | 86.2 |

| Group | Years | Cases Filed (n) | Cases Reviewed by Court (n) | Percent Accepted for Review | Cases Won (n) | Percentage of Accepted Cases Won (%) |
|---|---|---|---|---|---|---|
| NAACP LDF, petitioner, sponsorship[e] | 1930–1956 | — | 42 | — | 37 | 88 |
| NAACP LDF, petitioner, sponsorship[c] | 1947–1957 | 16 | 9 | 56 | — | — |
| The National Chamber Litigation Center, sponsorship and amicus filings[a] | 1920–1981 | — | 26 | — | 11 | 42 |
| National Right to Work Legal Defense Foundation, sponsorship and amicus filings[a] | 1956–1981 | — | 21 | — | 5 | 24 |
| OEO Legal Services Program | 1966–1974 | 164* | 119 | 73 | 74 | 62 |
| Petitioner | | 108* | 69 | 64 | 42 | 61 |
| Respondent | | 56 | 50 | 89 | 32 | 64 |
| States and Localities, sponsorship[f] | 1961–1967 | — | 242 | — | 57 | 31 |
| State and Local governments, petitioner, sponsorship[c] | 1947–1957 | 39 | 1 | 3 | — | — |
| U.S., Solicitor General, sponsorship[f] | 1961–1967 | — | 345 | — | 221 | 64 |
| U.S., Solicitor General, petitioner, sponsorship[g] | 1959–1982 | 1,054 | 723 | 69 | — | — |
| U.S., Solicitor General, respondent, sponsorship[g] | 1959–1982 | 18,046 | 1,237 | 4 | — | — |

| Group | Years | Cases Filed (n) | Cases Reviewed by Court (n) | Percent Accepted for Review | Cases Won (n) | Percentage of Accepted Cases Won (%) |
|---|---|---|---|---|---|---|
| Women's Right Organizations, sponsorship and amicus filings[h] | 1969–1980 | — | 46 | — | 29 | 63 |

*Note*: These groups were selected simply based on the availability of data in the interest group literature.

\* Includes one application for an injunction which was reviewed.

[a] Epstein, *Conservatives In Court*, pp. 77, 116.

[b] Sorauf, *Wall*, pp. 126–27, 251–53.

[c] Provine, *Case Selection*, pp. 96, 98, 201.

[d] Abraham, *The Judiciary*, p. 142.

[e] Hahn, ''NAACP Legal Defense and Education Fund,'' p. 394.

[f] Scigliano, *The Supreme Court and the Presidency*, pp. 177–79.

[g] Salokar, ''The Solicitor General,'' pp. 27–30.

[h] O'Conner and Epstein, ''Beyond Legislative Lobbying,'' p. 142.

# LSP Cases Remanded

| Remanded Cases | Win or Loss for LSP |
|---|:---:|
| *Carter v. Stanton* | win |
| *Crow v. California Dept. of Human Resources Development* | win |
| *Dillard v. Industrial Commission of Virginia* | loss |
| *Edelman v. Townsend* | win |
| *Fusari v. Steinberg* | win |
| *Givens v. W. T. Grant Co.* | win |
| *Glover v. McMurray* | win |
| *Gonzales v. Automatic Employees Credit Union* | loss |
| *Hackney v. Machado* | win |
| *Hagler v. Snow* | win |
| *Hutcherson v. Lehtin* | win |
| *Indiana Employment Division v. Burney* | win |
| *Jackson v. Dept. of Public Welfare* | win |
| *Kennerly v. District Court* | win |
| *Mazer v. Weinberger* | loss |
| *Metcalf v. Swank* | win |
| *Montgomery v. Kaiser* | loss |
| *Patterson v. Warner* | win |
| *Phillips v. Martin Marietta Corp.* | loss |
| *Richard S. v. City of New York* | win |
| *Richardson v. Wright* | win |
| *Roberts v. Harder* | win |
| *Russell v. Douthitt* | win |
| *Schmidt v. Lessard* | loss |
| *Shapiro v. Doe* | win |
| *Shevin v. Lazarus* | loss |

| Remanded Cases | Win or Loss for LSP |
|---|:---:|
| *Sloatman v. Gibbons* | win |
| *Stewart v. Chicago Housing Authority* | win |
| *Thorpe v. Housing Authority of Durham* | win |
| *Westby v. Doe* | win |
| *Wyman v. Rothstein* | loss |
| *Wynn v. Byrne* | loss |

# Agreement Rates between Justices in LSP Cases and the Court's Entire Docket, 1966–1974 Terms

| | White | Warren | Stewart | Rehnquist | Powell | Marshall | Harlan | Fortas | Douglas | Burger | Brennan | Blackmun |
|---|---|---|---|---|---|---|---|---|---|---|---|---|
| Black | *43.9*[a] | *66.6* | *58.5* | — | — | *46.2* | *48.8* | *62.5* | *45.0* | *74.2* | *50.0* | *52.6* |
| | 57.8[b] | 62.6 | 50.6 | — | — | 43.4 | 47.7 | 60.0 | 60.4 | 58.5 | 56.7 | 55.8 |
| Blackmun | *87.5* | — | *82.3* | *81.8* | *88.1* | *71.6* | *75.0* | — | *57.8* | *83.2* | *71.9* | |
| | 74.2 | — | 67.4 | 77.4 | 77.7 | 53.4 | 57.1 | — | 37.0 | 83.5 | 52.4 | |
| Brennan | *76.1* | *87.5* | *70.1* | *65.2* | *73.1* | *90.4* | *68.3* | *100.0* | *75.7* | *56.5* | | |
| | 67.7 | 92.5 | 63.8 | 43.6 | 54.5 | 86.2 | 53.9 | 81.2 | 68.9 | 47.5 | | |
| Burger | *74.1* | — | *77.8* | *84.9* | *82.1* | *53.8* | *62.5* | — | *41.2* | | | |
| | 71.7 | — | 66.6 | 85.4 | 81.8 | 50.3 | 64.5 | — | 35.8 | | | |
| Douglas | *60.7* | *66.7* | *57.1* | *54.1* | *58.1* | *77.1* | *48.8* | *75.0* | | | | |
| | 50.0 | 74.0 | 48.8 | 29.3 | 39.6 | 66.9 | 43.7 | 70.9 | | | | |
| Fortas | *87.5* | *87.5* | *87.5* | — | — | *100.0* | *62.5* | | | | | |
| | 66.3 | 84.7 | 59.5 | — | — | 85.6 | 52.9 | | | | | |
| Harlan | *73.8* | *77.8* | *66.7* | — | — | *65.0* | | | | | | |
| | 59.2 | 52.8 | 62.3 | — | — | 58.3 | | | | | | |
| Marshall | *74.8* | *87.5* | *67.8* | *58.5* | *65.2* | | | | | | | |
| | 64.6 | 89.3 | 65.0 | 44.3 | 56.6 | | | | | | | |
| Powell | *83.6* | — | *83.6* | *90.9* | | | | | | | | |
| | 72.6 | — | 74.1 | 78.2 | | | | | | | | |
| Rehnquist | *78.8* | — | *78.8* | | | | | | | | | |
| | 70.7 | — | 66.3 | | | | | | | | | |
| Stewart | *80.5* | *88.9* | | | | | | | | | | |
| | 65.6 | 60.0 | | | | | | | | | | |
| Warren | *77.8* | | | | | | | | | | | |
| | 72.8 | | | | | | | | | | | |

[a] Figures in italics represent agreement rates in LSP cases.

[b] Figures in roman represent agreement rates in all cases. Compiled from "The Supreme Court, 1966–74 Term: The Statistics."

# Bibliography

Abel, Richard L. "Informalism: A Tactical Equivalent to Law?" *Clearinghouse Review* 19 (1985): 375.

———. "Law Without Politics: Legal Aid Under Advanced Capitalism." *UCLA Law Review* 32 (1985): 474.

Abraham, Henry J. *The Judiciary: The Supreme Court in the Governmental Process.* 7th ed. Boston: Allyn and Bacon, Inc., 1987.

Adamany, David. "Law and Society: Realigning Elections and the Supreme Court." *Wisconsin Law Review* 1973 (1973): 790.

"Address of Chief Justice Vinson before American Bar Association," 7 September 1949. Quoted in Robert L. Stern and Eugene Gressman, *Supreme Court Practice*, 4th ed., p. 150. Washington, D.C.: Bureau of National Affairs, 1969.

Androskey, Lori. "Appointment of Counsel." Unpublished Senior Honors Thesis. Supervisor, Susan E. Lawrence. Rutgers University, 1989.

Armstrong, Virginia C., and Charles A. Johnson. "Certiorari Decisions by the Warren and Burger Courts: Is Cue Theory Time Bound?" *Polity* 15 (1982): 141.

Arnold, Mark. "Wither Legal Services." *Juris Doctor* (February 1971): 3.

Auerbach, Jerold S. *Unequal Justice: Lawyers and Social Change in Modern America.* New York: Oxford University Press, 1976.

Baker, Leonard. *Back to Back: The Dual Between FDR and the Supreme Court.* New York: The MacMillan Company, 1967.

Baker, Ross K., Gerald M. Pomper, and Wilson C. McWilliams. *American Government*, 2d ed. New York: MacMillan Publishing Company, 1987.

Baker, Stewart A., and James R. Asperger. "Foreword: Toward a Center for State and Local Legal Advocacy." *Catholic University Law Review* 31 (1982): 367.

Bamberger, E. Clinton. "Address to NLADA Annual Meeting." *Summary of Proceedings of the 43rd Annual Conference*, 1965. Quoted in Earl Johnson, Jr., *Justice and Reform: The Formative Years of the American Legal Services Program.* New Brunswick, N.J.: Transaction Books, 1978, p. 75.

Barber, Benjamin R. *Strong Democracy: Participatory Politics for a New Age.* Berkeley: University of California Press, 1984.

Barker, Lucius. "Third Parties in Litigation: A Systemic View of the Judicial Function." *Journal of Politics* 29 (1967): 41.

Barrett, Edward L., and William Cohen. *Constitutional Law Cases and Materials*, 6th ed. Mineola, N.Y.: Foundation Press, 1981.

Barron, Jerome A., and C. Thomas Dienes. *Constitutional Law: Principles and Policy, Cases and Materials.* New York: Bobbs-Merrill Law, 1982.

Baum, Lawrence. "Policy Goals in Judicial Gatekeeping." *American Journal of Political Science* 21 (1977): 13.

———. "The Judicial Gatekeeping Function: A General Analysis." In *American Court Systems: Readings in Judicial Process and Behavior*, p. 125. Edited by Sheldon Goldman and Austin Sarat. San Francisco: W. H. Freeman and Company, 1978.

Baum, Lawrence. "Judicial Demand-Screening and Decisions on the Merits: A Second Look." *American Politics Quarterly* 7 (1979): 109–19.

―――. *The Supreme Court*, 2d ed. Washington, D.C.: Congressional Quarterly Press, 1985.

―――. *American Courts: Process and Policy*. Boston: Houghton Mifflin Company, 1986.

―――. "Explaining the Burger Court's Support for Civil Liberties." *PS* 20, 1 (1987): 21.

Beck, Paul Allen. "Critical Elections and the Supreme Court: Putting the Cart After the Horse." *American Political Science Review* 70 (1976): 930.

Bell, Derrick. "Serving Two Masters: Integration Ideals and Client Interests in School Desegregation Litigation." *Yale Law Journal* 85 (1976): 470.

Bennett, Robert W. "The Burger Court and the Poor." In *The Burger Court: The Counter-Revolution That Wasn't*, p. 46. Edited by Vincent Blasi. New Haven, Conn.: Yale University Press, 1983.

Bentley, Arthur. *The Process of Government*. Chicago: University of Chicago Press, 1908.

Berry, Jeffrey M. *Lobbying for the People: The Political Behavior of Public Interest Groups*. Princeton, N.J.: Princeton University Press, 1977.

"A Bibliography of Critical Legal Studies." *Yale Law Journal* 94 (1984): 461.

Bickel, Alexander M. *The Supreme Court and the Idea of Progress*. New York: Harper and Row, 1970.

Black, Donald J. "The Mobilization of Law." *Journal of Legal Studies* 2 (1973): 125.

Blalock, Hubert M., Jr. *Social Statistics*, revised 2d ed. New York: McGraw-Hill Book Company, 1979.

Blasi, Vincent, ed. *The Burger Court: The Counter-Revolution That Wasn't*. New Haven, Conn.: Yale University Press, 1983.

Bradley, Robert C., and Paul Gardner. "Underdogs, Upperdogs and the Use of the Amicus Brief: Trends and Explanations." *Justice System Journal* 10 (1985): 78.

Breger, Marshall J. "Legal Aid for the Poor: A Conceptual Analysis." *North Carolina Law Review* 60 (1982): 282.

―――. "Accountability and the Adjudication of the Public Interest." *Harvard Journal of Law and Public Policy* 8 (1985): 349.

Brennan, William J. "Address, Conference of the Legal Services Program," 15 November 1966 (unpublished). Quoted in Sargent Shriver, "Law Reform and the Poor," *American University Law Review*, 17 (December 1967): 1.

Brenner, Saul. "The New Certiorari Game." *Journal of Politics* 41 (1979): 649.

Brest, Levinson. *Processes of Constitutional Decision-Making*. 2d ed. Boston: Little, Brown & Company, 1983.

Brill, Harry. "The Uses and Abuses of Legal Assistance." *Public Interest* 31 (1973): 38.

Brownell, Emery A. *Legal Aid in the United States*. Rochester, N.Y.: The Lawyers Co-operative Publishing Co., 1951.

―――. *Supplement to Legal Aid in the United States*. Rochester, N.Y.: The Lawyers Co-operative Publishing Co., 1961.

Bruer, Patrick J. "Washington Organizations and Public Policy Litigation: Explaining

Reliance on Litigation as a Strategy of Influence.'' Paper presented at the Annual Meeting of the Midwest Political Science Association, Chicago, 1987.

———. ''Washington Interest Group Organizations and Modes of Legal Advocacy.'' Paper presented at the Annual Meeting of the American Political Science Association, Washington, D.C., 3 September 1987.

———. ''Amicus Curiae and Supreme Court Litigation.'' Paper presented at the Annual Meetings of the Law and Society Association, Vail, Colo., 9–12 June 1988.

Bumiller, Kristin. *The Civil Rights Society: The Social Construction of Victims*. Baltimore: The Johns Hopkins University Press, 1988.

———. ''Victims in the Shadow of the Law: A Critique of the Model of Legal Protection.'' *Signs* 12 (1987): 421.

Burt, Robert A. ''The Burger Court and the Family.'' In *The Burger Court: The Counter-Revolution That Wasn't*, p. 92. Edited by Vincent Blasi. New Haven, Conn.: Yale University Press, 1983.

Cahn, Edgar S., and Jean C. Cahn. ''The War on Poverty: A Civilian Perspective.'' *Yale Law Journal* 73 (1964): 1317.

———. ''What Price Justice: The Civilian Perspective Revisited.'' *Notre Dame Lawyer* 41 (1966): 927.

———. ''Power to the People or to the Profession?—The Public Interest in Public Interest Law.'' *Yale Law Journal* 79 (1970): 1005.

Cain, Maureen. ''The General Practice Lawyer and the Client: Towards a Radical Conception.'' *International Journal of the Sociology of Law* 7 (1979): 331.

Calderia, Gregory A., and John R. Wright. ''Interest Groups and Agenda-Setting in the Supreme Court of the United States.'' Paper presented at the Annual Meetings of the Midwest Political Science Association, Chicago, 1987.

Campbell, Bruce, and Susette M. Talarico. ''Access to Legal Services: Examining Common Assumptions.'' *Judicature* 66 (1983): 313.

Camper, Diane, and Gerald C. Lubenow. ''The 'Truly Needed' Lawyers.'' *Newsweek*, 6 April 1981, pp. 82–83.

Canon, Bradley C., and S. Sidney Ulmer. ''The Supreme Court and Critical Elections: A Dissent.'' *American Political Science Review* 70 (1976): 1215.

Caplan, Lincoln. ''Annals of Law: The Tenth Justice.'' *The New Yorker*, 10 and 17 August 1987, pp. 29–58 and 30–62, respectively.

Cappell, Charles L. ''A Structural Analysis of the Changing Patterns of Agreement Among Supreme Court Justices, 1971–1985.'' Paper presented at the Annual Meetings of the Law and Society Association, Washington, D.C., 11–14 June 1987.

Cardozo, Benjamin N. *The Nature of the Judicial Process*. New Haven, Conn.: Yale University Press, 1921.

Carlin, Jerome, and Jan Howard. ''Legal Representation and Class Justice.'' *UCLA Law Review* 12 (1965): 381.

Carlin, Jerome E., Jan Howard, and Sheldon L. Messinger. *Civil Justice and the Poor*. New York: Russell Sage Foundation, 1967.

Casper, Gerhard, and Richard A. Posner. ''A Study of the Supreme Court's Caseload.'' *The Journal of Legal Studies* 3 (1974): 339.

Casper, Jonathan D. *Lawyers Before the Warren Court: Civil Liberties and Civil Rights*. Urbana, Ill.: University of Illinois Press, 1972.

Casper, Jonathan D. "The Supreme Court and National Policy-Making." *American Political Science Review* 70 (1976): 50.

Champagne, Anthony. "The Internal Operation of OEO Legal Services Projects." *Journal of Urban Law* 51 (May 1974): 649.

———. "Legal Services: A Program in Need of Assistance." In *The Attack on the Welfare State*, p. 131–48. Edited by Anthony Champagne and Edward J. Harphan. Prospect Heights, Ill.: Waveland Press, 1984.

Champagne, Anthony, Allan F. Wichelman, and Ronald P. Sokol. "The Impact of Courts on Society: Residency Requirements for Welfare Benefits As a Case Study." *Indiana Law Review* 8 (1975): 963.

Chase, Harold W., and Craig R. Ducat. *Constitutional Interpretation: Cases-Essays-Materials*. 2d ed. St. Paul, Minn.: West Publishing Co., 1979.

Chayes, Abram. "The Role of the Judge in Public Law Litigation." *Harvard Law Review* 89 (1976): 1281.

Choper, Jesse H. *Judicial Review and the National Political Process*. Chicago: University of Chicago Press, 1980.

Cloward, Richard, and Frances Fox Piven. "A Strategy to End Poverty." *Nation* (2 May 1966): 510–17.

Coates, Dan, and Steven Penrod. "Social Psychology and the Emergence of Disputes." *Law and Society Review* 15 (1980–81): 655.

Cobb, Roger W., and Charles D. Elder. *Participation in American Politics: The Dynamics of Agenda-Building*. Boston: Allyn and Bacon, Inc., 1972.

Cohen, Michael, James March, and John Olsen. "A Garbage Can Model of Organizational Choice." *Administrative Science Quarterly* 17 (1972): 1–25.

Cole, George F. "Clients of a Legal Services Program." Paper Prepared for Delivery at the 1971 Annual Meeting of the American Political Science Association. Quoted in Stuart A. Scheingold. *The Politics of Rights: Lawyers, Public Policy, and Political Change*. New Haven, Conn.: Yale University Press, 1974.

Community Progress, Inc. *Proposal*. 24 January 1964, pp. 2–3. Quoted in Earl Johnson, Jr., *Justice and Reform: The Formative Years of the American Legal Services Program*. New Brunswick, N.J.: Transaction Books, 1978, p. 26.

Cook, Beverly B. "Sentencing Behavior of Federal Judges: Draft Cases—1972." *University of Cincinnati Law Review* 42 (1973): 597–633.

———. "Public Opinion and Federal Judicial Policy." *American Journal of Political Science* 21 (1977): 567–600.

———. "Judicial Policy: Change Over Time." *American Journal of Political Science* 23 (1979): 208–14.

Cooper, Philip J. *Hard Judicial Choices: Federal District Court Judges and State and Local Officials*. New York: Oxford University Press, 1988.

Cortner, Richard C. "Strategies and Tactics of Litigants in Constitutional Cases." *Journal of Public Law* 17 (1968): 287–307.

Corwin, Edward S. "The 'Higher Law' Background of American Constitutional Law." *Harvard Law Review* 42 (1928–29): 149–85, 365–409.

Council for Public Interest Law. *Balancing the Scales of Justice: Financing Public Interest Law in America*. Washington, D.C.: The Council for Public Interest Law, 1976.

Council on the Role of Courts. "What Courts Do and Do Not Do Effectively." In *American Court Systems: Readings in Judicial Process and Behavior*, 2d edition, p. 18. Edited by Sheldon Goldman and Austin Sarat. New York: Longman, 1989.

Cowan, Ruth B. "Women's Rights Through Litigation: An Examination of the American Civil Liberties Union Women's Rights Project, 1971–1976." *Columbia Human Rights Law Review* 8 (1976): 373.

Cox, Archibald. "The Supreme Court 1965 Term." *Harvard Law Review* 80 (1966): 91.

————. *The Role of the Supreme Court in American Government*. New York: Oxford University Press, 1976.

Cramton, Roger C. "Promise and Reality in Legal Services." *Cornell Law Review* 61 (1976): 670–80.

Curran, Barbara A. *The Legal Needs of the Public: The Final Report of a National Survey*. Chicago: American Bar Foundation, 1977.

Dahl, Robert A. "Decision-Making in a Democracy: The Supreme Court As A National Policy-Maker." *Journal of Public Law* 6 (1957): 279.

————. "Further Reflections on 'The Elitist Theory of Democracy.'" *American Political Science Review* 60 (1966): 296.

Danziger, Sheldon H., and Daniel H. Weinberg, eds. *Fighting Poverty: What Works and What Doesn't*. Cambridge, Mass.: Harvard University Press, 1986.

"Developments." *Harvard Law Review* 82 (1969): 1065.

Dodyk, Paul M. *Law and Poverty: Cases and Materials*. St. Paul, Minn.: West Publishing Co., 1969.

Donahue, William A. *The Politics of the American Civil Liberties Union*. New Brunswick, N.J.: Transaction Books, 1985.

Dorsen, Norman. "The American Civil Liberties Union: An Institutional Analysis." *Tulane Law Journal* 6 (1984).

Douglas, William O. "The Supreme Court and Its Caseload." *Cornell Law Quarterly*, 45 (1960): 410. Quoted in Doris Marie Provine, *Case Selection in the United States Supreme Court*, p. 63. Chicago: University of Chicago Press, 1980.

Downs, Donald Alexander. *Nazis in Skokie: Freedom, Community, and the First Amendment*. Notre Dame, Ind.: University of Notre Dame Press, 1985.

Easton, David. *The Political System: An Inquiry into the State of Political Science*. New York: Knopf, 1953.

*Economic Opportunity Act of 1964, Amended, 1966, 1967. United States Code*, Title 42.

Egerton, Robert, and A. L. Goodhart. *Legal Aid*. Great Britain: Butler and Tanner, Ltd., 1945.

Ely, John Hart. "The Wages of Crying Wolf." *Yale Law Journal* 82 (1973): 920.

————. "Toward a Representation-Reinforcing Mode of Judicial Review." *Maryland Law Review* 37 (1978): 451.

————. *Democracy and Distrust: A Theory of Judicial Review*. Cambridge, Mass.: Harvard University Press, 1980.

Epstein, Lee. *Conservatives in Court*. Knoxville, Tenn.: The University of Tennessee Press, 1985.

Erlanger, Howard S. "Lawyers and Neighborhood Legal Services: Social Background and the Impetus for Reform." *Law and Society Review* 12 (Winter 1978): 253.

Estreicher, Samuel, and John Sexton. "The New York University Supreme Court Project." *New York University Law Review* 59 (1984): nos. 4–6.

Failinger, Marie A., and Larry May. "Litigating Against Poverty: Legal Services and Group Representation." *Ohio State Law Journal* 45 (1984): 1.

Federal Judicial Center. *Report of the Study Group on the Caseload of the Supreme Court.* Washington, D.C.: Administrative Office of the United States Courts, 1972.

Felstiner, William L. F., Richard L. Abel, and Austin Sarat. "The Emergence and Transformation of Disputes: Naming, Blaming, Claiming . . ." *Law and Society Review* 15 (1980–81): 631.

Fenno, Richard F., Jr. *Home Style: House Members in Their Districts.* Boston: Little, Brown & Company, 1978.

Finman, Ted. "OEO Legal Services Programs and the Pursuit of Social Change: The Relationship Between Program Ideology and Program Performance." *Wisconsin Law Review* 1971 (1971): 1001.

Fisher, K., and C. Ivie, *Franchising Justice: The Office of Economic Opportunity Legal Services Program and Traditional Legal Aid,* 1971. Quoted in Richard L. Abel, "Law Without Politics: Legal Aid Under Advanced Capitalism." *UCLA Law Review* 32 (1985): 474, 551.

Friedman, Lawrence M. "The Conflict Over Constitutional Legitimacy." In *The Abortion Dispute and the American System,* pp. 13–29. Edited by Gilbert Y. Steiner. Washington, D.C.: The Brookings Institution, 1983.

Fuller, Lon L. "The Forms and Limits of Adjudication." In *American Court Systems: Readings in Judicial Process and Behavior,* p. 42. Edited by Sheldon Goldman and Austin Sarat. San Francisco: W. H. Freeman and Company, 1978.

Funston, Richard. "The Supreme Court and Critical Elections." *American Political Science Review* 69 (1975): 795.

———. *Constitutional Counterrevolution?* New York: John Wiley and Sons, 1977.

Galanter, Marc. "Why the 'Haves' Come Out Ahead: Speculations on the Limits of Legal Change." *Law and Society Review* 9 (1974): 95.

———. "The Duty *NOT* to Deliver Legal Services." *University of Miami Law Review* 30 (1976): 929.

———. "Reading the Landscape of Disputes: What We Know and Don't Know (and Think We Know) About Our Allegedly Contentious and Litigious Society." *UCLA Law Review* 31 (1983): 4.

Garbus, Martin. "Mrs. Sylvester Smith v. Ruben King and George Wallace." In *Ready for the Defense,* 1971, pp. 149–52. Quoted in Jack Greenberg, "Litigation for Social Change: Methods, Limits and Role in Democracy." *Record of the Association of the Bar of the City of New York* 29 (1974): 370.

Gates, John B., and Wayne McIntosh. "Classical Liberalism, Interest Groups and Litigation: A Reevaluation." Paper presented at the Annual Meeting of the American Political Science Association, Washington, D.C., 3 September 1988.

George, Warren E. "Development of the Legal Services Corporation." *Cornell Law Review* 61 (1976): 681–730.

Gillers, Stephen. "Repeal by Indirection." *The Nation*, 27 December 1980, pp. 703–4.

Greenberg, Jack. "Litigation for Social Change: Methods, Limits and Role in Democracy." *Record of the Association of the Bar of the City of New York* 29 (1974): 320.

Gressman, Eugene. "Requiem for the Supreme Court's Obligatory Jurisdiction." *American Bar Association Journal* 65 (September 1979): 1325.

Griswold, Erwin N. "The Supreme Court's Caseload: Civil Rights and Other Problems." *Law Forum* 1973 (1973): 615.

———. "Rationing Justice—The Supreme Court's Caseload and What the Supreme Court Does Not Do." *Cornell Law Review* 60 (1975): 335.

Grossman, Joel B. "A Symposium: Social Science Approaches to Judicial Process." *Harvard Law Review* 79 (1965–66): 1551.

———. "A Model for Judicial Policy Analysis: The Supreme Court and the Sit-In Cases." In *Frontiers of Judicial Research*, pp. 405–60. Edited by Joel B. Grossman and Joseph Tanenhaus. New York: John Wiley and Sons, Inc., 1969.

———. "Access to Justice and the Resolution of 'Middle Range' Disputes." Paper presented at the Shambaugh Conference, "Political Science at Iowa," Iowa City, Iowa, 9–10 December 1982.

Grossman, Joel B., and Joseph Tanenhaus, eds., *Frontiers of Judicial Research*. New York: John Wiley and Sons, Inc., 1969.

Grossman, Joel B., Herbert M. Kritzer, Kristin Bumiller, Austin Sarat, Stephen McDougal, and Richard E. Miller. "Dimensions of Institutional Participation: Who Uses the Courts and How?" *Journal of Politics* 44 (1982): 86.

*Guidelines for Legal Services Programs*, 1966. Quoted in Earl Johnson, Jr., *Justice and Reform: The Formative Years of the American Legal Services Program*. New Brunswick, N.J.: Transaction Books, 1978, pp. 116, 321–22.

Gunther, Gerald. "Foreword: In Search of Evolving Doctrine on a Changing Court: A Model for a Newer Equal Protection." *Harvard Law Review* 86 (1972): 1.

———. *Cases and Materials on Constitutional Law*. 11th ed. Mineola, N.Y.: The Foundation Press, Inc., 1985.

Hahn, Jeanne. "The NAACP Legal Defense and Education Fund: Its Judicial Strategy and Tactics." In *American Government and Politics*, p. 367. Edited by Stephen L. Wasby. New York: Charles Scribner's Sons, 1973.

Hakman, Nathan. "Lobbying the Supreme Court—An Appraisal of 'Political Science Folklore.' " *Fordham Law Review* 35 (1966): 15.

———. "The Supreme Court's Political Environment: The Processing of Noncommercial Litigation." In *Frontiers of Judicial Research*, pp. 199–252. Edited by Joel Grossman and Joseph Tanenhaus. New York: John Wiley, 1969.

Halpern, Stephen. "Assessing the Litigative Role of ACLU Chapters." In *Policy and Policy-Making*, pp. 159–62. Edited by Stephen L. Wasby. Lexington, Mass.: Lexington Books, 1976.

Handler, Joel F., Ellen Jane Hollingsworth, and Howard S. Erlanger. *Lawyers and the Pursuit of Legal Rights*. New York: Academic Press, 1978.

Handler, Joel F. *Social Movements and the Legal System: A Theory of Law Reform and Social Change*. New York: Academic Press, 1978.

Hannon, Philip J. "The Leadership Problem in the Legal Services Program." *Law and Society Review* 4 (1969): 235.

———. "Law Reform Enforcement at the Local Level: A Legal Services Case Study." *Journal of Public Law* 19 (1970): 23.

———. "The Murphy Amendments and the Response of the Bar—An Accurate Test of Political Strength." *Legal Aid Briefcase* 28 (1970): 163.

Hanus, Jerome J. "Denial of Certiorari and Supreme Court Policy-Making." *American University Law Review* 17 (1967): 41.

Hazard, Geoffrey. "Social Justice Through Civil Justice." *University of Chicago Law Review* 36 (1969): 699.

———. "Law Reforming in the Anti-Poverty Effort. *University of Chicago Law Review* 37 (1970): 242.

Heclo, Hugh. "The Political Foundations of Antipoverty Policy." In *Fighting Poverty: What Works and What Doesn't*, pp. 312–40. Edited by Sheldon H. Danziger and Daniel H. Weinberg. Cambridge, Mass.: Harvard University Press, 1986.

Heumann, Milton. *Plea Bargaining*. Chicago: University of Chicago Press, 1978.

Holmes, Oliver Wendell. *The Common Law* (1881). Quoted in Jack Greenberg, "Litigation for Social Change: Methods, Limits and Role in Democracy," *Record of the Association of the Bar of the City of New York* 29 (1974): 320.

Howard, J. Woodford, Jr. "On the Fluidity of Judicial Choice." *American Political Science Review* 62 (1968): 43.

———. "Judicial Biography and the Behavioral Persuasion." *American Political Science Review* 70 (1971): 704.

———. "Discussant's Remarks: Is the Burger Court a Nixon Court?" *Emory Law Journal* 23 (Summer 1974): 745.

———. *Courts of Appeals in the Federal Judicial System: A Study of the Second, Fifth, and District of Columbia Circuits*. Princeton, N.J.: Princeton University Press, 1981.

*Index to Legal Periodicals*. Bronx, N.Y.: H. W. Wilson, Co., 1960–1984.

Jackson, Robert H. *The Struggle for Judicial Supremacy: A Study of Crisis in American Power Politics*. New York: Alfred A. Knopf, 1941.

Jacob, Herbert. *Debtors in Court: The Consumption of Government Services*. Chicago: Rand McNally & Company, 1969.

Johnson, Charles A., and Bradley C. Canon. *Judicial Policies: Implementation and Impact*. Washington, D.C.: CQ Press, 1984.

Johnson, Earl, Jr. "Refutation and Endorsement: A Reaction to Hannon's Analysis of the Murphy Amendment and the Bar." *Legal Aid Briefcase* 28 (1970): 257.

———. *Justice and Reform: The Formative Years of the American Legal Services Program*. New Brunswick, N.J.: Transaction Books, 1978.

———. Associate Justice. State of California Court of Appeal, Los Angeles, California. Letter, 14 March 1983. Interview (telephone), 10 July 1984.

*The Judiciary Act of February 13, 1925. Statutes at Large*, vol. 43 (1925). *United States Code*, vol. 28 (1970).

Kamisar, Yale. "The Warren Court (Was It Really So Defense-Minded?), the Burger Court (Is It Really So Prosecution-Oriented?), and Police Investigatory Practices,"

p. 62. In *The Burger Court: The Counter-Revolution That Wasn't*. Edited by Vincent Blasi. New Haven, Conn.: Yale University Press, 1983.

Katz, Jack. "Lawyers for the Poor in Transition: Involvement, Reform, and the Turnover Problem in the Legal Services Program." *Law and Society Review* 12 (Winter 1978): 275.

———. *Poor People's Lawyers in Transition*. New Brunswick, N.J.: Rutgers University Press, 1982.

———. "Caste, Class, and Counsel for the Poor." *American Bar Foundation Research Journal* 1985 (1985): 251.

Kessler, Mark. *Legal Services for the Poor: A Comparative and Contemporary Analysis of Interorganizational Politics*. Westport, Conn.: Greenwood Press, 1987.

Kingdon, John W. *Agendas, Alternatives, and Public Policy*. Boston: Little, Brown & Company, 1984.

Kluger, Richard. *Simple Justice*. New York: Vintage Books, 1975.

Krislov, Samuel. "The Amicus Curiae Brief: From Friendship to Advocacy." *Yale Law Journal* 72 (1963): 694.

———. "The OEO Lawyers Fail to Constitutionalize a Right to Welfare: A Study in the Uses and Limits of the Judicial Process." *Minnesota Law Review* 58 (1973): 211.

Kritzer, Herbert M. "Political Correlates of the Behavior of Federal District Judges: A 'Best Case' Analysis." *Journal of Politics* 40 (1978): 25–58.

———. "Federal Judges and Their Political Environments: The Influence of Public Opinion." *American Journal of Political Science* 23 (1979): 194–207.

Kuklinski, James H., and John E. Stanga. "Political Participation and Government Responsiveness: The Behavior of California Superior Courts." *American Political Science Review* 73 (1979): 1090–99.

Kurland, P. "1971 Term: The Year of the Stewart-White Court." *Supreme Court Review* 1972 (1972): 181–329.

Lasser, William. "The Supreme Court in Periods of Critical Realignment." *Journal of Politics* 47 (1985): 1174.

Lasswell, Harold D. *Politics: Who Gets What, When, How*. New York: McGraw-Hill, 1936.

Law, Sylvia A. "Economic Justice." In *Our Endangered Rights*, p. 134. Edited by Norman Dorsen. New York: Pantheon Books, 1984.

Lawrence, Susan E. "The Poor in Court: The Legal Impact of Expanded Access." Ph.D. Dissertation. The Johns Hopkins University, 1985.

———. "Participation Through Legal Mobilization: Structures of Representation." *Polity*, forthcoming.

*Lawyers' Edition of the U.S. Supreme Court Reports*. 2d Series. Vols. 18–45. Rochester, N.Y.: Lawyers Cooperative Publishing Co., 1966–76.

*Legal Services Corporation Act. United States Code Annotated*, vol. 42 (1980).

Lehne, Richard. *The Quest for Justice: The Politics of School Finance Reform*. New York: Longman, 1973.

Lenzer, Terry. "Legal Services Fights for the Poor, but Who Fights for Legal Services?" *Juris Doctor* (February 1971): 8.

Leuchtenburg, William. "Franklin Delano Roosevelt's Court-Packing Plan." *Supreme Court Review* 1966 (1966): 347.

Lewis, Anthony. *Gideon's Trumpet*. New York: Vintage Books, 1854.

———. "Conserving the Society." *New York Times*, 16 April 1981, p. 31.

Light, Paul C. *The President's Agenda: Domestic Policy Choice from Kennedy to Carter*. Baltimore: The Johns Hopkins University Press, 1982.

Lipsky, Michael. "Bureaucratic Dientitlement in Social Welfare Programs." Paper presented at the Annual Meeting of the Western Political Science Association, Seattle, Wash., 26 March 1983.

Lockhart, William B., Yale Kamisar, and Jesse H. Choper (and Steven H. Shiffrin). *Constitutional Rights and Liberties: Cases-Comments-Questions*. 5th and 6th eds., St. Paul, Minn.: West Publishing Co., 1980 and 1986.

Loomis, Burdett A., and Allan J. Cigler. "Introduction: The Changing Nature of Interest Group Politics." In *Interest Group Politics*, 2d ed., pp. 1–26. Edited by Allan J. Cigler and Burdett A. Loomis. Washington, D.C.: CQ Press, 1986.

Maguire, John MacArthur. "Poverty and Civil Litigation." *Harvard Law Review* 36 (1922–23): 361.

———. *The Lance of Justice: A Semi-Centennial History of the Legal Aid Society, 1876–1926*. Cambridge, Mass.: Harvard University Press, 1928.

Manwaring, David R. *Render Unto Caesar: The Flag Salute Controversy*. Chicago: University of Chicago Press, 1962.

———. "The Flag Salute Case." In *The Third Branch of Government: Eight Cases in Constitutional Politics*, pp. 29–31. Edited by C. Herman Pritchett and Alan F. Westin. New York: Harcourt, Brace & World, 1963.

Mason, Alpheus Thomas. "New Foundations for Liberty and Authority in the Old World." In *Free Government in the Making*, 3d ed., p. 3. Edited by Alpheus Thomas Mason and Gordon E. Baker. New York: Oxford University Press, 1965.

Mason, Alpheus Thomas, and William M. Beaney. *The Supreme Court In A Free Society*. New York: W. W. Norton and Company, Inc., 1968.

Mayhew, David R. *Congress: The Electoral Connection*. New Haven, Conn.: Yale University Press, 1974.

Mayhew, Leon H. "Institutions of Representation: Civil Justice and the Public." *Law and Society Review* 9 (1975): 401.

McIntosh, Wayne V. "Supreme Court Impact on Third Parties: An Exploration of Amicus Participation in the Federal Appeals Courts." Paper presented at the Annual Meetings of the American Political Science Association. Washington, D.C., 30 August–2 September 1984.

McIntosh, Wayne V., and Paul E. Parker. "Amici Curiae in the Court of Appeals." Paper presented at the Annual Meetings of the Law and Society Association, Chicago, 29 May–1 June 1986.

McWilliams, Wilson Carey. "Democracy and the Citizen: Community, Dignity, and the Crisis of Contemporary Politics in America." In *How Democratic is the Constitution?* p. 79. Edited by Robert A. Goldwin and William A. Schambra. Washington, D.C.: American Enterprise Institute, 1980.

Mead, Lawrence M. "Comment." In *Fighting Poverty: What Works and What*

*Doesn't*, pp. 283–86. Edited by Sheldon H. Danziger and Daniel H. Weinberg. Cambridge, Mass.: Harvard University Press, 1986.

Mendelson, Wallace. "From Warren to Burger: The Rise and Decline of Substantive Equal Protection." *American Political Science Review* 66 (1972): 1226.

Michelman, F. "Foreword: On Protecting the Poor Through the Fourteenth Amendment." *Harvard Law Review* 83 (1969): 7–59.

Miller, Richard E., and Austin Sarat. "Grievances, Claims, and Disputes: Assessing the Adversary Culture." *Law and Society Review* 15 (1980–81): 525.

Moynihan, Daniel P. *Maximum Feasible Misunderstanding: Community Action in the War on Poverty*. New York: Free Press, 1969.

—————. *Family and Nation*. New York: Harcourt Brace Jovanovich, Inc., 1987.

Murphy, Walter F. *Elements of Judicial Strategy*. Chicago: University of Chicago Press, 1964.

—————. "The Art of Constitutional Interpretation: A Preliminary Showing." In *Essays on the Constitution of the United States*. Edited by M. Judd Harmon. Port Washington, N.Y.: Kennikat Press, 1978.

Murray, Charles. *Losing Ground: American Social Policy, 1950–1980*. New York: Basic Books, Inc., Publishers, 1984.

Nagel, Stuart A. "Court-Curbing Periods in American History." *Vanderbilt Law Review* 18 (1965): 925.

National Legal Aid and Defender Association, Executive Committee, *Resolution*, 16 December 1964. Quoted in Earl Johnson, Jr., *Justice and Reform: The Formative Years of the American Legal Services Program*. New Brunswick, N.J.: Transaction Books, 1978, p. 49.

Nelson, Barbara J. *Making an Issue of Child Abuse: Political Agenda Setting for Social Problems*. Chicago: University of Chicago Press, 1984.

Neustadt, Richard E. *Presidential Power: The Politics of Leadership From FDR to Carter*. New York: John Wiley and Sons, Inc., 1980.

Note. "Beyond the Neighborhood Office—OEO's Special Grants in Legal Services." *Georgetown Law Journal* 56 (1969): 742.

Note. "Federal Judicial Review of State Welfare Practices." *Columbia Law Review* 67 (January 1967): 84.

Note. "Neighborhood Law Offices: The New Wave in Legal Services for the Poor." *Harvard Law Review* 80 (1967): 805.

Note. "Private Attorneys-General: Action in the Fight for Civil Liberties." *Yale Law Journal* 58 (1949): 574.

Note. "The Right to Counsel in Civil Litigation." *Columbia Law Review* 66 (1966): 1322.

Note. "Suitable Home Tests Under Social Security: A Functional Approach to Equal Protection." *Yale Law Journal* 70 (1961): 1192.

Nowak, John E., Ronald D. Rotunda, and J. Nelson Young. *Constitutional Law*. 3d ed. St. Paul, Minn.: West Publishing Co., 1986.

O'Brien, David M. University of Virginia, Charlottesville, Virginia. Interview, 19 August 1983.

—————. *Storm Center; The Supreme Court in American Politics*. New York: W. W. Norton and Company, 1986.

O'Connor, Karen. *Women's Organizations' Use of the Courts*. Lexington, Mass.: Lexington Books, 1980.

O'Connor, Karen, and Lee Epstein. "Amicus Curiae Participation in U.S. Supreme Court Litigation: An Appraisal of Hakman's 'Folklore.' " *Law and Society Review* 16 (1982): 311.

―――. "Court Rules and Workload: A Case Study of Rules Governing Amicus Curiae Participation." *Justice System Journal* 8 (1983): 35.

―――. "The Rise of Conservative Interest Group Litigation." *Journal of Politics* 45 (May 1983): 432.

―――. "Beyond Legislative Lobbying: Women's Rights Groups and the Supreme Court." *Judicature* 67 (1983): 134.

―――. "Rebalancing the Scales of Justice: Assessment of Public Interest Law." *Harvard Journal of Law and Public Policy* 7 (1984): 483.

Olson, Susan M. *Clients and Lawyers: Securing the Rights of Disabled Persons*. Westport, Conn.: Greenwood Press, 1984.

―――. "Interest Group Litigation in Federal District Court." Paper presented at the Annual Meetings of the Law and Society Association, Vail, Colo., 1988.

Pacelle, Richard, Jr. "The Supreme Court Agenda Across Time: Toward a Theory of Agenda-Building." Paper presented at the Annual Meeting of the Midwest Political Science Association, Chicago, 1986.

―――. "The Supreme Court and the Growth of Civil Liberties: The Process and Dynamics of Agenda Change." Paper presented at the Annual Meetings of the American Political Science Association, Chicago, 1987.

Pateman, Carole. *Participation and Democratic Theory*. New York: Cambridge University Press, 1970.

Patterson, James T. *America's Struggle Against Poverty, 1900–1985*. Cambridge, Mass.: Harvard University Press, 1986.

Perry, H. W., Jr. Washington University, St. Louis, Mo. Interview, 10 November 1984.

―――. "Indices and Signals in the Certiorari Process." Paper presented at the Midwest Political Science Association Meetings, Chicago, 9–11 April 1986.

―――. "Deciding to Decide: Agenda-Setting in the U.S. Supreme Court." Ph.D. Dissertation. University of Michigan, 1987.

Perry, Michael. *The Constitution, the Courts, and Human Rights*. New Haven, Conn.: Yale University Press, 1982.

Peterson, Mark A. *Legislating Together: The White House and Capitol Hill from Eisenhower to Reagan*. Cambridge, Mass.: Harvard University Press, 1990.

Pious, Richard M. "Policy and Public Administration: The Legal Services Program in the War on Poverty." *Politics and Society* 1 (May 1971): 365.

―――. "Congress, the Organized Bar, and the Legal Services Program." *Wisconsin Law Review* 1972 (1972): 418.

Pitkin, Hanna Fenichel. *The Concept of Representation*. Berkeley: University of California Press, 1967.

Piven, Frances Fox, and Richard A. Cloward. *Regulating the Poor: The Functions of Public Welfare*. New York: Pantheon, 1971.

Pole, J. R. *The Pursuit of Equality in American History*. Berkeley: University of California Press, 1978.

Polsby, Nelson W. *Political Innovation in America: The Politics of Policy Initiation*. New Haven, Conn.: Yale University Press, 1984.

"Poverty Law Developments." *Clearinghouse Review*, 1–10 (1967–77).

*Poverty Law Reporter*, 2: 9787. Quoted in Stuart A. Scheingold. *The Politics of Rights: Lawyers, Public Policy, and Political Change*, p. 192. New Haven, Conn.: Yale University Press, 1974.

Powell, Doug. West Publishing Co., St. Paul, Minn. Interview, 8 May 1983.

Provine, Doris Marie. *Case Selection in the United States Supreme Court*. Chicago: University of Chicago Press, 1980.

Puro, Steven. "The United States as *Amicus Curiae*." In *Courts, Law, and Judicial Process*, p. 220. Edited by S. Sidney Ulmer. New York: The Free Press, 1981.

Pye, A. Kenneth. "The Role of Legal Services in the Anti-Poverty Program." *Law and Contemporary Problems* 31 (1966): 211.

Rabin, Robert L. "Lawyers for Social Change: Perspectives on Public Interest Law." *Stanford Law Review* 28 (1976): 207.

Rathjen, Gregory J. "Lawyers and the Appellate Choice: An Analysis of Factors Affecting the Decision to Appeal." *American Politics Quarterly* 6 (October 1978): 387.

Rathjen, Gregory J., and Harold L. Spaeth. "Denying Access in Plenary Cases: The Burger Court." In *Courts, Law, and Judicial Process*, p. 265. Edited by S. Sidney Ulmer. New York: The Free Press, 1981.

"Reagan Names Interim Board for Legal Services Corp." *Washington Post* 24 (November 1984): A1.

Redlich, Allen. "The Art of Welfare Advocacy: Available Procedures and Forums." *Albany Law Review* 36 (1971): 57.

Reich, Charles. "Midnight Welfare Searches and the Social Security Act." *Yale Law Journal* 72 (1963): 1347.

———. "The New Property." *Yale Law Journal* 73 (1964): 733.

———. "Individual Rights and Social Welfare: The Emerging Legal Issues." *Yale Law Journal* 74 (1965): 1245.

Rosenblatt, Rand E. "Legal Entitlements and Welfare Benefits." In *The Politics of Law*, p. 262. Edited by David Kairys. New York: Pantheon Books, 1982.

Rosenthal, Douglas E. *Lawyer and Client: Who's In Charge?* New Brunswick, N.J.: Transaction Books, 1977.

Rothstein, Lawrence E. "The Myth of Sisyphus: Legal Services Efforts on Behalf of the Poor." *University of Michigan Journal of Law Reform* 7 (Spring 1974): 493–515.

Salokar, Rebecca M. "The Solicitor General Before the U.S. Supreme Court, 1959–1982: A Descriptive Analysis." Paper presented at the Annual Meeting of the Law and Society Association, Washington, D.C., 13 June 1987.

Schardt, Arlie. "Legal Services: Round II." *Civil Liberties Review* 2 (1975): 39.

Schattschneider, E. E. *The Semisovereign People*. Hinsdale, Ill.: The Dryden Press, 1975.

Scheingold, Stuart A. *The Politics of Rights: Lawyers, Public Policy, and Political Change*. New Haven, Conn.: Yale University Press, 1974.

Schmidhauser, John R. *Constitutional Law in Politics*. Monterey, Calif.: Brooks/Cole Publishing Company, 1984.

Schwarz, John E. *America's Hidden Success: A Reassessment of Public Policy From Kennedy to Reagan, Revised*. New York: W. W. Norton & Company, 1988.

Scigliano, Robert. *The Supreme Court and the Presidency*. New York: The Free Press, 1971.

Shapiro, Martin. *Law and Politics in the Supreme Court*. New York: The Free Press, 1964.

———. "Stability and Change in Judicial Decision-Making: Incrementalism or Stare Decisis?" *Law in Transition Quarterly* 2 (1965): 134.

———. *Courts*. Chicago: University of Chicago Press, 1981.

*Shepard's Citations*. Colorado Springs, Colo.: McGraw Hill, 1966–83.

Shriver, Sargent. "Law Reform and the Poor." *American University Law Review* 17 (1967): 1.

Silver, Carol Ruth. "How to Handle a Welfare Case." *Law in Transition Quarterly* 87 (1967): 95.

Simon, William H. "Legal Informality and Redistributive Politics." *Clearinghouse Review* 19 (1985): 384.

Smith, Reginald Heber. *Justice and the Poor*. New York: Carnegie Foundation, 1919.

———. "Introduction." *Legal Aid in the United States*. By Emery A. Brownell. Rochester, N.Y.: The Lawyers Co-operative Publishing Co., 1951.

———. *Justice and the Poor*. New York: Carnegie Foundation, 1919. Quoted in Earl Johnson, Jr., *Justice and Reform: The Formative Years of the American Legal Services Program*, p. 13. New Brunswick, N.J.: Transaction Books, 1978.

Smith, Rogers. "All Critters Great and Small: Critical Legal Studies and Liberal Political Theory." *Law, Courts, and Judicial Process Section Newsletter* (American Political Science Association) 3, 3 (1986): 1.

Songer, Donald R. "Concern for Policy Outputs as a Cue for Supreme Court Decisions on Certiorari." *Journal of Politics* 41 (1979): 1184.

Sorauf, Frank J. *The Wall of Separation: The Constitutional Politics of Church and State*. Princeton, N.J.: Princeton University Press, 1976.

Sosin, Michael R. "Legal Rights and Welfare Change, 1960–1980." In *Fighting Poverty: What Works and What Doesn't*, pp. 260–83. Edited by Sheldon H. Danziger and Daniel H. Weinberg. Cambridge, Mass.: Harvard University Press, 1986.

Spaeth, Harold J. *Supreme Court Policy Making: Explanation and Prediction*. San Francisco: W. H. Freeman and Company, 1979.

———. "The Attitudes and Values of Supreme Court Justices." In *Courts, Law, and Judicial Process*, p. 387. Edited by S. Sidney Ulmer. New York: The Free Press, 1981.

Sparer, Edward V. "The Role of the Welfare Client's Lawyer." *UCLA Law Review* 12 (1964): 361.

———. "Social Welfare Law Testing." *The Practical Lawyer* 12 (1966): 12.

———. "The Right to Welfare." In *The Rights of Americans*, pp. 65–127. Edited by Norman Dorsen. New York: Pantheon Books, 1970.

―――. "Welfare Testing Memo." Quoted in Jack Greenberg, "Litigation for Social Change: Methods, Limits, and Role in Democracy." *Record of the Association of the Bar of the City of New York* 29 (1974): 320.

Sprague, John D. *Voting Patterns of the United States Supreme Court, Cases in Federalism, 1889–1959.* New York: The Bobbs-Merrill Company, Inc., 1968.

Steiner, Gilbert Y. "Introduction: Abortion Policy and the Potential for Mischief." In *The Abortion Dispute and the American System,* pp. 1–12. Edited by Gilbert Y. Steiner. Washington, D.C.: The Brookings Institution, 1983.

Stern, Robert L., and Eugene Gressman. *Supreme Court Practice.* 4th ed. Washington, D.C.: Bureau of National Affairs, 1969.

Stiegler, Mayo H. "All for the Sake of Statistics." *Legal Aid Briefcase* 28 (1970): 101.

Sullivan, Lawrence A. "Law Reform and the Legal Services Crisis." *California Law Review* 59 (1971): 1.

"The Supreme Court, 19xx Term: The Statistics." *Harvard Law Review*, 1967–75.

Supreme Court of the United States, Revised Rules. *United States Code*, vol. 28, Appendix (1967).

"Supreme Court Supports Jurisdiction Act." *American Bar Association Journal* 65 (September 1979): 1328.

Synder, Eloise. "A Quantitative Analysis of Supreme Court Opinions from 1921–1953: A Study of the Responses of an Institution Engaged in Resolving Social Conflict." Ph.D. Dissertation, Pennsylvania State University, 1956.

Tanenhaus, Joseph, Marvin Schick, Matthew Muraskin, and Daniel Rosen. "The Supreme Court's Certiorari Jurisdiction: Cue Theory." In *American Court Systems: Readings in Judicial Process and Behavior*, p. 130. Edited by Sheldon Goldman and Austin Sarat. San Francisco: W. H. Freeman and Company, 1978.

Teger, Stuart H., and Douglas Kosinski. "The Cue Theory of Supreme Court Certiorari Jurisdiction: A Reconsideration." *Journal of Politics* 42 (1980): 834.

Trattner, Walter I., ed. *Social Welfare or Social Control? Some Historical Reflections on "Regulating the Poor."* Knoxville: University of Tennessee Press, 1985.

Tribe, Laurence H. *American Constitutional Law.* Mineola, N.Y.: The Foundation Press, 1978.

Trubeck, David M., Joel B. Grossman, William L. F. Felstiner, Herbert M. Kritzer, and Austin Sarat. *Civil Litigation Research Project Final Report.* Madison, Wis.: University of Wisconsin Law School, 1983.

Truman, David M. *The Governmental Process.* New York: Alfred A. Knopf, 1951.

Turner, Wallace. "Proposal by Reagan Opens an Old Wound." *New York Times*, 15 March 1981, p. 25.

Tushnet, Mark V. *The NAACP's Legal Strategy Against Segregated Education, 1925–1950.* Chapel Hill, N.C.: The University of North Carolina Press, 1987.

Ulmer, S. Sidney. "Supreme Court Justices as Strict and Not-So-Strict Constructionists: Some Implications." *Law and Society Review* 8 (1973): 13.

―――. "Selecting Cases for Supreme Court Review: An Underdog Model." *American Political Science Review* 72 (1978): 902.

―――. "Selecting Cases for Supreme Court Review: Litigant Status in the Warren and Burger Courts." In *Courts, Law, and Judicial Process*, p. 284. Edited by S. Sidney Ulmer. New York: The Free Press, 1981.

———. "Conflict with Supreme Court Precedent and the Granting of Plenary Review." *Journal of Politics* 45 (1983): 474.

———. "The Supreme Court's Certiorari Decisions: Conflict as a Predictive Variable." *American Political Science Review* 78 (1984): 901.

———. "Government Litigants, Underdogs, and Civil Liberties in the Supreme Court: 1903–1968 Terms." *Journal of Politics* 47 (1985): 899.

Ulmer, S. Sidney, William Hintz, and Louise Kirlosky. "The Decision to Grant Certiorari as an Indicator to Decision 'On the Merits.' " *Polity* 4 (1972): 429.

———. "The Decision to Grant or Deny Certiorari: Further Consideration of Cue Theory." *Law and Society Review* 7 (1972): 637.

U.S. Commission on Revision of the Federal Court Appellate System, Structure and Internal Procedures. *Recommendations for Change: A Preliminary Report*, pp. A-33–A-41. Washington, D.C.: April 1975.

U.S. Comptroller General. "Report to Congress: The Legal Services Program—Accomplishments Of and Problems Faced By Its Grantees, B-130515." Washington, D.C.: Government Printing Office, 1973.

U.S. Congress. House. Committee on Education and Labor. *Hearings on H.R. 8311 Before the House Committee on Education and Labor*. 90th Cong., 1st sess., 2016, 1967, p. 2130. Quoted in Richard Pious, "Congress, the Organized Bar, and the Legal Services Program." *Wisconsin Law Review* 1972 (1972): 418, 427.

U.S. Congress. House. Committee on Health, Education, and Welfare. *Establishment of a Legal Services Corporation, Hearings before the Subcommittee on Education and Labor on H.R. 3147, H.R. 3175, and H.R. 3409*. 93d Cong., 1st sess., February and March 1973.

U.S. Congress. Senate. Committee on Labor and Public Welfare. *Examination of the War on Poverty, Hearings before the Subcommittee on Employment, Manpower, and Poverty on S. 1545, Part 8*. 90th Cong., 1st sess., June 1967.

U.S. Congress. Senate. Committee on Labor and Public Welfare. S. Rept. 563. 90th Cong., 1st sess., 1967.

U.S. Congress. Senate. *Congressional Record* 113 (1967): 27871. 90th Cong., 2d sess., 1968.

U.S. Congress. Senate. Committee on Labor and Public Welfare. *Legal Services Program of the Office of Economic Opportunity, Hearings before the Subcommittee on Employment, Manpower, and Poverty*. 91st Cong., 2d sess., October 1970.

U.S. Department of Commerce. *Statistical Abstract of the United States, 1972*, Table 486, p. 299. Washington, D.C.: Government Printing Office, 1972.

U.S. Office of Economic Opportunity. "The Legal Services Program." *Annual Reports*. Executive Office of the President, 1966–72.

Van Alstyne, William. "The Demise of the Right-Privilege Distinction in Constitutional Law." *Harvard Law Review* 81 (1968): 1439.

———. "Cracks in 'The New Property': Adjudicative Due Process in the Administrative State." *Cornell Law Review* 62 (1977): 445.

Verba, Sidney, and Gary R. Orren. *Equality in America: A View From the Top*. Cambridge, Mass.: Harvard University Press, 1985.

Verba, Sidney, and Norman H. Nie. *Participation in America: Political Democracy and Social Equality*. Chicago: University of Chicago Press, 1972.

Vose, Clement E. "Litigation as a Form of Pressure Group Activity." *The Annals of the American Academy of Political and Social Science* 319 (1958): 20.

—. *Caucasians Only: The Supreme Court, the NAACP, and the Restrictive Covenant Cases*. Berkeley: University of California Press, 1959.

—. *Constitutional Change: Amendment Politics and Supreme Court Litigation Since 1900*. Lexington, Mass.: Lexington Books, 1972.

Walker, Jack L. "A Critique of the Elitist Theory of Democracy." *American Political Science Review* 60 (1966): 285.

—. "Setting the Agenda in the U.S. Senate: A Theory of Problem Selection." *British Journal of Political Science* 7 (1977): 423–45.

Wasby, Stephen L. "Interest Groups in Court: Race Relations Litigation." In *Interest Group Politics*, p. 251. Edited by Allan J. Cigler and Burdett A. Loomis. Washington, D.C.: Congressional Quarterly Press, 1983.

—. "How Planned Is 'Planned Litigation'?" *American Bar Foundation Research Journal* 1984 (1984): 83–138.

—. "Civil Rights Litigation by Organizations: Constraints and Choices." *Judicature* 68 (1985): 337.

Way, Frank. "Stability and Change in Constitutional Litigation: The Public Piety Cases." *Journal of Politics* 47 (1985): 910.

Wells, Richard S., and Joel B. Grossman. "The Concept of Judicial Policy-Making: A Critique." *Journal of Public Law* 15 (1966): 286–310.

Westwood, H. C. "Getting Justice for the Freedman." *Howard Law Journal* 16 (Spring 1971): 492.

Wexler, Stephen. "Practicing Law for Poor People." *Yale Law Journal* 79 (1970): 1049.

Woodward, Bob, and Armstrong, Scott. *The Brethren: Inside the Supreme Court*. New York: Simon and Schuster, 1979.

Zemans, Frances Kahn. "Framework for Analysis of Legal Mobilization: A Decision-Making Model." *American Bar Foundation Research Journal* 1982 (1982): 989.

—. "Legal Mobilization: The Neglected Role of the Law in the Political System." *American Political Science Review* 77 (1983): 690.

—. "Fee Shifting and the Implementation of Public Policy." *Law and Contemporary Problems* 47 (1984): 187.

# Table of Cases Cited

To aid the reader, this table also includes all 164 LSP sponsored cases, set in italics, that formed the data base for this work, irrespective of whether they are cited in the text. The twenty-four cases in which the LSP only participated through the filing of an amicus curiae brief are also included. They are designated by an asterisk (*).

# Index

National Legal Aid and Defender Association
(NLADA), 19, 21, 25, 28; and opposition to
the LSP, 25–27
National Right to Work Legal Defense Foun-
dation, 168
National Welfare Rights Organization, 49
Native Americans. *See* Indian rights litigation
Neighborhood Legal Services Project, Wash-
ington, D.C., 24, 27
neighborhood social service centers, Ford
Foundation's, 23, 24, 25, 28
Nelson, Barbara J., 96
Neustadt, Richard E., 159
New South Wales, 19
New York, 60, 137; City, 33
New Zealand, 19
Nie, Norman H., 3, 8, 154–55
Nixon Court, 53, 58, 86–87, 104–7, 119. *See
also* Burger Court
Nixon, Richard M., 12, 114–15, 116, 126
North Dakota, 36
Northern Ireland, 19
Nowak, John E., 133, 137, 164

O'Brien, David, 71, 106
O'Connor, Karen, 6, 7, 40, 41, 52, 62, 63,
101, 102, 118, 119–20, 169
Office of Economic Opportunity (OEO), 9, 12,
23–29, 34, 37, 42, 65, 66–67, 71, 115,
117, 126, 162. *See also* Great Society and
War on Poverty
Oklahoma City, Oklahoma, 36
Old Age Assistance, 145
Olson, Susan M., 7, 17, 58, 67, 121, 149
Oregon, 67
Orren, Gary R., 115, 155

Pacelle, Richard, Jr., 22, 39, 90, 91, 94, 113
Parker, Paul E., 63
Pateman, Carole, 153, 154
Patterson, James T., 8, 20, 22, 92, 96, 114,
115–16, 118, 122, 126
Penrod, Steven, 4
Perry, H. W., Jr., 71, 73, 75, 76, 78, 83, 84,
86, 87, 88, 91, 94
Perry, Michael, 95
personal well-being litigation, 135–36, 139,
141, 142–44; of the LSP, 49, 59, 60, 64,
80, 103–4, 135–37
Peterson, Mark A., 96
philosophies of legal assistance, 17; of the

projects preceding the LSP, 23–25, 37. *See
also* legal aid societies and Legal Services
Program
Pious, Richard M., 13, 33, 36, 42, 66, 116,
117
Piper and Marbury, 26–27
Pitkin, Hanna Fenichel, 17
Piven, Frances Fox, 10, 35, 49, 87, 89, 96–
97, 150
Pole, J. R., 115
political and legal climate, 97, 112–22, 126,
158–59; and abortion litigation, 120; and
church-state litigation, 120; effect on judicial decision making, 11, 112–21; role in
shaping judicial conceptions of the proper
work of the court, 91–96. *See also* Legal
Services Program, political and legal climate
political participation, 154–55, 157; litigation
as a form of, 3–4, 7–8, 13–15, 24–25, 65–
68, 90–91, 152–59
political rights litigation of the LSP, 59, 80,
90, 103–4
politics of rights, 4
Polsby, Nelson W., 96
Pomper, Gerald M., 157
Posner, Richard A., 73
poverty, rediscovery of, 8, 22–23, 37, 92,
96–97, 115, 117, 149; policy on, 114–15;
statistics on, 87, 89
Powell, Lewis F., 105–12, 126, 135, 143,
172; as American Bar Association President, 26, 71
president, 3, 92, 96–97, 115, 116–17, 122,
150, 152, 157, 158, 159
President's Committee on Juvenile Delinquency, 23
pretermination hearings, 49, 126, 133–35,
137, 150
*pro bono publico*, 5, 7, 41, 157
professional dominance, 65–68; by lawyers,
17, 58, 66–67, 149, 154
property rights, 90
Protective Agency for Women and Children,
18
Protestants and Other Americans United for
Separation of Church and State, 6
Provine, Doris Marie, 71, 73, 75, 76, 78, 80,
82, 84–85, 86, 87, 90, 169
public utilities litigation of the LSP, 59, 89.
*See also* shelter litigation

**DUE DATE**

| | | |
|---|---|---|
| MAY 1 1992 | MAY 0 7 1995 | |
| | DEC 1 1 1996 | |
| NOV 3 3 1992 | | |
| APR 2 2 1993 | | |
| MAY 1 1 1993 | | |
| | | |
| NOV 1 7 1994 | | |
| MAY 1 1 1995 | MAY 0 9 1994 | |
| DEC 1 0 1997 | | |

Printed
in USA